£30
Sept 1

TRAINING EDUCATORS OF ADULTS

THEORY AND PRACTICE OF ADULT EDUCATION IN NORTH AMERICA SERIES

Edited by Peter Jarvis, University of Surrey

TRAINING EDUCATORS OF ADULTS

The Theory and Practice of Graduate Adult Education

Edited by
STEPHEN BROOKFIELD

ROUTLEDGE
London and New York

First published in 1988 by
Routledge
a division of Routledge, Chapman and Hall
11 New Fetter Lane, London EC4P 4EE

Published in the USA by
Routledge
a division of Routledge, Chapman and Hall, Inc.
29 West 35th Street, New York NY 10001

Printed and bound in Great Britain by
Biddles Ltd, Guildford and King's Lynn

British Library Cataloguing in Publication Data

Training educators of adults : the theory
    and practice of graduate adult education.
    — (Croom Helm series on theory and
    practice of adult education in North
    America).
    1. Adult education teachers — Training of
    — United States
    I. Brookfield, Stephen II. Series
    370′.7′120973   LC5225.T4

ISBN 0-415-00564-7

CONTENTS

CONTENTS

PART SIX
CRITERIA OF GOOD PRACTICE IN
GRADUATE ADULT EDUCATION

PART SEVEN
CURRICULA AND PROGRAMS OF
GRADUATE ADULT EDUCATION

PART EIGHT
CONCLUSION

EDITOR'S NOTE

The Croom Helm Series of books on the Theory and Practice of Adult Education in North America provides scholars and students with a collection of studies by eminent scholars of all aspects of adult education throughout the whole continent. The series already includes books on planning, history and learning in the workplace. It is intended that many others will be added to the list from all the sub-disciplines of adult education. They will cover both theoretical and practical considerations and each will constitute a major contribution to its own specific field of study. Some of these will be symposia while others will consist of single authored treatises.

Among the first books in this series was Stephen Brookfield's collection of papers from Lindeman, Learning Democracy: Eduard Lindeman on Adult Education and Social Change. Lindeman needed no introduction to scholars of adult education and neither will the topic of his second collection of papers. In this collection he examines the history of graduate education in the United States. Training adult educators does occur throughout the world of adult education and in each country there are different systems. In the United Kingdom, as Brookfield points out, there is a system of preparation of adult educators that takes place before they actually begin teaching: it is practical rather than theoretical and it is not at graduate level, but there are also post-graduate diplomas and degrees. Hence, he has included an important comparative chapter of his own in this collection. Among the great advantages of this volume is that now well known studies on this topic will once again be easily accessible.

It is hoped that over the next few years this series will include studies on areas that are of concern and interest to all scholars and among the next books to appear will be a study of adult education in multi-cultural America.

Peter Jarvis
Series Editor

ACKNOWLEDGEMENTS AND SOURCES OF SELECTIONS

Acknowledgement is gratefully made to the following organizations and individuals for their granting of permission to use the materials contained in this book:

The American Association for Adult and Continuing Education, the International Council for Adult Education, the Commission of Professors of Adult Education, Taylor and Francis Limited, Betty Leonard Lindeman, Lynn Davie, Sharan Merriam, Roger Boshier, Reynold Willie, Harlan Copeland and Howard Williams.

"Training Adult Educators in North America" by Sharan Merriam. From Convergence, Vol. 18, No's 3-4, 1985. Reprinted by permission of the International Council for Adult Education and Sharan Merriam.

"A General Theory of the Doctorate in Education" by Malcolm Knowles. From Adult Education, Vol. 12, No. 3, 1962. Reprinted by permission of the American Council for Adult and Continuing Education.

"The Nature and Aims of Adult Education as a Field of Graduate Education" by A.A. Liveright. From Adult Education: Outlines of an Emerging Field of University Study. G. Jensen, A.A. Liveright and W.C. Hallenbeck (eds), Washington D.C.; Adult Education Association of the United States, 1964. Reprinted by permission of the American Association for Adult and Continuing Education.

"A Conceptual Framework for Analyzing the Training of Trainers and Adult Educators" by Roger Boshier. From Convergence, Vol. 18, No's 3-4, 1985. Reprinted by permission of the International Council for Adult Education and Roger Boshier.

ACKNOWLEDGEMENTS & SOURCES OF SELECTIONS

"Preparing Leaders in Adult Education" by Eduard Lindeman. Speech to the Pennsylvania Association for Adult Education, November 18th, 1938. Reprinted by permission of Betty Lindeman Leonard.

"The Making of the Makers" by Harry O. and Bonaro W. Overstreet. From Leaders For Adult Education. H.O. and B.W. Overstreet. New York; American Association for Adult Education, 1941. Reprinted by permission of the American Association for Adult and Continuing Education.

"Training Adult Educators" by Wilbur C. Hallenbeck. From Handbook of Adult Education in the United States. M.L. Ely (ed.). New York; Center for Adult Education, Teachers College, 1948. Reprinted by permission of the Center for Adult Education, Teachers College.

"The Education of Adult Educational Leaders" by Cyril O. Houle. From Handbook of Adult Education in the United States. M.S. Knowles (ed.). Washington DC; Adult Education Association of the United States, 1960. Reprinted by permission of the American Association for Adult and Continuing Education.

"The Emergence of Graduate Study in Adult Education" by Cyril O. Houle. From Adult Education: Outlines of an Emerging Field of University Study. G. Jensen, A.A. Liveright and W.C. Hallenbeck (eds), Washington, DC; Adult Education Association of the United States, 1964. Reprinted by permission of the American Association for Adult and Continuing Education.

"The Competencies of Adult Educators" by Martin N. Chamberlain. From Adult Education, Vol. 11, No. 2, 1961. reprinted by permission of the American Association for Adult and Continuing Education.

"Knowledge and Skills for the Adult Educator: A Delphi Study" by Mark H. Rossman and Richard L. Bunning. From Adult Education, Vol. 28, No. 3, 1978. Reprinted by permission of the American Association for Adult and Continuing Education.

"Comparative Study of Adult Education Practitioners and Professors on Future Knowledge and Skills Needed by Adult Educators" by Richard Daniel and Harold Rose. From Adult Education, Vol. 32, No. 2, 1982. Reprinted by permission of the American Association for Adult and Continuing Education.

ACKNOWLEDGEMENTS & SOURCES OF SELECTIONS

"Life Crises and Career Change in Adult Educators" by Lynn E. Davie. From Adult Education Research Conference Proceedings, No. 20. Ann Arbor, Michigan, 1979. Reprinted by permission of Lynn E. Davie.

"The Adult Education Professoriat of the United States and Canada" by Reynold Willie, Harlan Copeland and Howard Williams. From International Journal of Lifelong Education, Vol. 4, No. 1, 1985. Reprinted by permission of Taylor and Francis Ltd. and Reynold Willie, Harlan Copeland and Howard Williams.

"Philosophical Orientations of Adult Educators" by Leon McKenzie. From Lifelong Learning, Vol. 9, No. 1, 1985. Reprinted by permission of the American Association for Adult and Continuing Education.

"Criteria for the Education of Adult Educators" by C.O. Robinson. From Adult Education, Vol. 12, No. 4, 1962. Reprinted by permission of the American Association for Adult and Continuing Education.

"Principles of Good Practice in Continuing Education" by Jack Mezirow. From Lifelong Learning, Vol. 8 No. 3, 1984. Reprinted by permission of the American Association for Adult and Continuing Education.

"Some Further Thoughts on Principles of Good Practice in Continuing Education" by Michael Collins. From Lifelong Learning, Vol. 8, No. 8, 1985. Reprinted by permission of the American Association for Adult and Continuing Education.

"Standards for Graduate Programs in Adult Education". Document presented to and approved by the Commission of Professors of Adult Education Annual Meeting, Hollywood, Florida, October 1986. Reprinted by permission of the Commission of Professors of Adult Education.

"Objectives for Graduate Programs in Adult Education". From Adult Education: Outlines of an Emerging Field of University Study. G. Jensen, A.A. Liveright and W.C. Hallenbeck (eds), Washington DC; Adult Education Association of the United States, 1964. Reprinted by permission of the American Association for Adult and Continuing Education.

PREFACE

The purpose of this book is to provide readers with an understanding of the history, organization, conduct and underlying intellectual orientations of graduate adult education in the United States. Graduate adult education is defined as the provision of diploma, masters and doctoral degrees in adult education within university departments or programs of adult education. For the purposes of this book, the term graduate adult education will be used throughout to describe what in Britain is called postgraduate adult education. To Americans, the term postgraduate is unwieldy and unfamiliar. When used it most likely refers to post-doctoral study; that is, study after doctoral graduation. Since the book is describing the American system, it seems appropriate to employ the American usage and to use the term graduate adult education to refer to the provision of diploma, masters and doctoral degrees in adult education.

The book is organized into seven major sections, and for internal consistency the selections within each section are presented in chronological order. The first section is an overview of theory and practice in American adult education. The two essays in this section are intended to orient readers to the prevailing concepts and practices both within the wider field of adult education, and within the specific practice of graduate adult education. In the first essay I review the most common approaches to conceptualizing adult education, I describe the major providing agencies, and I outline the chief professional roles played by adult educators. The purpose of this essay is to introduce to the reader unfamiliar with the field of American adult education some of the major organizing concepts and practices within the field. In the second selection in this section Sharan Merriam discusses some of the chief issues involved in training adult educators in the United States, and gives an overview of some of the ways in which graduate programs in adult education are organized.

The second section on 'Conceptual Issues in Training Educators of Adults' contains three discussions of some

1

conceptual matters pertaining to graduate adult education.
Malcolm Knowles proposes a rationale for the organization of
the doctorate in education (the EdD). For graduate programs
in adult education in the United States, the EdD is the chief
degree provided. The PhD, although available at many institutions, tends to be awarded much less frequently within
American university departments of adult education than is
the case with the EdD. The generalist orientation described
by Knowles as endemic to EdD programs is argued by him to
be particularly appropriate to graduate adult education, which
he views as essentially interdisciplinary in character. A.A.
Liveright, in a paper which has subsequently been highly
significant in discussions regarding the form and content of
American graduate adult education, summarizes some of the
most cogent contributions to the debate on these matters
which had been made up to the time the paper was written
(1964). He sets forth a framework for examining the aims and
patterns of graduate adult education. Finally, Roger Boshier,
in a lead article in a recent issue on 'Training of Trainers
and Adult Educators' of the international journal of adult
education - Convergence - presents a conceptual framework
for analyzing this activity. Boshier speaks to the need, as he
sees it, to unify the field, and then erects a model to classify
adult educational roles and functions. The implications of this
model for the content and method of graduate adult education
are discussed.

The third section - 'Historical Perspectives' - contains
five pieces published or written between 1938 and 1964 which
were influential in shaping the debate regarding the method,
purposes and content of graduate adult education. In a
speech to the Pennsylvania Association for Adult Education in
1938, Eduard Lindeman draws a distinction between what he
describes as mechanistic and organic conceptions of adult
education. In favouring the organic conception Lindeman
argues that the goals of adult education are irredeemably
social and that adult educators need particular knowledge and
skills to help them achieve these goals. In 'The Making of the
Makers', two legendary figures within American adult education - Harry and Bonaro Overstreet - present a variety of
case histories of adult educators and then comment on the
commonalities they observe amongst this variety. In a chapter
initially published within the 1948 Handbook of Adult
Education Wilbur C. Hallenbeck, the recipient of the first
ever doctoral degree in adult education within the United
States, provides a brief description of issues, methods and
content in the training of adult educators. The section is
completed by two pieces by Cyril Houle, published in 1960
and 1964. The first of these - 'The Education of Adult
Educational Leaders' - initially appeared in the 1960 edition of
the Handbook of Adult Education. In this piece Houle sets out
a pyramid of leadership within adult education and then

describes training programs for lay leaders, for part-time leaders, and for specialists in adult education. With regard to this last category, Houle proposes six central objectives for training. In the 1964 selection drawn from the Commission of Professors of Adult Education book on Adult Education: Outlines of an Emerging Field of University Study, Houle reviews the emergence of graduate adult education in the United States from the 1930's to the 1960's.

The section on 'Proficiencies of Adult Educators' contains three selections, all of which are intended to give readers a sense of the professional circumstances, working conditions and required skills and knowledge of American adult educators. Only if such circumstances, conditions, skills and knowledge are fully understood can any judgments regarding the suitability of graduate adult education be made. The section begins with a presentation by Martin Chamberlain of the results of a survey of ninety prominent adult educators who responded to an instrument in which they were asked to rate 45 different concepts, skills and values for their appropriateness to the practice of adult education. These 45 statements of competency are then rank ordered according to the frequency of response to each statement. Some interesting discrepancies are revealed in this survey between some generally accepted givens of adult education (for example, that group methods are especially suitable as teaching methods with adult learners) and their actual importance as rated by respondents. The selections in this section by Rossman and Bunning and by Daniel and Rose continue this attempt to delineate what experts see as uniquely appropriate knowledge and skills for adult educators. The Rossman and Bunning study used a delphi technique to assess the views of 141 American and Canadian university professors of adult education on these required skills and knowledge. Beginning with an open ended question on adult educational skills and knowledge needed for the next decade, the authors moved the respondents through three successively refined questionnaires in which these professors were asked to generate an emerging consensus on this theme, and to outline implications for practice deriving from the skills and knowledge specified. The Daniel and Rose study took this process one stage further by presenting some of the skills and knowledge specified by professors in Rossman and Bunning's study to a sample of practitioners and then asking these practitioners to comment on the relevance of these skills and knowledge for their own work efforts. Taken together these three selections comprise an interesting cumulative record of changing perceptions of appropriate adult educational skills and knowledge.

The section on 'Characteristics and Orientations of Adult Educators' contains three short pieces all of which deal with the attitudes and activities of practising adult educators. In the first of these Lynn Davie interviewed 69 adult educators in the Toronto area concerning the connections between their work activities and what they perceived as their major life changes. Although this study was conducted with a Canadian sample, it is included in the present book for two reasons. First, a case can be made that the actual work experiences, activities and conditions of Canadian adult educators are sufficiently similar to those of their American counterparts to allow for some meaningful comparisons. Second, it is difficult to locate any studies of American adult educators which explore the connections investigated by Davie. The piece by Willie, Copeland and Williams does address the issues of adult educators' career satisfactions, professional activities and the connections between these satisfactions and activities and other life changes, though their sample is restricted to 177 professors of adult education within university departments of adult education. Their study reveals that these professors find their careers satisfying and that respondents generally affirmed their career choice as the correct one. The authors suggest that their study reveals a sombre scenario of an increasingly aging and conservative professoriat. They cite their findings as strong justification for increased institutional attention to faculty development programs, sabbatical leaves, and for support for research activities and for professors' involvements with professional networks and associations. Finally, McKenzie's survey of the philosophical orientations of adult educators reveals the progressive orientation to be the most common among three very differing groups of practitioners.

The section on 'Criteria of Good Practice in Graduate Adult Education' contains four papers, all of which discuss various criteria by which good practice in adult education, including graduate adult education, can be discussed. The first paper is a small scale attempt to establish such criteria with 24 adult educators in the Mountain Plains region in 1961. The two following papers, those by Mezirow and Collins, discuss the attempt by the Council on the Continuing Education Unit (CCEU) to generate indicators by which good practice in adult education can be recognized. After setting out these principles, Mezirow argues that they are overly reductionist and neglectful of major domains of adult learning. Collins reinforces these criticisms, arguing that they 'infantilize' both learners and educators. The section concludes with the most recent attempt by the American Commission of Professors of Adult Education to develop standards for graduate programs in adult education. This document was approved at the annual general meeting of the Commission at the national adult education convention in Florida, October 1986. It stands as the most concerted effort in the last two decades by American professors of adult education to specify the organization, method and content of graduate adult education.

The sixth section on 'Curricula and Programs of Graduate Adult Education' contains data on the organization and functioning of graduate programs. Dickerman's essay (which first appeared, like other pieces by Liveright and Houle in this book, in the landmark Adult Education: Outlines of an Emerging Field of University Study) attempts to build theory regarding graduate adult education from its practice. In my own analysis of programs of graduate adult education I draw on several recent surveys to present a picture of the operational procedures, faculty and student characteristics and curricula of American graduate adult education. The last paper in this section undertakes a cross cultural analysis of graduate adult education in the United States and Great Britain. In this paper I analyse graduate programs according to five analytical categories; (1) historicity, (2) political content, (3) philosophical orientation, (4) specified competencies of adult educators and (5) paradigms of appropriate research. The argument is made that graduate programs must be understood as socio-cultural products; that is, as reflective of, and sustaining to, dominant cultural values and ideologies.

The book concludes with an attempt to propose a philosophical rationale for graduate adult education. This paper argues that graduate programs should develop critically reflective practitioners - adult educators who can be aware of the assumptions underlying their practice, who can identify the 'theories in use' they employ, who can place their practice as adult educators within a wider socio-political context, and who can scrutinize critically the myths, givens and folk wisdoms regarding the conduct of adult education. The paper is personal and prescriptive and does not represent the views of the Commission of Professors of Adult Education or any other persons or organizations.

Several individuals and organizations have been helpful to me during the writing of this book. For their financial assistance I have to thank two foundations. In 1985 the Spencer Foundation awarded me a grant which enabled me to begin the research for this book. In 1987 the Kellog Foundation awarded me a grant which allowed me to bring this project to fruition. Throughout this time Kimerly Miller worked as my research assistant for the project and I wish to thank her for her efforts in locating materials, analyzing data and editing the manuscript. Conversations with a number of adult educators in America, France and England were invaluable to me in framing the book, and for their advice on this matter I wish to thank Harold Noah (of Teachers College, Columbia University, New York), Ettore Gelpi, John Ryan, and Paul Bertelsen (of UNESCO), John Lowe (of OECD), Arthur Stock (of the British National Institute of Adult

Continuing Education) and Colin Titmus (formerly of Gold-smiths' College, University of London). Needless to say, none of them are to be held in any way responsible for any inaccuracies, errors or poor judgments contained in the following pages. Finally, my thanks go to all the individuals and organizations which allowed me to use their materials within this collection. Full acknowledgments of those con-cerned are made elsewhere in this volume.

PART ONE

OVERVIEW: THEORY AND PRACTICE IN AMERICAN ADULT EDUCATION

Chapter One

ORGANIZING CONCEPTS AND PRACTICES IN ADULT EDUCATION IN THE UNITED STATES

Stephen Brookfield (1988)

CONCEPTUALIZING ADULT EDUCATION IN THE UNITED STATES

To many engaged in the practice of adult education in the United States, conceptualizing their activities might seem to be something of an annoying irrelevance; an irritating example of the tendency of academics to debate the number of angels which can fit on to the head of the adult educational pin. The pragmatic tenor of American culture is as apparent in the theory and practice of adult education as it is in other areas, and spending time conceptualizing practice may be considered to be unnecessary by many in this field. Indeed, some adult educators believe that trying to identify some definitional characteristics which are unique to adult education is a fruitless endeavour. Campbell (1977) declares that trying to impose a single definition on the kaleidoscopic range of activity and approaches comprising adult education is unproductive and tedious. Verduin, Miller and Greer (1977) observe that adult education is a mulitfaceted and complex process, encompassing subject and interest areas as broad as those of the population it serves.

Many practitioners protest that conceptualizing adult education is unnecessary, principally because the activity defines itself in terms of its clientele. Put simply, adult education is often seen as the education of adults. It becomes defined in primarily operational terms; that is, as the provision of opportunities for adults to acquire skills and knowledge in a systematic, purposeful manner. An example of this operational approach is Long's belief that adult education "includes all systematic and purposive efforts by the adult to become an educated person" (1987, p. viii). To many American educators, the idea that adult education is equivalent to the education of adults is appealing for its democratic associations. It is a generous, broad and all encompassing concept of educational provision. It allows for flexibility in terms of format and setting, and is sufficiently generic to include activities as diverse as military education, training in business and industry, adult basic education, recreational programmes, liberal arts discussion groups and community action initiatives.

CONCEPTUALIZING THROUGH 'ADULTHOOD'

Alternatives to the broadly operational approach to the conceptualization of adult education discussed above do exist. One approach grounds the practice of adult education in notions of adultness. This approach presumes that if we can identify the essential characteristics of adulthood, in particular the manner in which adults differ from children and the uniquely adult roles they play in society, then we can derive the essential nature of adult education from a consideration of these characteristics. Derived from this analysis of adulthood, so the argument goes, will come a specification of the curriculum, methods and purposes of adult education. Sworder (1955) for example, identified the responsibilities of adulthood as participating in political affairs, maintaining economic stability, assuming parenthood status, and providing a cultural and spiritual environment for future generations. Schwertman (1955) believed that adults' accumulation of experience meant that adult education was fundamentally different from secondary education and that the task of adult education was the "constant expansion of experience in desirable directions" (p. 41). Such directions would be to increase knowledge in general, to develop intellectual skills, and to increase aesthetic and spiritual sensibility.

Verner (1964) defined the adult as a person with responsibility for himself or herself and for others, who had accepted a functionally productive role in the community. He did not, however, develop a curricular agenda based upon the nature and requirements of this responsibility. To Liveright and Haygood (1968), adult education was a process whereby persons no longer attending school on a regular and full time basis consciously undertook sequential and organized activities to bring about specified psychomotor, affective or cognitive changes, or to solve community problems. Darkenwald and Merriam (1982) view adult education as a process whereby individuals performing the social roles of adulthood undertake systematic and sustained learning to bring about changes in knowledge, attitudes, values or skills. These attempts to develop a conceptualization of adult education all suffer from their cultural specificity. What are conceived as the social roles of adulthood, or the cultural characteristics of adultness, are reflective of a particular sub-cultural milieu. Definitions of adultness which focus on the performance of social roles such as being a parent or holding down a regular job do betray the class and cultural orientation of the definer. According to these ideas, people who are unemployed, who do not have children, or who live as single parents, are not fulfilling the social roles of adults.

CONCEPTUALIZATION THROUGH FUNCTIONAL ANALYSIS

An alternative approach to conceptualizing adult education is through a form of quasi-functional analysis. Seeking to understand the significance of certain behaviours or institutional structures through an analysis of their functions is a well attested analytic exercise in the social sciences. Functional analysis as developed in anthropology and sociology attempts to ascertain the extent to which an institution, ritualistic behaviour or system of received codes and values serves to maintain the larger whole of which it is a part. To this extent, a functional analysis of an adult education system would explore the manner in which that system sought to inculcate values, transmit knowledge and develop skills which contributed to the continued and effective functioning of the society of which it was a part. Functional analysis is a post-facto approach to conceptualization in which we seek to understand how an institution, set of behaviours or value system contributes to the maintenance of an existing order. It is both analytic and descriptive and is devoid of prescriptive elements. The purpose of functional analysis is to understand the functioning of social wholes through a fragmentation and compartmentalization of those wholes into their component parts.

Empirical analyses of the functioning of adult education systems, or of the manner in which the adult education system contributes to the maintenance of the social whole, are rare in the North American literature. Instead, a form of quasi-functional analysis is evident in which prescriptive and descriptive elements are mixed together. Hence, analysts present as 'functions' of adult education descriptions of purposes for which adult education programmes are established, estimations of actual achievements of programmes, and statements regarding preferred purposes for adult education.

An early example of this is Bryson's (1936) analysis. Bryson, a professor in the first ever university department of postgraduate adult education created in the United States (at Columbia University Teachers College in New York City) declared that adult education performed five functions in the pursuit of one overarching purpose defined as "the enlargement of the personality and quickening of life" (p.39). These functions were (1) to provide remedial education so that everyone possessed the minimum skills needed for life in American society (for example, literacy or child care skills), (2) occupational training, (3) relational education, in which the study of emotions, attitudes and psychological habits would help us understand ourselves and our relations with others, (4) liberal education (defined as activities pursued for their own sake), and (5) political education, including the study of politics as a subject discipline and training for political action. Bryson saw the performance of these functions as resulting in "an increase in the student's own power of self-direction.... a constant growth in independent thinking power and in the capacity for the management of one's own program" (1936, p.31).

Writing after the Second World War another Teachers College professor, Paul Essert (1951), outlined a similarly broad ranging and wholly prescriptive analysis of functions for adult education. Adult education was charged with achieving five purposes, all of which were considered to be innately desirable. It had to enhance adults' sense of occupational achievement so that they took a pride and satisfaction in their work. It had to restore and revive in people the experience of scientific inquiry so that they could enjoy the beauties of their existence. It had to grant the experience of self-government, so that a fundamental task of the adult educator became helping people find or establish laboratories through which they could share in the determination and responsibilities of government. It had to set education within the groups (such as neighbourhood and community groups or work groups) in which adults acquired basic daily behaviour patterns. Finally, it had to encourage the experience of intermittent solitude so that adults could contreract the unwholesome group demands of American culture and build a personal philosophy.

As conceived by Essert, the functions of adult education in America can be seen to be infused with a moral imperative. This same prescriptive spirit informs Hallenbeck's (1960) essay on The Function and Place of Adult Education in American Society. Hallenbeck (also a Teachers College professor!) identified five characteristics of American culture - the rapidity of change, the dominance of technology, the intensity of specialization, the compexity of relationships, and the vastness of opportunity - which framed the way in which adult educators used their special position to develop learners for life in that culture. Specifically, adult educators were (1) to expand adults' communication skills, (2) to develop in students qualities of flexibility for change, (3) to improve human relations, (4) to facilitate people's participation in democratic activities, and (5) to nurture personal growth.

The historically significant analyses of Bryson, Essert and Hallenbeck are not functional analyses in the technical sense in which these are found in the social science literature. In most of these cases we might better substitute the term 'purposes' for that of 'functions'. Hence, the functions of adult education described are more statements of desired outcomes - favoured aims which the writers concerned feel adult educators should pursue. Even in Hallenbeck's analysis of social conditions, the functions outlined are in no sense descriptive of empirical reality. These personal statements are essentially philosophical charters; prescriptive visions of what purposes adult education might serve. A simple change of preposition - replacing 'of' by 'for' - is a more accurate indication of the nature of these analyses. They are statements of functions 'for' adult education (in the sense of being prescribed purposes) rather than analyses of the functions 'of' adult education (in the sense of being empirical assessments of the contributions made by adult education to the maintenance of the social whole). Elements of strong personal preference are evident in these three contributions. Perhaps the nearest to an empirically based analysis of adult education functions in the American literature is Darkenwald and Merriam's (1982) declaration that "the basic functions of adult education are instruction, counseling, program development, and administration" (p.6). This analysis, however, is set within the context of a discussion of professional roles. It is a role analysis of adult educators' typical tasks, rather than an account of how adult education structures and behaviours contribute to the maintenance of the larger society.

One final point should be made regarding the efforts to conceptualize adult education through functional analysis. Many American writers ascribe to adult education some form of political function, either through adult education assisting adults to make informed, responsible political (primarily electoral) choices, or in terms of participation in adult education classes comprising a training laboratory for democratic activity. Bryson (1936) described the political function of adult education as being the provision of accurate, trustworthy information to citizens and the creation of opportunities for adults to discuss issues of public concern with other citizens. Teachers of adults were urged to inculcate principles of rational scepticism in their students and to urge them "to stand firmly against the winds of doctrine" (p.64). He declared that "a constant and stubborn effort to help those students who work with him to acquire a more alert attitude toward their already accepted and verbalized beliefs, and toward all new things offered them, is the hallmark of a fit teacher for grown men and women" (p.65). As a result of their encouraging an attitude of alert scepticism Bryson warned teachers of adults that they would likely encounter the enmity of political leaders and conventional thinkers. Because rational scepticism served as a corrective to the simplistic solutions and propaganda offered by political leaders, teachers who nurtured such scepticism would open themselves to public opprobrium.

Bryson's colleague at Columbia University, Eduard Lindeman (1926, 1945) believed that adult education was

integral to the democratic struggle and necessary to counter-
act the influence of demagogues. Participation by adults in a
network of neighbourhood discussion groups examining issues
of racial discrimination, the merits of free enterprise and
socialist economic systems, the democratization of educational
facilities, and the role of the United States in world affairs,
would ensure the future of democracy. More recently,
Knowles and Klevins (1982) declare that "adult education is,
or ought to be, a highly political and value laden activity.
When individuals are involved in education they tend to
expand: their awareness of self and environment, their range
of wants and interests, their sense of justice, their need to
participate in decision-making activities, their ability to think
critically and reason rationally, their ability to create
alternative courses of action, and, ultimately, their power or
control over the forces and factors which affect them - this is
political action" (p.16).

CHARACTERISTICS OF AMERICAN ADULT EDUCATION

The range of providing agencies, programmes, settings, institutional forms, client groups and curricular areas identified
as typical by American adult educators is bewilderingly wide
ranging. A review of handbooks on adult education (Ely,
1948; Knowles, 1960; Smith, Aker and Kidd, 1970; Boone,
Shearon, White and Associates, 1980) published decennially by
the chief professional organization in the field (most recently
called the American Association for Adult and Continuing
Education), of foundations texts (Darkenwald and Merriam,
1982; Klevins, 1982; Brookfield, 1986) and of historical or
contemporary reviews of practice (Knowles, 1977; Peterson
and Associates, 1979; Brookfield, 1983; Long, 1987), yields
the following breakdown of distinctive fields of practice and
of major providing agencies:

DISTINCTIVE FIELDS OF ADULT EDUCATION PRACTICE

Adult Basic Education
Labour (Trade Union) Education
Women's Education
Continuing Professional Education
Citizen Education
Parent Education
Leisure Education
Education for the Handicapped
Education for Home and Family Life
Training in Business and Industry
Community Action
Community Education
Educational Brokering

Correctional Education
Armed Forces Education
Health Education
Liberal Education
Intercultural Education
Consumer Education
Education for the Elderly
Human Relations Training
Workers' Education
Adult Religious Education
Community Development
Crafts Education
Educational Counseling

Providing Agencies

Public (State) Schools	Non-Profit Agencies
Community Colleges	Parents' Groups
Universities	Community Organizations
Professional Organizations	Self-Help Groups
The Military	Cooperative Extension
Corporations and Businesses	Prisons
Cultural Institutions	Hospitals
(Libraries/Museums)	The Mass Media
Proprietary Schools	Voluntary Organizations
Community Development Agencies	Free Universities
Labour Unions	

The American Association for Adult and Continuing Education (AAACE), the chief national professional body for adult education in the United States, allows members to affiliate with many of 35 programme units within the organization which they choose. Units are grouped into seven categories: (1) those with interests in theory, research and evaluation, (2) those concerned with one or more special populations or issues (the elderly, the learning disabled, international adult education, social justice and human rights, women's issues and volunteerism), (3) those concerned with particular ocupational and professional groups (business and industry, computer literacy, continuing professional education, human resource development, labour education, religious adult education and vocational or career education), (4) those employed as state directors or administrators of community education programmes, (5) those providing particular services (colleges, universities, cooperative extension service, correctional institutions, educational media and technology, home and family living, and libraries), (6) those interested in what are called 'life skills' programmes (adult basic education, competency based education, bilingual education, community education), and, (7) those in the military (the armed services and veterans associations). As is evident from this list of programme units, those who define themselves as adult educators to the extent that they join the major professional organization in the field work and locate themselves in a very wide range of settings, providing agencies and activities.

Attempts have been made to introduce some classificatory order into this variety of fields, activities and agencies. In his historical survey of adult educational forms and functions Knowles (1977) attempted an inductive derivation of what he called the 'genetic principles' of American adult education. These were that (a) adult education institutions emerge in response to specific needs, (b) adult education develops episodically, (c) adult education programmes survive best when attached to agencies established for other purposes, (d) adult education programmes usually occupy a secondary status within the host institution, (e) adult education programme

15

stability is related to differentiation in administration, finance, curriculum and methodology, and (f) adult education segments crystallize without reference to any conception of a general movement.

Schroeder (1970) established the following fourfold typology of providing agencies:

1. Agencies established primarily to serve the educational needs of adults (for example, proprietary schools, independent residential and non-residential adult education centres, free universities, learning exchanges).

2. Agencies established to serve the educational needs of young people, with an added, secondary function of providing some educational opportunities for adults (for example, public schools, junior colleges, community colleges, universities).

3. Agencies established to serve both educational and non-educational community needs, in which adult education is an allied function undertaken only to serve needs recognized as being beyond the scope of the agency (for example, libraries, museums, health and welfare programmes).

4. Agencies established to serve the needs of special groups in which adult education is subordinate to the furthering of the agency's interests (for example, corporations, labour unions, voluntary associations, government).

Schroeder's typology was further refined and elaborated in his essay on a <u>Typology of Adult Learning Systems</u> (1980). Using a systems theory approach Schroeder defined adult education as "a developmental process used to link various agent and client systems for the purpose of establishing directions and procedures for adult learning programs" (p. 42). Endemic to this process were six major decision points: deciding on educational needs, programme objectives and programme procedures (macro-level decisions) and deciding on learning needs, learning objectives and learning experiences (micro-level decisions). Variables considered by participants in these decisions were agency and clients' values, institutional goals and resources (on the macro-level) and performance standards and capabilities (on the micro-level).

Another tri-dimensional model of adult education has been proposed by Boyd and Apps (1980, pp. 1-13) who argue that three components of adult education practice are the transactional modes of adult education (individual, group and community), the client focus of particular programmes, and the personal, cultural and social systems affecting adult education. These three components are explained as follows:

1. TRANSACTIONAL MODES OF ADULT EDUCATION

Adult learning efforts can be located in one of three mutually exclusive modes of adult educational practice. These are (a) the individual mode, in which adults learn on their own without the assistance of formal education, (b) the group mode, in which groups of people explore some common concern, and (c) the community mode in which adults engage in the collaborative resolution of some community problem.

2. CLIENT FOCUS

The client focus of an adult education programme is, quite simply, the individual (s) or group (s) who will benefit from participation in the activity. The foci most frequently evident are individuals, groups and communities.

3. PERSONAL, SOCIAL AND CULTURAL SYSTEMS

The 'personal' system affecting adult education is the distinctive experiences, abilities, learning styles, cultural background and personality characteristics of the individual learner which affects that person's learning activities. The 'social' system comprises the patterns of interrelated roles played by members of learning groups, the statuses these different individuals hold, and the norms generated by the group. The 'cultural' system is evident in the sets of beliefs, values, rules, principles and customs guiding the conduct of group members.

Carlson (1980) has criticized this model on two counts. Firstly, that it neglects informal, unorganized adult education; that conducted by "peers, poets, propagandists, priests, peddlers, politicians, performers, publishers, pamphleteers, playwrights, publicans and practitioners of the plastic arts" (p.178). The alliterative allure of this sentence should not be allowed to obscure Carlson's basic point; that is, that the Boyd-Apps model applies chiefly to adult education occurring within designated educational institutions. Yet to Carlson, the bulk of adult education is "unorganized, unplanned learning and spontaneous independent adult education" (p.178). Secondly, Carlson feels that the model is primarily adaptive and that it casts the adult educator in the role of salesman or physician, affiliated with an institution whose task it is to foster coping skills for solving problems within the existing power structure.

In their response to Carlson's criticisms, Boyd and Apps (1980) claim that unorganized education is a contradiction in terms, in that a self-defining characteristic of education is that it is planned and purposeful. They declare that "only

17

people who consciously plan for learning are conducting adult education, according to our definition" (p.186). To the criticism that their model of adult education is primarily adaptive and that it leaves existing structures unchallenged, Boyd and Apps maintain that endemic to conceiving education as transactional is the belief that transactional relationships are cooperative and allow for the possibility of change.

Several criticisms of the Boyd-Apps model are advanced by Cookson (1983). He criticises Boyd and Apps for trying to generate a "sui generis" conceptual framework for understanding adult education practice, when a wealth of legitimate contributions have been made to understanding adult education by adapting concepts drawn from other disciplines. He views the notion of transactional modes as vague and points out that there is an ambiguous boundary between the transactional modes and client focus dimensions of the model. He argues that a separate conceptual dimension focusing on client motivations and expectations is unwarranted, given that clients' motivations are so heterogeneous and difficult to discern. He also criticises the conceptualization of personal, social and cultural systems, for being premised on individual motivations within small groups.

The catalogue of criticisms advanced by Carlson and Cookson is formidable and Cookson suggests that the overstatement made by Boyd and Apps for their model is partly responsible for its lack of influence on the theoretical analysis in the field. For example, Boyd and Apps claim that their model demarcates the essential nature and parameters of adult education, that it provides a framework for identifying and organizing problems in adult education, and that through it we can assess the usefulness of theories and concepts drawn from other fields. They also claim that the model accounts for instructional and curriculum development activities, and for the analysis of the different components of educational programmes (Boyd and Apps, 1980, p.13). As Cookson observes, "even if the three dimensional model were adequate in terms of specificity, mutual exclusiveness, and precision, it is doubtful that it - or any other single model - could yield so many significant contributions" (1983, p.52).

Any single act or episode of adult learning is likely to be too complex to be compressed into one or other of the three transactional modes outlined by Boyd and Apps. Indeed, much adult learning will cross the neat delineations of the three modes. Individual learning efforts, for example, will frequently make substantial use of groups as learning resources, will regard intra-group forces as important supports to individual learning, and will be orientated toward community development or community action. Such efforts are demonstrably cross-transactional and cast doubt on the mutual exclusivity of the model's categories. The Boyd-Apps 'model' is not a model in the classic sense; that is, an analytical construct comprised of commonly recurring, empirically observed features and processes which are included owing to their level of generality and abstraction. It is, rather, a classificatory grid or matrix which can be imposed on the complex myriad of adult educational encounters in an attempt to try and understand their interconnections and relationships.

In fact the quest for a classically Aristotelian classificatory schema covering adult education, in which the categories are both mutually exclusive and comprehensive, is probably doomed to failure. Adult educational interactions are multi-layered and multi-faceted, and they belie simply classification. Those seeking to introduce conceptual order into the field might be better advised to concentrate on those features of adult learning which are in some way more observable in adult life than in other periods. Having identified these capacities, and in particular that of critical reflection (Brookfield, 1987), an empirical base exists upon which an elaboration of appropriate practices can be built.

ADULT EDUCATIONAL ROLES

Paralleling the diversity of providing agencies, distinctive areas of practice and client groups observed in American Adult Education is a similar multiplicity of roles. In the analyses of Darkenwald and Merriam (1982) and Knox (1979, 1980) the chief roles of adult educators identified are those of teachers (frequently called instructors), programme developers, administrators and counselors. To educators who locate themselves within a business and industrial context (Nadler, 1979, 1984; Du Bois, 1982), the roles of trainer and human resource developer are most important. A major emphasis within the field is placed on the role of the adult educator as a facilitator of learning (Knowles 1980, 1984; Brockett, 1983; Brookfield, 1986). To those who locate the practice of adult education within a context of community education, development and action, the roles of change agent (Alinsky, 1971) and animateur (Kidd, 1971) are crucial. Some brief elaboration of the components of these roles is necessary if the range of subject areas and methods evident in American graduate adult education programmes are to be fully understood. For clarity, these roles are grouped into four categories; teaching roles, programme developmental roles, training and human resource developmental roles and community action roles.

(1) TEACHING, FACILITATION AND INSTRUCTION

The concept of teaching, in the United States, has fallen out of favour, at least where the education of adults is concerned. The reason for this may be the association made by most people between the act of teaching and education within schools. 'Teaching' is a term which conjures up images of elementary and secondary schooling in which figures of authority espouse their views in front of serried rows of dutiful pupils. This Norman Rockwell vision of school life is as far removed from what happens within many public schools as can be imagined, yet to many adult educators 'teaching' according to this image is what happens in schools. Facilitation or instruction, on the other hand, is what happens with adults. In reality, however, the majority of practitioners in fields such as adult basic education, public school adult education, community college education, university education and continuing education are performing teacher roles. Specifications of exemplary performance of the teaching role, and qualities of exemplary teachers can be found in Heath (1980), Apps (1981) and Draves (1984).

Within the generic role of teacher several alternative conceptions of teaching can be distinguished (Brookfield, 1987); the teacher as artist, the teacher as facilitator and the teacher as critical analyst. Teachers as artists develop creative, improvisational responses to person and context specific situations. In the teacher as artist conception the qualities of creativity, innovation, improvisation and sensitivity are paramount (Lenz, 1982). Teachers as facilitators see themselves as resource persons and enablers of learning who are in helping relationships with learners. At the basis of these relationships is assisting learners to attain goals set by the learners themselves. In the teacher as facilitator conception the qualities of empathy, supportiveness, caring and nurturing are emphasized (Tough, 1979; Brundage and Mackeracher, 1980; Brockett, 1983). Teachers as critical analysts are concerned to place before learners alternatives to their current ways of thinking and living, to point up contradictions in personal, community and social life, and to prompt a critical scrutiny of learners' value frameworks and the assumptions they have uncritically assimilated. In the teacher as critical analyst conception the purpose of teaching is to bring adults to the realization that the world is malleable; that assumptions, beliefs and values about one's personal and social worlds are culturally created rather than divinely ordained (Shor, 1980; Mezirow, 1981; Brookfield, 1987).

The concept of instructional roles rather than teaching roles is emphasized in many graduate programmes, particularly those where a management-style orientation to adult education is apparent. Eisner (1985) links the popularity of this approach to the preeminence in the earlier part of this century of modes of practice focused on technical rationality in industry and on prediction and control of training outcomes in the military. As Giroux (1983) notes, "the technological and behaviorist models that have long exercised a powerful influence on the curriculum were, in part, adapted from the scientific-management movement of the 1920's" (p. 44). In this orientation the purpose of educational encounters becomes to take learners through a series of activities sequenced according to their progressive levels of complexity. Success is evident when learners have attained the pre-defined objectives which were established at the outset (Dickinson, 1979). In reviews of the research literature on instructor effectiveness, Pratt (1981) has deplored the simplistic search for common exemplary charac- teristics which all instructors should possess. The emphasis on the adult educator as instructor is strong, however, particularly in those departments of graduate adult education where the influence of Ralph Tyler (1949) holds sway.

(2) PROGRAMME DEVELOPMENT

In terms of employment possibilities for graduates of adult education programmes in the United States, being employed in some form of programme development is the most likely outcome of their having attained a graduate degree in the field. As a result, courses in programme development are among those most frequently featured in the curricula of graduate adult education. The texts typically used in such courses (Houle, 1972; Knox and Associates, 1980; Boyle, 1981) include within the programme developmental role a wide range of functions including conducting needs assessments (qualitative and quantitative), managing committees, developing curricula, designing instruction, counseling current and potential learners, preparing and administering budgets, marketing courses, developing staff, evaluating programme effectiveness and conducting public relations activities. Courses in programme development concentrate on developing all these capacities in students.

(3) TRAINING AND HUMAN RESOURCE DEVELOPMENT

Concepts of training and human resource development are familiar within American adult education. In various analyses of adult education within business and industry, Nadler (1978, 1984) has distinguished between training (preparing workers for specific current jobs), education (preparing workers for future jobs), and development (encouraging workers to explore non job-related activities). Human resource development is defined as "a series of organized activities, conducted within a specified time, designed to produce behavioral change" (Nadler, 1979, p.3). Du Bois (1982) views the human resource developer working within

21

business and industrial organizations as something close to an improved version of an adult educator. He writes that "the emerging role of the human resource developer encompasses much more than that of the traditional adult educator. This professional is a new professional on the educational scene; an adult educator with new and more expansive expertise, cognizant of the dynamics of human behavior and the workings of the organization" (p.376).

Nadler (1979) breaks the role of human resource developer into three sub-sets: (1) being a learning specialist involved in instruction, curriculum development, developing materials, designing methods and developing staff, (2) being an administrator involved in personnel development, super-vision, improving community relations, and budgeting, and (3) being a consultant involved in changing organizational behaviours, stimulating others to learn, and advocating un-popular or little known views. In a task analysis of the activities of 125 human resource developers in business Shipp (1985) identified programme development (especially needs assessment), budgeting, report writing and dissemination, evaluation, supervision, planning organizational change, managing information and forecasting future manpower needs as the chief activities of these professionals.

(4) COMMUNITY EDUCATION

The community dimension to adult education activities has long been recognized by American adult educators. Indeed, the American Association for Adult Education (established in 1926) and its successor organization, the Adult Education Association of the United States (established in 1953), were both imbued from the outset with a strong sense of community service. Fundamental to good practice as conceived in these organizations' mission statements was the need for adult education to contribute to community problem-solving, com-munity development and the building of democratic habits of community participation (Pell, 1953; Herring, 1953; Hallenbeck, Verner, London and Bergevin, 1962). Operation-ally, many providing agencies have traditionally described themselves as departments, programmes or centres of adult and community education. Local professional organizations are often titled associations of adult and community education. At times, in fact, the word 'adult' is dropped, and adult edu-cation programmes are simply subsumed under the general rubric of 'community education'. In analyses of community education practice in the United States, (Seay, 1979; Warden, 1979; Minzey and Le Tarte, 1979; Williams and Robins, 1980; Kerensky, 1981) the emphasis is placed firmly on neighbour-hood schools opening their doors to the adult population in the evenings and at weekends, to become educational centres serving all community residents.

A number of roles are identified within the literature of community adult education, such as activators, animateurs, change agents, and community activists. Community activators (Hiemstra, 1985) concentrate on alerting persons and agencies not defined as being primarily involved in education (such as banks, the media, trade unions) to the adult educational possibilities inherent in their activities. Having alerted these persons and agencies, activators suggest specific ways in which they could add an adult educational dimension to their efforts. Animateurs (Blondin, 1971; Kidd, 1971) intervene in communities to assist community groups to achieve commonly defined goals. They help develop people's skills of community action, they nurture a sense of cohesion among group members, and they help people locate relevant resources (human and material) in the community. The overall aim is "to achieve self-determination in a group of people, so that it becomes autonomous; that is, freed from its besetting automatisms and determinisms. Autonomy means the ability to make decisions and choices freely and to take the consequences" (Blondin, 1971, p. 160). Hence, "the process of animation gives rise to a process of self-education, the essence of which is a heightening of the capacity for self-determination" (ibid).

Animateurs and change agents in community settings draw on Alinsky's (1971) concept of the revolutionary organizer in which the organizer's responsibility to the members of his or her community is to "shake up the prevailing patterns of their lives - agitate, create disenchantment and discontent with the current values, to produce, if not a passion for change, at least a passive, affirmative, non-challenging climate" (p. xxi). In the United States, the activities of the Highlander Folk School (Adams, 1975; Clark, 1978; Lovett, 1980; Kennedy, 1981; Gaventa and Horton, 1981) have inspired many adults educators to place their practice within a context of community action and community change. At Highlander, generations of adult educators have been encouraged to work with emerging social movements (such as the civil rights movement, or the ecology movement) who are committed to democratic participation and decision-making. Educators have the responsibility "to help people deal collectively with community and workplace problems which reflect the maldistribution of power in society" (Highlander Research and Education Center, 1980, p.4).

CONCLUSION

As is evident from this introductory review of prevailing conceptualizations of adult education, the range of providing

23

agencies, and the varying orientations evident towards defining the role of adult educators, the field of adult education in the United States is characterized by a paradigmatic plurality. Indeed, adult education as a body of knowledge, theory or research can itself be thought of as multi-paradigmatic or, perhaps even more accurately, as pre-paradigmatic. No agreement exists on a central body of research insights, theoretical tenets or philosophical axioms. This means that, depending on the agency or practitioner concerned, adult education can be defined as an effort in collective consciousness raising, a means by which workers can be 're-tooled' to help the American economy become more competitive, or a way of assisting people in their personal spiritual development. The most well known and influential theorists and researchers in the field (Malcolm Knowles, Paulo Freire, Cyril Houle) and the writers from whom they draw most strongly (Eduard Lindeman, Carl Rogers, Karl Marx, Erich Fromm, Ralph Tyler) operate according to directly antithetical assumptions about the purpose of education and the nature of the wider society within which educational activities are grounded.

The organization of graduate programmes of adult education reflect this paradigmatic plurality as much as do the research journals and the most influential texts in the field. In any one faculty group there will probably be those who regard themselves as confirmed behaviourists, andragogues, humanistic psychotherapists and those who see adult education as the conscientization of the oppressed. Weaver and Kowalski (1987) note that programmes differ greatly according to the extent to which they are dominated by professors espousing training and human resource development as the chief area of adult education practice, and those insisting that adult education be retained within departments and schools of professional education. These competing paradigms, not surprisingly, give rise to a certain amount of conceptual and curricular confusion. In a recent survey of adult education syllabi, for example, Cross (1985) noted that "while there is modest agreement on course titles, there is little consensus on what constitutes a basic reading list for graduate students preparing for careers in adult and continuing education" (p.1). This should not necesarily be regarded as a sign of professional immaturity where the practice of adult education is concerned. Given the diversity of settings and agencies involved in helping adults learn in the United States, and the contrasting purposes towards which these efforts are directed, it is no surprise to find such paradigmatic plurality. Indeed, in a pluralistic society such as the United States, in which no one centralized statutory governing or providing adult education body exists, such conceptual and curricular confusion may well be a professional given in the field.

REFERENCES

Alinsky, S.D. (1971) Rules for Radicals, Random House, New York.

Adams, F. (1975) Unearthing Seeds of Fire, John F. Blair Publishers, Winston-Salem, North Carolina.

Apps, J.W. (1981) The Adult Learner on Campus, Cambridge Books, New York.

Blondin, M. (1971) "Animation Sociale." in J.A. Draper (ed.), Citizen Participation: Canada, New Press, Toronto.

Boon, E.J., Shearon, R.W., White, E.E. and Associates (1980) Serving Personal and Community Needs Through Adult Education, Jossey-Bass, San Francisco.

Boyle, P.G. (1981) Planning Better Programs, McGraw Hill, New York.

Boyd, R.D., Apps, J.W. and Associates (1980) Redefining the Discipline of Adult Education, Jossey-Bass, San Francisco.

Brockett, R. (1983) "Facilitator Roles and Skills." Lifelong Learning, 6 (5), 7-9.

Brookfield, S.D. (1983) Adult Learners, Adult Education and the Community, Open University Press, Milton Keynes, (Published in the United States by Jossey-Bass Publishers).

Brookfield S.D. (1986) Understanding and Facilitating Adult Learning, Open University Press, Milton Keynes, (Published in the United States by Jossey-Bass Publishers).

Brookfield, S.D. (1987) Developing Critical Thinkers, Open University Press, Milton Keynes, (Published in the United States by Jossey-Bass Publishers).

Brookfield, S.D. (1988). "Teacher Roles and Teacher Styles." in C.J. Titmus and J.R. Kidd (eds.). Lifelong Education for Adults. Pergamon, Oxford

Brundage, D.H. and Mackeracher, D. (1980) Adult Learning Principles and Their Application to Program Planning. Ministry of Education Ontario, Toronto.

Bryson, L. (1936) Adult Education. American Book Company, New York.

Campbell, D.D. (1977) Adult Education as a Field of Study and Practice: Strategies for Development. Center for Continuing Education, University of British Columbia Vancouver.

Carlson, R.A. (1980) "The Foundations of the Boyd-Apps Model." in R.D. Boyd, J.W. Apps and Associates. Redefining the Discipline of Adult Education. Jossey-Bass, San Francisco.

Clark, M. (1978) "Meeting the Needs of the Adult Learner: Using Nonformal Education for Social Action." Convergence, 11 (2), 44-53.

Cookson, P. (1983) "Boyd and Apps Conceptual Model of Adult Education: A Critical Examination." Adult Education, 34 (1), 48-53.

Cross, K.P. (1985) "Adult/Continuing Education." Unpublished paper, Graduate School of Education, Harvard University, Boston.

Darkenwald, G. and Merriam S.B. (1982) Adult Education: Foundations of Practice. Harper and Row, New York.

Dickinson, G. (1979) Teaching Adults. Don Mills, General Publishing, Ontario.

Draves, W.A. (1984) How to Teach Adults. Learning Resources Network, Manhattan, Kansas.

Du Bois, E.E. (1982) "Human Resource Development: Expanding Role." in C. Klevins (ed.). Materials and Methods in Adult and Continuing Education. Klevens Publications, Canoga Park, California.

Eisner, E.W. (1985) The Educational Imagination. Macmillan, New York.

Ely, M.L. (ed.) (1948) Handbook of Adult Education in the United States. Center for Adult Education, Teachers College, New York.

Essert, P.L. (1951) Creative Leadership of Adult Education. Prentice Hall, New York.

Gaventa, J. and Horton, B.D. (1981) "A Citizen's Research Project in Appalachia, USA." Convergence, 14 (2), 30-42.

Giroux, H.A. (1983) Theory and Resistance in Education. Bergin and Garvey, South Hadley, Massachussetts.

Hallenbeck, W.C. (1960) "The Function and Place of Adult Education in American Society." in M.S. Knowles (ed.). Handbook of Adult Education in the United States. Adult Education Association of the United States, Chicago.

Hallenbeck, W.C., Verner, C., London, J. and Bergevin, P. (1962) Community and Adult Education. Adult Education Association of the United States, Washington D.C.

Heath, L.L. (1980) "Role Models of Successful Teachers of Adults." in A.B. Knox (ed.). Teaching Adults Effectively. San Francisco, Jossey-Bass.

Herring, J.W. (1953) "Adult Education: Senior Partner to Democracy." Adult Education, 3 (2), 53-59.

Hiemstra, R. (1985) The Educative Community. Hi Tree Press Baldwinsville, New York.

Highlander Research and Education Center. (1980) Highlander Reports: October 1980. Highlander Research and Education Center, New Market, Tennessee.

Houle, C.O. (1972) The Design of Education. Jossey-Bass, San Francisco.

Kennedy, W.B. (1981) Highlander Praxis: Learning With Myles Horton." Teachers College Record, 83 (3), 105-119.

Kerensky, V.M. (1981) "Ten Educational Myths: A Community Educator's Perspective." Community Education Journal, 8 (2), 9-13.

Kidd, J.R. (1971) "Adult Education, the Community and the Animateur." in J.A. Draper (ed.). Citizen Participation: Canada. New Press, Toronto.

Klevins, C. (ed.) (1982) Materials and Methods in Adult and Continuing Education. Klevens Publications, Canoga Park, California.

Knowles, M.S. (ed.) (1960) Handbook of Adult Education in the United States. Adult Education of the United States, Chicago.

Knowles, M.S. (1977) A History of the Adult Education Movement in the United States. Robert Krieger Publishers, Malabar, Florida.

Knowles, M.S. (1980) The Modern Practice of Adult Education. Cambridge Books, New York.

Knowles, M.S. and Associates. (1984). Andragogy in Action. Jossey-Bass, San Francisco.

Knowles, M.S. and Klevins, C. (1982) "Historical and Philosophical Perspectives." in C. Klevins (ed.). Materials and Methods in Adult and Continuing Education. Klevens Publications, Canoga Park, California.

Knox, A.B. (1979) Enhancing Proficiencies of Continuing Educators. Jossey-Bass, San Francisco.

Knox, A.B. and Associates (1980) Developing, Administering, and Evaluating Adult Education. Jossey-Bass, San Francisco,

Lenz, E. (1982) The Art of Teaching Adults. Rinehart and Winston, New York, Holt.

Lindeman, E.C. (1926) The Meaning of Adult Education. New Republic, New York.

Lindeman, E.C. (1945) "World Peach Through Adult Education." The Nation's Schools, 35 (3), 23.

Liveright, A.A. and Haygood, D. (eds.) (1964) The Exeter Papers. Boston University Center for the Study of Liberal Education for Adults, Boston.

Long, H.B. (1987) New Perspectives on the Education of Adults in the United States. Croom Helm, London.

Lovett, T. (1980) "Adult Education and Community Action." in, J. Thompson (ed.). Adult Education For a Change. Hutchinson, London.

Mezirow, J. (1981) "A Critical Theory of Adult Learning and Education." Adult Education, 32 (1), 3-27.

Minzey, J.D. and Le Tarte, C. (1979) Community Education: From Program to Process to Practice. Pendell, Midland, Michigan.

Nadler, L. (1979) Developing Human Resources. Learning Concepts Ltd., Austin, Texas.

Nadler, L. (ed.). (1984) The Handbook of Human Resource Development. Wiley, New York.

Pell, O.A.H. (1953) "Social Philosophy at the Grass Roots." Adult Education, 2 (4), 123-137.

Peterson, R.E. and Associates (1979) Lifelong Learning in America: An Overview of Current Practices, Available Resources, and Future Prospects. Jossey-Bass, San Francisco.

Pratt, D.D. (1981) "Teacher Effectiveness - Future Directions for Adult Education." Studies in Adult Education, 13 (2), 112-119.

Seay, M.F. and Associates (1979) Community Education: A Developing Concept. Pendell, Midland, Michigan.

Shipp, T.R. (1985) "The HRD Professional: A Macromotion Study." in Lifelong Learning Research Conference Proceedings. Department of Agriculture and extension Education. University of Maryland, No. 6. College Park, Maryland.

Shor, I. (1980) Critical Teaching and Everyday Life. South End Press, Boston.

Schroeder, W.L. (1970) "Adult Education Defined and Described." in R.M. Smith, G.A. Aker and J.R. Kedd (eds.). Handbook of Adult Education in the United States. Macmillan, New York.

Schroeder, W.L. (1980) "Typology of Adult Learning Systems." in J.M. Peters and Associates. Building an Effective Adult Education Enterprise. Jossey-Bass, San Francisco.

Schwertman, J.B. (1955) "What is Adult Education?" Adult Education, 5 (3), 131-145.

Smith, R.M., Aker, G.F. and Kidd, J.R. (eds.) (1970) Handbook of Adult Education in the United States. Macmillan, New York.

Sworder, S. (1955) "What is Adult Education?" Adult Education, 5 (3), 131-145.

Tough, A.M. (1979) The Adult's Learning Projects. Learning Concepts Ltd., Austin, Texas.

Tyler, R.W. (1949) Basic Principles of Curriculum and Instruction. University of Chicago Press, Chicago.

Verduin, J.R., Miller, H.G. and Greer, C.E. (1977) Adults Teaching Adults: Principles and Strategies. Learning Concepts Inc., Austin, Texas.

Verner, C. (1964) "Definition of Terms." in G. Jensen, A.A. Liveright, and W.C. Hallenbeck (eds.). Adult Education: Outlines of an Emerging Field of University Study. Adult Education Association of the United States, Washington D.C.

Warden, J.W. (1979) Process Perspectives: Community Education as Process. Mid-Atlantic Community Education Consortium, Charlottesville.

Williams, W. and Robins, W.R (1980) "Observations on the Californian Case." in C. Fletcher and N. Thompson (eds.) Issues in Community Education. Falmer Press, Lewes, Sussex.

Chapter Two

TRAINING ADULT EDUCATORS IN NORTH AMERICA

Sharan Merriam (1985)

NATURE OF THE FIELD

Organized adult education activities can be traced back to colonial experience in the United States and Canada, but the awareness of adult education as a field of professional practice usually is dated with the founding of the American Association for Adult Education in 1926. By then, the characteristics of adult education, some of which are peculiarly American, and all of which affect professional practice, had become firmly established. Long (1983) discusses five characteristics that capture, to some extent, the nature of adult education in the United States. Historically, adult education has been (i) creative in meeting the needs of its clientele, (ii) pragmatic in that most adult learners participate for some specific reason and wish to immediately apply new knowledge or skills, (iii) voluntary, that is directly dependent upon an adult's free choice to enroll and continue in a learning experience, (iv) pluralistic in the audiences served, in the delivery systems of adult education, and in the philosophical orientations, and (v) dynamic, for adult education responds to change by developing innovative practices.

The dynamic and creative responsiveness of the field has lead to the pluralism or diversity that is both a strength and a limitation. The plethora of institutions and agencies, programs and settings in adult education offer a range of opportunities for adults to continue to learn not found in most other parts of the world.

On the other hand, such diversity seems to preclude any single, unified approach to the preparation of those working in adult education. It is even difficult to estimate how many people work in adult education. An informal survey estimated that 'perhaps a half million persons - probably more if one counts all the part-time people - work with adult learners' (Wilson, 1984). The ten areas surveyed included business and industry, professors of adult education, adult basic education teachers, cooperative extension, colleges and universities, community colleges, public schools, trade and technical schools, community based groups, and recreation and parks.

An even bigger problem is the range of philosophical orientations that coexist under the rubric of adult education. On one end of the continuum one can employ adult education to change oppressive social conditions as Paulo Freire and others espouse, or, one can focus on individual development without attending to social issues. Boshier's model (this issue) proposes four 'outcomes' or philosophical orientations that create a need for adult education. Numerous programs exemplifying each of these outcomes - social integration, social responsibility, social change, and technical competency - can be found in the United States and Canada. In Canada, the Frontier College labourer-teacher model is a good example of education designed to foster social integration, whereas the Antigonish movement in Nova Scotia sought social change, and the vocational institutes engender technical competence.

Who Are the Adult Educators?

The nature of adult education has resulted in a situation where even the full-time leadership - the apex of Houle's (1970) pyramid discussed by Boshier (1985) lack a professional identity. Twenty years ago, Liveright (1964) described adult education leaders as follows.

1. Few of them have participated in an organized program of graduate study in adult education or hold advanced degrees therein.
2. Most come from other occupations and have moved into adult education after other kinds of employment.
3. Many look upon adult education as a stepping stone rather than as a permanent career.
4. During the past ten years many have moved from adult education to other posts in the educational or community field-many to other administrative posts in education.
5. Their conceptions of the ideal adult educator and of competencies required for the professional adult educator vary widely.
6. Many are oriented to action rather than to research; few have made major research contributions to the field.
7. Many are concerned about their status and position as adult educators and do not feel completely identified with the field; if they do so, they feel themselves second-rate citizens in the academic hierarchy.
8. There is as yet no clearly defined set of values or ethics subscribed to by all.

TRAINING ADULT EDUCATORS IN NORTH AMERICA

Little appears to have changed when one looks at the results of a 1983 survey of adult educators conducted by the Learning Resources Network (LERN) in the United States. 'The typical practicing adult educator,' it found, 'is new to the position, has little or no course work in adult education, comes from a field outside of adult education and is likely to leave it in five years, and works very hard' (Hartman, 1983-84). Calling adult education, 'a come-and-go profession', Hartman observed that most practicing adult educators are largely untrained for the field in which they are working. Liveright's observations and the results of the LERN survey bring to the surface several issues which confound a systematic approach to the training of adult educators. Three issues concern the lack of a collective identity, career structure, and evidence that training makes a difference in performance.

ISSUES IN PREPARING ADULT EDUCATORS

The lack of a common identity among adult educators hinders the development of the field as well as the establishment of even tentative guidelines for professional preparation. Most American adult educators identify themselves with some entity other than the profession itself. Many administrators, for example, join organizations that represent their employing institution, such as library, hospital, or university extension division, rather than their national or local adult education association. Those who fill an instructional role in adult education often identify with the content area of their institution, or with the clintele who they teach. Others group together on the basis of the medium they employ, such as educational television or correspondence study organizations. Without a common identificaiton as adult educators, many are likely to lack the incentive to be trained as adult educators.

A second issue is the lack of a career structure within the field. Nowhere is this more obvious that in the above-mentioned LERN survey of professional development. Most of the respondents held degrees in fields other than education, fewer than one third had worked professionally in adult education prior to their present job, most expected to stay in adult education less than five years, and most anticipated their next job to be outside adult education. 'One educator speculated that there is nowhere up to go, so advancement can only come by going outside of adult education' (Hartman, 1983-84). Without a defined career structure, it is difficult to determine what knowledge, skills, or competencies a person needs to prepare for a career in adult education.

A third problem is the lack of evidence that training makes a difference. Griffith (1983) observed that:
'Today we have over 200 professors of adult education.

We have over 2,038 people with doctorates in the field of adult education, scattered all over the world. The cold, hard facts are that we don't have any empirical evidence that people who have been trained academically in the field of adult education do any better in carrying out the roles of adult educators than those who have not been professionally trained.'

The LERN survey also found 'the general trend' in written responses to a question on formal preparation to be that 'academic study had little effect on one's ability to work in the field.' This question plagues other professions as well. Training may very well make a difference but until we have evidence to that effect, it will be difficult to convince some practitioners of the need for formal preparation.

A trained cadre of adult educators would have a common identity, might well delineate appropriate career patterns, and could make a measurable difference in the practice of adult education. This argument leads into a discussion of the professionalism of the field. Boshier identifies the heart of the issue as being how to recruit and train personnel and avoid the undesirable aspects of professionalism. While it is not within the scope of this article to debate the benefits and perils of professionalization, some aspects of the debate have a bearing on the preparation of people to be adult educators and trainers. In order for adult education to be visible as an emerging profession or as an 'occupation in the process of becoming more professionalized' (Darkenwald & Merriam, 1983), those in the field must share common knowledge and possess 'a certain minimal vision' (Griffith, 1983). Cervero (1982) identified three goals that an occupational group such as adult educators could seek in becoming more professsional:

1. Develop a common understanding of the function, values, and philosophies of the field and continually discuss and review these.
2. Develop an understanding and ability to use the knowledge base of adult education to solve the practical problems in our work.
3. Develop a collective identity with other adult educators.

These three goals could be met through pre-service and in-service trianing. Achieving these goals would bring some coherence to the field while avoiding the regulatory and exclusionary aspects of professionalism.

WHAT TRAINING, FOR WHOM?

The training of adult educators in North America is based upon several assumptions. First, it is assumed that a trained person performs more effectively than one who has had no training. As noted earlier, there is no empirical evidence that this is so, at least with respect to academic preparation. If training is broadly conceived to include on-the-job experience, apprenticeship/mentor relationships, and short-term skill development activities, then most practitioners would agree that 'training' enhances performance. A second assumption is that a body of knowledge about adult education exists that can be conveyed through training. This unique body of knowledge concerns the history and philosophy of adult education, adult learning patterns, instructional techniques for adults, and program planning in adult education. A third assumption is that appropriate mechanisms can be developed and levels of competency established in training people to work in the field. Such processes and levels are beginning to emerge as differentiations among short-term training needs, undergraduate, master's and doctoral level preparation.

Boshier's model (1985) is particularly helpful in clarifying the training enterprise. It suggests that the content and process of training depends upon one's role in the field, whether it is primary or secondary, and what outcomes are being sought. More about how this model applies to the training situation in North America will be discussed shortly.

Analysis of Training Needs

Assumptions that underlie the preparation of adult educators have stimulated efforts by several writers to delineate who should be trained and what competencies should be obtained through training. Most identify specific competencies for specific roles and settings in adult education. There are desirable competencies for teachers, administrators, counselors, industrial trainers, professors, and so on. In reviewing these studies, Grabowski (1976) was able to extract ten competencies. Competent adult educators should:

understand and take into account the motivation and participation patterns of adult learners;
understand and provide for the needs of adult learners;
be versed in the theory and practice of adult learners;
know the community and its needs;
know how to use various methods and techniques of instruction;
possess communication and listening skills;
know how to locate and use education materials;
have open minds and allow adults to pursue their own interests;
continue their own education;
be able to evaluate and appraise a program.

One of the most thorough analyses of training needs of adult educators was presented in Knox's (1979) monograph, 'Enhancing Proficiencies of Continuing Educators'. He preferred the concept of proficiency over competency because proficiency means being capable of performing well in a situation and 'links understanding and performance,' whereas competency implies some minimum standard. For all practitioners in continuing education, Knox proposes three 'core' proficiencies.

The first proficiency is an understanding of the field of continuing education. This involved knowledge of the variety of agencies and institutions offering continuing education opportunities, particularly knowledge of the organization for which one works; an understanding of societal trends and issues that invariably have an impact upon adult education; and an awareness of resources such as literature, people, organizations, that might be useful to practice.

A second core proficiency requires an understanding of adult development and learning. As Knox noted, 'The coherence of the field stems from the common function of helping adults learn.' Thus the understanding of adults as learners is of critical importance, including understanding the adult life cycle and how it relates to participation and motivation in adult education. A recent study of adult learners, for example, found that 83% engage in learning activities because of some change in their lives (Aslanian & Bricknell, 1980). 'To know an adult's life cycle,' the authors concluded, 'is to know an adult's learning schedule.' Knowledge of how people learn and the dynamics of a learning environment is also important.

The third core proficiency involves personal qualities and effectiveness in relationships with others, and an approach to practice that is innovative and creative.

Primary Roles and Functions

As with most training models, Knox looks additionally at the needs of the field through its primary roles and functions. Most full-time continuing educators are administrators who come from diverse backgrounds. Areas of proficiency important for administrators in particular are the art and science of administration, program development and familiarity with research as either producer or consumer. Those in counsellor or teacher roles, most of whom work part-time, typically receive less training than administrators, even though they are in closest contact with the adults that the field purports to serve. For teachers, counsellors and other resource persons, two areas of proficiency are important: knowledge of subject matter and the process of helping adults learn. As Knox states, such persons 'are knowledgeable and use their expertise to take the content into account throughout the process; but they must combine this expertise with an under-standing of adult learners and of effective instructional procedures.'

The third role is that of policy-maker. Many people, in and out of agencies and organizations, make decisions and policies that affect continuing educators. Most policy-makers are either administrators in the parent organization, board members, government and foundation administrators, legis-lators, or leaders of associations and community organizations. Policy-makers are having an increasing impact and, thus, an adequate knowledge of desirable direction for agency development is a necessary proficiency - in addition to the core proficiencies.

In summary, the training of North American adult edu-cators is based upon the assumptions that trained personnel are more effective than untrained, that a body of knowledge about adult education exists that can be shared, and that training processes and needs can be identified. Most of the needs are specific to one's role in the field, although some writers have delineated generic competencies and proficiencies as well

HOW TRAINING OCCURS

Most training of adult educators is unsystematic and episodic, as discussed earlier. The reasons include the fact many persons involved in the education of adults identify them-selves with the institution for which they work or with their content area. Closely related is the fact that adult education, although pervasive throughout North American society, is not a highly visible field with its own separate identity. There is a lack of discernible career patterns. One may become employed, and assume leadership in the field, with little or no preparation. Training is, nevertheless, occurring, and at least in several areas, substantially increasing.

Boshier's model (1985) provides a good reference point for discussion. The amount, nature, and type of training that someone is likely to receive depends upon whether the person is a planner or teacher, whether adult education is a primary or secondary concern, and whether one is involved in edu-cation designed to foster social responsibility, social integration, social change, or technical competence. A teacher of English as a Second Language, for example, is likely to be part-time and striving to develop students' language ability to allow them to become socially integrated. The training of this teacher is likely to be limited to on-the-job experience or short-term workshops organized by the employer. An admin-istrator of a public school adult education program, on the other hand, is probably full-time, interested in several 'outcomes,' and may be engaged in graduate study in adult education.

Thus, from Boshier's grid several forms of training emerge that are characteristic of North American adult education. Training can occur through experience in the field, through short-term, in-service opportunities, and through graduate study.

Most observers of training in adult education would have to cite on-the-job experience as the major means through which practitioners become 'competent' or 'proficient.' As many have noted, most enter adult education through a 'back door' from some other field, role, or agency. Once in a continuing education or training position much needs to be learned quickly. Proficiency in the role thus develops through trial-and-error, through modelling another's behaviour, through consulting with colleagues and co-workers, and through self-directed study. Self-directed study is, of course, appropriate for those involved in a field that strives to assist adults in their own learning. In self-directed study an individual may take advantage of learning packages, competency-based materials, consultation with experts, audio-visual resources, field visits, and so on.

A second major way that the training of trainers and adult educators occurs is through short-term, in-service activities. This is particularly the case for the large cadre of volunteers and part-time people. In-service training activities typically are sponsored by the employing institution or agency, professional associations, resource centers, colleges and universities, and private consultants. They are short-term, seek to achieve specific goals which are usually job-related or situation-specific, and may offer Continuing Education Units or other credit.

In a discussion of the training of paraprofessional adult educators, Yerka (1981) reviewed the model found in most settings that employ paraprofessionals. This model, which consists of orientation, core and in-service components, also applies to the training of volunteers and part-time adult educators. Orientation training seeks to acquaint the trainee with the work situation, and work expectations. Core training focuses on the 'development of basic functional skills needed to perform a job.' In-service education is synonymous with on-the-job training and is 'considered an extension of the core,' or, 'involved training in the specific requirements of a job.'

Given the wide variety of delivery systems for short-term training activities, it would be virtually impossible to estimate what percent and to what degree adult educators receive training in this manner. One can speculate that it is through these short-term activities that the bulk of formal training occurs in North America. It is certainly greater than training conducted through graduate degree programs, the third means of preparing trainers and educators. The relative prevalence of training through short-term activity versus credit coursework can only be viewed indirectly. A national assessment of adult basic education, English as a Second Language and General Equivalency Diploma programs in the 50 American states and the District of Columbia, for example, found that 30% of the teachers had engaged in credit coursework, while 75% had participated in in-sevice staff development activities related to adult education (Development Associates, 1980).

Graduate degree programs in adult education are the third mechanism by which persons prepare for or become trained in adult education. Since the first doctorate was awarded in 1935 by Columbia University, this area of training has grown substantially. Now at least 80 institutions, including several in Canada, offer degrees in adult and continuing education. Most students are employed full-time in adult education and most, at the doctoral level at least, as administrators and have worked in the field prior to enrolling in a graduate program (Ingham & Hanks, 1981). 'Unlike agency activities and self-directed study,' Knox (1979) wrote, 'graduate programs tend to emphasize exposure to concepts and procedures from throughout the field of continuing education and from related fields and scholarly disciplines that can broaden the perspective and enrich the performance of practitioners.'

A typical graduate program consists of three types of core courses: adult learning, organization of the field, and program development and administration; research courses; and special courses in related areas. As with other forms of training, numerous issues with regard to graduate training have yet to be resolved. These include identifying the knowledge base unique to adult education, differentiating between a master's degree and a doctoral degree (and more recently an undergraduate degree), determining the best combination of theory and practice and of basic and applied research, determining what preparation professors in these programs should have, and establishing autonomy and identity as a field of study both within and outside the university.

THE PERSPECTIVE IN SUMMARY

To capture in a short overview the nature of training of trainers and adult educators in North America is a bit like trying to explain the nature of gravity or the concept of love. Such phenomena are pervasive and elusive, simple and complex. This article has attempted to describe the preparation of adult educators from the perspective of issues and problems. The dynamic and pluralistic nature of the field, with its numerous philosophical orientations, gives rise to issues and problems that pervade the training enterprise. Three issues - lack of a collective identity, lack of a definite career structure, and lack of evidence that preparation makes a difference - were explored in terms of the larger issue of professionalization. The final section presented an overview of three major forms of training: on-the-job experience; short-term, structured learning activities; and graduate degree programs.

REFERENCES

Aslanian, C.B., and Brickell, H.M. (1980) Americans in Transition: Life Changes as a Reasons for Adult learning. Future Directions for a Learning Society, College Entrance Examination Board, New York.

Boshier, R. (1985) A Conceptual Framework for Analyzing the Training of Trainers and Adult Educators. Convergence, Conveyances. Vol 18, Nos 3-4.

Cervero, R. (1982) The Predicament of Becoming a Professional. Speech given at the Northern Area Adult Education Service Center Fall Conference, October. Available from the author, Adult Education Department, University of Genjia, Atheus, Seugic, U.S.A.

Darkwnwald, G. & Merriam, S. (1982) Adult Education: Foundations of Practice. Harper and Row, New York.

Development Associates, Inc. (1980) An Assessment of the State-Administered Programme of the Adult Education Act, Final Report. Office of Program Evaluation, Department of Education, Washington, D.C.

Gradowski, S. (1976) Training Teachers of Adults: Models and Innovative Programs. National Association for Public Continuing and Adult Education, and ERIC Clearing house in Career Education, Syracuse, New York.

Gradowski, S. (1981) Preparing Educators of Adults. Jossey-Bass, San Francisco.

Griffith, W. (1983) "Personnel Preparation" in Power and Conflict in Continuing Education. Wadsworth Publishing Co. Belmont (Ed.).

Hartman, M. (1983/84) "Some Surprises Found in National Survey of Adult Educators", The Learning Connection, (1), December 1983-January 1984.

Houle, C.O. (1970) "The Educators of Adults" in R.M. Smith, G.F. Aker and J.R. Kidd (eds.) Handbook of Adult Education. The Macmillan Company, New York.

Ingham, R.J. and Hanks, G. (1981) "Graduate Degree Programs for Professional Adult Educators" in S. Grabowski (ed.) Preparing Educators of Adults. Jossey-Bass, San Francisco.

Knox, A.B. (1979) Enhancing Proficiencies of Continuing Educators. Jossey-Bass, San Francisco.

Liveright, A.A. (1964) "The Nature and Aims of Adult Education as a Field of Graduate Education" in G. Jensen, A.A. Liveright and W. Hallenbeck, (eds.). Adult Education: Outlines of an Emerging Field of University Study. Adult Education Association of the U.S.A., Washington, D.C.

Long, H.B. (1983) Adult and Continuing Education. College Press, New York.

Wilson, G. (1984) "Where the Jobs are in Adult Education?" The Learning Connection, 5 (5), June 1984.

Yerka, B.L. (1981) "Training Paraprofessional Instructors of Adults" in S. Grabowski (ed.) Preparing Educators of Adults. Jossey-Bass, San Francisco.

PART TWO

CONCEPTUAL ISSUES IN TRAINING
EDUCATORS OF ADULTS

Chapter Three

A GENERAL THEORY OF THE DOCTORATE IN EDUCATION

Malcolm S. Knowles (1962)

The need for a coherent theory to undergird any graduate degree programs cannot be overemphasized. If a faculty is not agreed on and clear about the rationale of a given degree, certain consequences are predictable: (1) Society will have confused or mistaken expectations toward the holders of degrees. (2) Prospective students will have inadequate criteria for deciding whether or not to enter into a degree program and, having entered, will be at a disadvantage in participating on a basis of mutuality with the faculty in planning their programs. (3) The faculty will lack adequate criteria for building curriculums that have continuity, sequence, and integration. (4) The faculty will lack security about their individual areas of freedom to take into account individual differences. (5) The institution will lack an adequate basis for evaluating the excellence of its products.

PURPOSE OF A THEORY

The purpose of a theory of graduate degree programs, therefore, is to provide guide lines for the development of a program for each degree which will (1) result in a clear image of what the degree stands for; (2) provide a consistent basis for planning by students and faculty; (3) promote functional evaluation and program improvement; and (4) define areas of freedom for individualization.

An adequate theory would delineate clearly between the "core characteristics" in the model of the product the degree is intended to symbolize (Figure 3.1).

According to this construct, Theory A says, "The holders of our EdD are uniform; when you hire one of them, you know what you're getting." Theory B says, "Our doctors of education have a basic equipment that is common but about an equal area of competencies that varies with each individual; when you hire one of them you can be sure of getting a good all-round educator, but you have a choice among

Figure 3.1

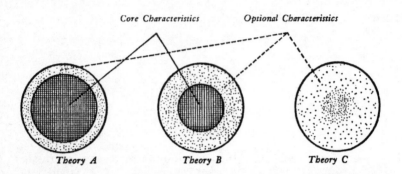

Core Characteristics   Optional Characteristics

Theory A   Theory B   Theory C

specialized competencies." Theory C says, "Our EdD's are all different; before hiring any of them you'll have to find out what each has to offer."

The theory proposed (Figure 3.1) is of the "B" type. Whether or not it survives the process of faculty examination is less important to its author than that it contribute to the evolution of a common and coherent theory by the faculty.

A "ROLE THEORY" OF THE EdD

This theory assumes that there is a generalized role of "educator" to which society assigns certain expectations. It further assumes that some specialization of function takes place within this role, so that specialized sub-roles must be provided for within the general role of educator. Thus, it is assumed that all educators must possess certain common competencies as educational generalists, but that each educator also has certain differentiated competencies as an educational specialist, such as teacher, administrator, counselor, etc.

According to this theory, an adequate graduate curriculum can be evolved only by following a diagnostic procedure involving these steps:

1. Analyzing the functions required in the roles of
   (a) educational generalist and
   (b) each kind of educational specialist.
2. Determining the competencies required to perform each function.
3. Diagnosing the learnings (knowledges, understandings, skills, attitudes, interests, and values) that make up each competency.

Figure 3.2: A model for the development of competencies for the role of educational generalist

Required Functions	Relevant Competencies	Appropriate Learning Activities
A. The formulation of educational policies, objectives and programs	1. An understanding of the role of education in the social order	Systematic inquiry into the historical, anthropological, sociological, and philosophical factors affecting the role of education in society.*
	2. An ability to identify and think philosophically about educational issues	Guided practice in diagnosing, clarifying, analyzing, and resolving educational issues.**
	3. An understanding of the process of human growth and learning	Systematic inquiry into the dynamics of individual behavior, the psychology of learning, and learning theory.
	4. An ability to evaluate institutional effectiveness and educational outcomes	Study of measurement principles and methods and practices in applying them.**
	5. An ability to use and to involve others in orderly decision-making processes	Laboratory experience in the practice of human relations and problem-solving skills.**
B. Obtaining public understanding and support of education	1. An understanding of the dynamics of community behavior	Study of sociological and social psychological research findings.**
	2. Skill in planning and executing strategies of community involvement and communication	Study of change theory and laboratory practice of communication skills and strategy planning.**
C. The planning supervising, and evaluating of learning activities	1. Same as A-3	Same as A-3
	2. An understanding of principles of curriculum development	Study of principles of curriculum development.*
	3. Skill in performing a helping role in supervision and collaboration	Laboratory practice in performing a helping role in a variety of situations.*
	4. Ability to select and use a variety of methods to achieve particular educational objectives	Study of and practice in using various educational methods*
	5. Ability to measure learning outcomes	Study of measurement procedures and practice in constructing and using evaluation devices*

Required Functions	Relevant Competencies	Appropriate Learning Activities
	6. An accepting attitude toward learners and skill in motivating and guiding their learning	Study of principles of guidance and practice in applying them.*
	7. An understanding of and skill in using group process in learning	Study of dynamics of group behavior and laboratory practice in group leadership.*
D. Participation in the advancement of education	1. Ability to interpret and apply research findings in the social sciences and particular subject areas	Study of and practice in using research methods; laboratory experience in creative experimentation.*
	2. Ability to conduct and report original research	Guided experience in conducting and reporting original research.**
	3. Skill in providing leadership in professional activities	Study of leadership theory and practice in performing leadership functions; clarification of personal and professional value system.**

*Most appropriate at the master's level.
**Most appropriate at the doctor's level.

4. Formulating objectives in terms of behavioral changes to be sought in these learnings.
5. Planning a program of learning activities that will achieve these objectives according to a design that provides for continuity, sequence, and integration of the learnings.

An illustration of the kind of pattern that might result from such a process in regard to the role of generalist is provided in Figure 3.2; and a projected supplemental pattern for the role of adult educational specialist is provided in Figure 3.3.

SOME IMPLICATIONS

1. Regarding the planning of programs for individual students. Within this theoretical framework such concepts as "core curriculum," "required courses," and, indeed, a fixed "minimum credits" have no place. Instead, each student's personal doctoral program would be constructed by: (a) assessing which of the generalist and specialist competencies have already been developed through previous education and experience; (b) figuratively constructing a template in which these competencies are placed in the same positions in which they appear in each model; and (c) superimposing each template on its corresponding model in such a way that missing competencies will show through. A program of learning experiences would then be scheduled, including course work, field experience, independent reading, research

Figure 3.3: A model for the development of competencies for the role of adult education specialist

Required Functions	Relevant Competencies	Appropriate Learning Activities
A. The formulation of policies, objectives, and programs in institutions of adult education	1. An understanding of the function of adult education in society	Study of the nature and scope of the adult educational field.*
	2. Ability to diagnose adult educational needs and translate these into objectives and programs	Practice in using basic program planning processes.*
	3. An understanding of the unique characteristics and processes of adults as learners	Systematic inquiry into research findings about adult psychology and developmental process.*
	4. Ability to plan and execute strategies of institutional and community change	Laboratory experience in performing the role of change agent.**
B. The organization and administration of programs of adult education	1. Same as A-2	Same as A-2.*
	2. An understanding of the theory and dynamics of organization	Study of organizational theory and dynamics.*
	3. Skill in the selection, training, and supervision of leaders and teachers	Laboratory and field experience in practice of supervisory skills.*
	4. Skill in institutional management	Study and practice of principles and methods of financing, staffing, interpreting, etc.*
C. The performance of special functions required in particular adult educational roles	5. Such specialized competencies as use of mass media, preparation of materials, organizational and community consultation, human relations training, etc.	Guided independent study, supervised field experience, systematic study in related fields, group projects, skill exercises, research projects, etc.

projects, theses, and exercises, which would be completed when all required competencies have been developed. Admittedly, the principal weakness in this procedure at the present time is the inadequacy of the measures of competency. Hopefully some better device for measuring competencies than the Graduate Record Exam can be devised. But until then the assessment of competencies by the judgment of faculty members would at least be no more damaging to sound program construction than the present process of attempting to attach meanings to grades in previous courses and scores of aptitude tests.

2. Regarding the curriculum and methodology of the graduate program. A curriculum organized wholly in accordance with a role theory of the doctoral degree would be competency-centered rather than subject centered. Units of instruction (or, better, of learning) would be defined in terms of competencies to be developed; and the knowledges, understandings, skills, attitudes, and values included in each unit would be those required for the development of a particular competency. Presumably less reliance would be placed on the instructional course as the primary instrumentality of learning, and more emphasis would be placed on project teams, guided individual study, seminars, field experience, and the like. The appropriate methodologies would be those less directed toward the transmission of doctrine and information and more directed toward the stimulation and guidance of mutual inquiry by students and teachers together. The relevant role for the teacher to perform according to this approach to graduate study is that of consultant and resource person, not that of inculcator and judge; and the relevant role for the student is that of responsible inquirer, not that of dependent receptor.

3. Regarding the master's degree program. A theory which requires graduate programs to be based on preparation for role performance by inference requires a clear differentiation between the roles of a master of education and a doctor of education. For example, if the role of a master is defined as that of an educational craftsman and the role of a doctor is defined as that of a professional leader, some clues are provided as to the types and levels of competencies that are appropriate for each role. This line of reasoning would require, therefore, that generalist and specialist models that define competencies required at the master's level be constructed through the same diagnostic procedure described for the doctoral degree.

4. Regarding the autonomy of the individual professor. This theory requires agreement among the faculty as to what competencies are required for the performance of the generalized role of "educator" and how these competencies are to be assessed. Given this agreement, then each faculty member is wholly responsible for developing programs with their advisees through which missing competencies will be developed. The theory assumes, of course, that there is prior agreement by the faculty that there is such a thing as a generalized role of educator, and that the function of a graduate program is to develop competencies in performing this generalized role as well as specialized roles.

A SPECIAL THEORY OF THE EdD

Graduate degrees in particular educational specialties must symbolize the development of those competencies required not only for the performance of the role of educational generalist but also for the performance of a particular specialist role. An adequate theory of graduate training in the specialist role of adult educator must be based on a similar assumption that there are certain generalized competencies that differ with the various sub-specialties within the adult educational role. The former type of competencies is illustrated in categories A and B of Figure 3.2, while the latter are illustrated in category C.

This special theory assumes, however, that the adult educational role is essentially interdisciplinary in character, and that therefore the bulk of an individual student's program will be directed toward the development of generalized competencies, although many of these (e.g., Figure 3.2, function D, competency 2: "Ability to conduct and report original research") may be pursued in the context of the adult educational specialty.

Chapter Four

THE NATURE AND AIMS OF ADULT EDUCATION
AS A FIELD OF GRADUATE EDUCATION

A. A. Liveright (1964)

actually

The field of adult education has not yet reached the point at which it is either possible or desirable to describe the content or organization of a graduate program in specific terms. Actually, adult education cannot yet be truly classified as a profession, although it evidences many of the characteristics of an occupation moving rapidly in that direction. Nevertheless, though no firmly defined discipline of adult education exists at this time, it is possible to suggest the kind of program appropriate for graduate education in the field and what, in general, should be included therein.

As described in earlier chapters, adult educators carry on such varied tasks and work for so many different kinds of organizations and institutions that they do not as yet share common aims, nor do they all look upon adult education as a career. Even experts in the field hold widely differing views of the most desirable competencies for the full-time practitioner in adult education.

In view of this lack of organization and current flux and movement, it would be unwise, even if it were possible, to establish rigid qualifications for entry into the field or to insist on a highly standardized and uniform pattern of graduate study. However, as adult education develops and follows the cycle of growth already in evidence, it is inevitable that some minimum standards for a program of graduate education will be established and a system for accrediting qualified practitioners emerge.

Toward that end, the immediate task is obviously that of reaching some agreement as to the objectives of a graduate program of education for adult educators and then working consciously toward the patterns and curricula which will best achieve these aims. This chapter therefore makes an attempt to examine the characteristics of the field, and based on this examination, to suggest such objectives and patterns.

ADULT EDUCATION AS A PROFESSION

Definitions of a Profession
There are almost as many ways of defining and describing a profession as there are persons who have written about it. Nevertheless, it is possible to draw from such different statements some patterns which can provide clues and guide-posts in determining to what extent adult education is indeed a profession.*

Even though definitions of a profession vary considerably, they do so more in terms of specificity and number of criteria that with respect to the nature of criteria. Almost all include Ralph Tyler's (1) two essential characteristics: existence of a recognized code of ethics, and techniques of operation based upon some general principles.

Beyond Tyler's simple statement of the characteristics of a profession, the definition by T.H. Marshall as quoted by Everett Hughes (2) is useful in looking at the field of adult education: professions are "... those occupations in which caveat emptor cannot be allowed to prevail and which, while they are not pursued for gain, must bring their practitioners income of such a level that they will be respected and such manner of living that they may pursue the life of the mind."

A more detailed attempt to define a profession was made by Byron Horton of the Graduate Faculty of St. Johns University, writing in the Scientific Monthly (3). He sets forth the following ten criteria:

1. A profession must satisfy an indispensable social need and be based upon well-established and socially acceptable principles.
2. It must demand an adequate preprofessional and cultural training.
3. It must demand the possession of a body of specialized and systematized knowledge.
4. It must give evidence of needed skills which the general public does not possess, that is, skills which are partly native and partly acquired.
5. It must have developed a scientific technique which is the result of tested experience.
6. It must require the exercise of discretion and judgment as to the time and manner of the performance of duty. This is in contrast to the kind of

---

* For another analysis of adult education as a profession see Lawrence A. Allen, "The Growth of Professionalism in the Adult Education Movement, 1925-1958: A Context Analysis of the Periodical Literature," Doctoral dissertation, Department of Education, University of Chicago, 1961.

work which is subject to immediate direction and supervision.

7. It must be a type of beneficial work, the result of which is not subject to standardization in terms of unit performance or time element.

8. It must have a group consciousness designed to extend scientific knowledge in technical language.

9. It must have sufficient self-impelling power to retain its members throughout life. It must not be used as a mere stepping-stone to other occupations.

10. It must recognize its obligations to society by insisting that its members live up to an established and accepted code of ethics.

Using these selected definitions of a profession as bench marks, it is apparent that the field of adult education today does not meet even the simplest definition of a profession. Applying Tyler's definition, adult education may lay claim to techniques based on "general principles" but it cannot cite a generally accepted code of ethics. Using Marshall's definition, we must admit a lack of control of practitioners and we might question whether most adult educators "pursue a life of the mind" as characteristics of their field of activity. Moving on to Horton's definition, we can at best claim that adult education meets five of his ten criteria.

At the moment, therefore, adult education cannot be properly classified as a profession in the true sense of the word.

However, more important than determining whether adult education is now a profession is examining the extent to which it is consciously moving toward professionalization.

Everett Hughes, who has concerned himself with a study of professionalization, writing on professions in transition (4), says that "The practitioners of many occupations - some new, some old - are self-consciously attempting to achieve recognition as professionals ... The old service or function, formerly performed by amateurs or for pay by people of little or no formal training, comes to be the live work of a large and increasing number of people." He notes that the first people in this emerging profession come from other occupations; the first to take graduate training are already in the field; the early teachers tend to be enthusiastic leaders of a movement or protagonists of a new technique; they find their colleagues in the movement, rather than in the academic world; there is increasingly a new wave of late seekers of special training. He also points out that this development toward a profession continues in the direction of standard terms of study - eventually leading to higher degrees, research in the field considered proper to the field - and a continuing corps of people who teach rather than practice the profession directly. Finally, he says that in the successful case standardized schooling and training become effectively the license to work at the occupation.

Examining this picture of a profession in transition it becomes obvious that adult education is moving along the lines defined by Hughes, with persons already in the field becoming increasingly involved in special training, a corps of continuing teachers, some research properly suited to the field, and a concerted effort to define standardized schooling and training.*

Although adult education cannot now be classified as a profession it clearly meets the criteria of a profession in transition or an emerging profession.

In examining adult education as a profession it is also important to determine in what direction it is moving. Is adult education becoming a "helping" or a "facilitating" profession, to use the words of William J. McGlothlin (5)?

> According to McGlothlin, all professions can be said to fall into two major groups defined by the focus of their work ... Some focus mainly on people, usually working directly with them ... Although these professions often work with the environment, their major focus is on direct contact with people themselves, as patients, students, or clients, each with a problem to be solved and wishing help to solve it. Because of their focus, these professions have come to be known as "helping" professions ... Practitioners in the other professions ... all work for the benefit of people, but they deal more directly with things and each is more directly concerned with supplying goods and services which benefit people than it is with helping people directly. For this reason, I have called the second group "facilitating professions."

Law, medicine, general education, and social work are all clearly professions which fall into the "helping" category; examples of "facilitating" professions are architecture and engineering.

As an emerging profession, adult education falls into the category of a "helping" rather than a "facilitating" profession.

OBJECTIVES SUGGESTED BY PROFESSIONAL STATUS OF ADULT EDUCATION

From this analysis of adult education as a profession certain ends emerge as appropriate for a graduate program. Such a

---

* See also Lawrence A. Allen's conclusions about the status of adult education op. cit., pp. 152-155.

program should attempt to develop a sense of values and a broad philosophy for the entire field of adult education and should move toward establishing a code of ethics for those working in the field. Considering adult education as an emerging profession, a graduate program in the field should increasingly teach techniques based on general principles and inculcate in its students a feeling of commonality and purpose, and a belief that adult education represents a continuing career. To arrive at the desired degree of professionalization the graduate program should develop an understanding of the social needs for adult education and the social role to be performed by its practitioners. It should also work consciously toward the development of a sound body of research concerned primarily with the practice of adult education.

Viewing adult education as a field moving in the direction of the "helping" professions, graduate education should provide an understanding on the part of the practitioner of his own behavior as well as that of the persons with whom he works, a sense of values and a high degree of sensitivity with respect to teacher-student relations, and a mastery of the skills involved in intergroup and interpersonal relations.

ADULT EDUCATION AS A DISCIPLINE

Definitions of a Discipline

There is probably almost as much discussion and disagreement about adult education as a discipline as about its right to be called a profession. If we accept the definition of a discipline in Webster's New Collegiate Dictionary as "a branch of knowledge involving research" adult education would seem to qualify as a discipline. More important, however, than a discussion of whether or not adult education is a true discipline is an examination of the kind of discipline it is likely to become as it moves toward professional status.

In this context a paper by Gale Jensen (6) is of special interest. Although his subject is education as a whole, his conclusions are applicable to adult education. He points out three aspects of education as a discipline: first, it is a factual or descriptive discipline; second, it is a normative discipline; and third it is an art, a practice, an engineering.

As a descriptive study, education is concerned with discovering how psychological factors influence human behavior and how sociological factors govern it. "It is," Jensen says, "the findings from investigations in these areas which provide the foundation of education as a descriptive or factual discipline." He summarizes this aspect as follows: "When we speak of education as a factual or descriptive discipline, we are speaking about the biological, psychological and sociological descriptions of human behavior and development which enable us to know what is humanly possible, and the conditions that must be present if stipulated behaviors are to be realized." In the case of adult education, this means the investigation of the conditions and limits within which the objectives of adult education programs can be achieved".

When Jensen calls education a normative discipline, he means that it is concerned with those problems of what "should or ought to be." If it is true of general education to say that education is a deliberate attempt to develop people in certain ways, it is especially true of adult education. When we establish and achieve behavioral objectives in adult education programs, we not only have a direct impact on the students themselves, but also on their families, their communities, and their occupations. Summarizing this point, Jensen states: "The truth of the matter is that we always educate in some direction; that if we educate at all we develop some kind of character. In this we have no choice; but we do have choice as to the kind of behavior we should develop. We can make these choices consciously and intellegently in the sense that we are aware of the ways by which we arrive at them."

When we discuss education as an art, a practice, or an engineering, Jensen suggests that we are concerned with the task of organizing the bio-psycho-sociological elements of the human organism's environment in keeping with the requirements laid down by the factual or descriptive phases of the discipline, in such a way that they will most effectively bring about the realization of the proposed behaviors.

In Jensen's terms, adult education should be looked upon as a practical discipline concerned with factual and descriptive elements and with normative elements; it should be looked on as an art, a practice, and an engineering.

OBJECTIVES SUGGESTED BY KIND OF DISCIPLINE

To view adult education as a field of graduate education which is rapidly building and organizing a body of content, and to believe that it will emerge as a practical discipline in Jensen's terms, clearly implies certain aims. As a factual and descriptive discipline a program of graduate education must continue to accelerate research in the areas of adulthood and adult learning; it must develop greater understanding of human behavior and interpersonal relations, in order to evolve adult education programs which have most likelihood of working; and it must concern itself with the historical and social role of adult education in modern society. As a normative discipline, the graduate program should investigate learning situations and educational processes so that behavioral changes may best be brought about. It should concern itself with a philosophy and code of ethics for the field so that practitioners will develop a sense of personal and social responsibility about the scope and limits of programs which try to bring about changes in individuals. And finally, as "an art, a practice, and an engineering," the graduate program must be involved with the skills which make possible a sound program of adult education within the descriptive and normative limits which characterize the discipline.

ADULT EDUCATION IN TERMS OF REQUIRED COMPETENCIES

Analysis of Competencies Required of Adult Education

A search for the objectives of a graduate program for adult educators leads us next to an examination of the extent and kinds of agreement within the field about the desired competencies required of a full-time adult educator.

Martin Chamberlain has provided us with useful material along this line in his recent doctoral dissertation, "The Professional Adult Educator (7)." In this study he asked some 135 adult educators (including professors, deans, students, observers, and others in the field) to rate, in order of their importance, forty-five different competencies which were felt by the respondent to be important to adult educators. For this rating he described the prototype professional adult educator as one of the following:

> A full-time administrator of a program of adult education, for example an evening college dean or assistant, the educational director of a labor union, the director of adult education of a public school, the training director of an industrial organization, the head of an adult education department of a library, the senior staff member of a co-operative extension division. The administrator may also be a teacher or act as a consultant, but we are primarily interested in his role as an administrator.*

> Chamberlain discovered - as might be expected in a profession in transition - that wide variances appeared in high-ranking competencies, both within the entire group of respondents and between various groups of respondents, such as the professors, the deans, and the other subgroups.

---

* It may be worthy of note in this discussion to emphasize that Chamberlain, like most authors, looks upon the developing professional adult educator as an administrator rather than as a teacher.

Utilizing the total mean scores derived from all of the ratings, he identified the following as the top ten competencies:

1. A belief that most people have potentiality for growth.
2. Imagination in program development.
3. Ability to communicate effectively in both speaking and writing.
4. Understanding of the conditions under which adults are most likely to learn.
5. Ability to keep on learning.
6. Effectiveness as a group leader.
7. Knowledge of his own values, strengths, and weaknesses.
8. Open-mindedness - i.e., willingness to accept others' ideas.
9. Understanding of what motivates adults to participate in programs.
10. Strong commitment to adult education.

Thus, although there are a number of disagreements and variations among adult educators as to what constitutes the competencies required of a professional adult educator, it is possible to identify a cluster of competencies which are felt by a majority of experts in the field to be important.

OBJECTIVES SUGGESTED BY REQUIRED COMPETENCIES

Mr. Chamberlain himself lists the objectives for a graduate program of education which stem from his list of the top fifteen high-rated competencies. In his view a graduate program of adult education should aim at developing practitioners who meet the following qualifications:

1. They must believe in the potentiality for growth of most people, have strong commitments to adult education, and practice this by continual personal learning projects. They must have open minds and be willing to accept others' ideas. They must believe in freedom of thought and expression and have a dynamic, rather than a static, concept of the field of adult education.
2. They must possess certain skills, especially the ability to write and speak well, to lead groups effectively, to organize and direct complex administrative activities, and to provide imagination in the development of programs.
3. They must understand the conditions under which adults learn, and the motivations which bring them to programs. They must also know their community,

its structure and organization, and know themselves, including their strengths and weaknesses
and personal philosophies.

THE PRACTITIONERS OF ADULT EDUCATION

Description of the Practitioners

The variety of organizations and institutions involved in the
field of adult education and the different tasks performed by
its practitioners have been described by Mr. Knowles in
Chapter III,* and in Chapter IV* Mr. Houle discussed the
varied and frequently unplanned manner in which most of
today's leaders have entered the field. Such wide diversity in
backgrounds, in employers, and in the tasks performed in
adult education make it especially difficult either to describe
the typical adult educator or to suggest what the ideal practitioner should be.

However, in an article in the Adult Education Handbook
(8), Mr. Houle has given us a method of looking at practitioners in the field. His so-called "pyramid of leadership,"
mentioned by Knowles in Chapter III of this volume,**
describes three kinds of leaders: (1) volunteer leaders; (2)
leaders who have a definite adult education responsibility,
though not themselves primarily adult educators; and (3)
those whose primary concern and responsibility is for adult
education.

The diversity of tasks and levels of responsibility
represented in this pyramid of leadership make it apparent
that various kinds of training and education are required for
these three levels of leadership. As suggested by Mr. Houle,
and also set forth in a recent pamphlet, "Adult Education, A
New Imperative for Our Times" (9), the major responsibility
for training the first group in the pyramid, lay leaders, lies
with the agencies and institutions using them, aided and
abetted on occasion by graduate professors of adult education. Responsibility for in-service training of the second
group rests partly with the agencies and organizations concerned and partly, at least for basic and general education in
the field, with the professors of adult education. For the
education of the third and top level, major responsibility
rests with the professors. This is the group with which we
are primarily concerned in discussing a program of graduate
education.

Let us look more closely at this latter group, in connection with both defining the aims of a graduate program

---

* These refer to the book in which this chapter first
appeared (ed).
** Reference to original volume (ed).

and determining a curriculum. Various studies of the adult education leaders at the apex of the triangle suggest the following conclusions:

1. Few of them have participated in an organized program of graduate study in adult education or hold advanced degrees therein.
2. Most come from other occupations and have moved into adult education after other kinds of employment.
3. Many look upon adult education as a stepping stone rather than as a permanent career.
4. During the past ten years, many have moved from adult education to other posts in the educational or community field - many to other administrative posts in education.
5. Their conceptions of the ideal adult educator and of the competencies required for the professional adult educator vary widely.
6. Most of them are action rather than research oriented, and few have made major research contributions to the field of adult education.
7. Many are concerned about their status and position as adult educators and do not as yet feel completely identified with the field or if they do, they feel themselves "second-rate citizens" in the academic hierarchy.
8. There is as yet no clearly defined set of values or code of ethics subscribed to by all of them.

This brief overview of the practitioners of adult education suggest some major differences between personnel in the field of adult education and those in the professions of medicine, law, and the church. It supports the position developed earlier in this chapter, that adult education at this time is clearly not a mature profession but rather a collection of practitioners, some of whom are moving toward professional status.

The fact that the practitioners of adult education - even at the apex of the pyramid - vary so in the organizations and institutions they represent, their tasks and responsibilities, background, prior education and training, and the fact that they hold such differing images of the field, has special implications for a graduate program.

Objectives Suggested by Analysis of Practitioners

The foregoing analysis of the practitioners now active in the field of adult education suggests the following aims for a graduate program: (1) the development of a set of values and philosophy of adult education which will provide a feeling of commonality and a sense of belonging to an important and growing field; (2) the development of a sound code of ethics which can serve as a base of operations for all practitioners; (3) agreement, as rapidly as possible, on a common body of knowledge to be required; and (4) the involvement of many practitioners and students in significant and related research.

AIMS AND PATTERNS OF A GRADUATE PROGRAM OF EDUCATION

Framework for Examining Pattern of Graduate Education

We have now considered some of the aspects which determine the nature and the goals of a graduate program for adult educators. We have also suggested a number of aims which logically grow out of these different aspects. It is now necessary to bring them together in some order which will permit comparison with programs of graduate education in other professions or emerging professions. To accomplish this purpose we shall utilize a framework developed by William J. McGlothlin and used by him in studying the patterns of professional education for ten professions.*

In analyzing these graduate programs of education McGlothlin says: "Basically, professional education has two related aims: one, to supply enough professional people; and two, to assure society that they are competent to practice their professions. The first is the aim of quantity; the second is the aim of quality."

For most professions the question of quantity is one of supplying enough graduates to fill the needs of the profession caused by loss of its members by death, retirement, and defection, and also to meet expanding demands. Professional schools are considered the only, or at least the only desirable, channel for entrance into the professions.

By contrast, in the field of adult education, as we have seen, professional or graduate education is now now looked upon as a precondition of employment. Entry into this field is not controlled by government legislation, inspection, control, or rigid requisites established by the profession itself. The field is still fairly wide open and uncontrolled. As a result, professors of adult education are less concerned with pre-employment requirements and the quantity aspect than is McGlothlin.

In discussing this very point in Chapter IV Mr. Houle states: "Even though most of the existing universities which offer programs of graduate education have fewer students than they would like ... the growth in curricula will help to

---

* A major portion of this section is based on the framework and theory developed by William J. McGlothlin, footnote 5.

establish the field, to make graduate study more essential to practitioners, to enlarge the content, and to demonstrate new curricular approaches which may later be adopted."

In other words, with respect to the objective of quantity, we can probably depend on the institutions now offering graduate programs to supply the need for persons with graduate education for some years to come.

It is a question of quality - the competence to serve as effective practitioners - that concerns us most.

McGlothlin lists five attributes or objectives common to all programs of professional study, or graduate education for an emerging profession. According to his framework their graduates will have the following attributes:

1. Competence to practice his profession, with sufficient knowledge and skill to satisfy its requirements.

2. Social understanding with sufficient breadth to place his practice in the context of the society which supports it, and capacity for leadership in public affairs.

3. Personality characteristics which make possible effective practice.

4. Zest for continued study which will steadily increase knowledge, and such reading, investigating, and research skills as are necessary to translate the zest into action.

5. Enough competence in conducting or interpreting research to enable him to add to human knowledge through either discovery or the application of new truths.

In discussing the patterns of graduate education we propose to use McGlothlin's formulations as stated, slightly modifying one of them. For our purposes, we shall change his third attribute, "Personality characteristics which make possible effective practice," to "Philosophy and set of values which make possible effective practice."

In an attempt to organize the patterns of a graduate program for adult education we propose, therefore, to examine these attributes as they apply to the field of adult education.

1. Competence to practice his profession, with sufficient knowledge and skill to satisfy the requirements.

The major question to be raised here is the relative emphasis and amount of time to be placed on education concerned with knowledge or skills. Closely related to this is the question as to whether such graduate education should train a person to do a specific job upon graduation, or whether he should have the broad knowledge and understanding that will prepare him for the field, permitting him, in general, to specialize on the job.

There seems to be some agreement that a graduate program for adult educators should emphasize general knowledge rather than specific skills, especially since in most cases students are already working in the field. They are thus daily practicing the skills and are thoroughly familiar with their own specialities. Where graduate students have had no experience in adult education this skill must be provided through additional field work.

Even when students in a graduate program are preparing for future careers in adult education, specific aspects of the program should be subordinated to the general; the basic theoretical background which underlies selection of the most appropriate methods should be developed, with some opportunity for demonstration and practice included in the curriculum. Opportunity to develop skills in the various methods of adult education might well be provided through supervised field work, off campus internship situations, or on the job itself, with opportunities for clinics and evaluation sessions back in the classroom.

2. Social Understanding - placing the practice of adult education in the context of the society which supports it, and developing a capacity for leadership in public affairs.

In dealing with this area McGlothlin writes as follows:

A professional man ... must understand the significance and relationships of his profession. Furthermore, as he achieves status and influence within his profession, he will constantly be faced with decisions which surmount the bounds of the technical knowledge of his profession and which must be based upon knowledge and understanding made available by many fields. In addition, as a professional man, he will be called upon for leadership in public affairs, often wholly outside his profession. At the very least, enlightened citizenship requires social understanding.

As a minimum standard in considering patterns of graduate education for adult educators, and also in planning the curriculum, we should subscribe to the statement of the Association of Colleges for Teacher Education (10) which describes the professionally educated graduate as one who "expresses carefully considered, rather than impetuous judgments of public events. Views his own affairs and those of his profession in the light of real understanding of the social, economic, and political factors operating in his community, nation, and world."

If this objective is sound for teachers of youth, it is even more so for teachers of adults, who are confronted in every program and every class with the direct impact of the society and community in which their students must operate. The substance of their programs is, in fact, built upon the daily experiences and understandings of their students in the world in which they live. While secondary school and college students ordinarily live in a special and protected world, adult students are already a functioning part of society. It is therefore essential that adult educators have a sound understanding of the social forces and factors which impinge upon the lives and thoughts of their students.

3. Philosophy and set of values which make possible effective practice.

Commenting on this aspect of professional education, Charlotte Towle (11) has said: "A profession has an ideology, an ethic system, by which its members are inspired and governed. A student entering a profession has both the need and the wish for a set of values to give direction and limits to his striving. What I am to think and feel in order to act as I should is a prominent anxiety of a neophyte in a profession." McGlothlin adds to Miss Towle's point the statement that "To some extent, he who chooses a profession chooses a personality."

A major aim of graduate education for adult educators must therefore be to develop the image, the code of ethics, the values, and the scope and limit of adult education, and these in turn will develop the personality of the adult educator.

Almost all professions have set as an objective for themselves the development and inculcation of a code of ethical conduct. In view of the possibilities for adult educators to further all kinds of political, social, community, group, and social movements, it is especially incumbent upon them to develop such ethical codes. A program of graduate education must therefore consider the kinds of situations in which professional adult educators can operate, the kinds of groups and organizations which will call upon them for assistance, and the methods they should use, in terms of the extent to which these methods develop or inhibit individual insight, thinking, and strengths.

Although it is not in order here for us to determine these ethical codes, it is proper to emphasize that any sound program of professional education must include a careful and intelligent consideration of either a code of ethics or a process whereby each individual adult educator can consciously decide on his own values and code.

The extent to which graduate education for adult education should move beyond this and attempt to develop a "professional personality," as suggested by both Towle and McGlothlin, is probably a moot question. If this should lead to an aim such as the one expressed in the field of teacher education, that of being "personally desirable," it may be better to avoid any attempt to develop a "professional personality." On the other hand, if the aim is "to develop feelings and attitudes that will make it possible for the student to think and act appropriately," as it is in social work education, a program of graduate education for adult educators does have a task to perform in developing a "professional personality." A program which works toward an inner understanding and an attitude which permits the adult educator to think and act appropriately is a desirable one, whereas one which aims at developing a particular kind or stamp of personality is to be rigorously avoided.

4.   Zest for continued study which will steadily increase knowledge and skill required by practice.

The entire field of adult education is based upon the premise that, for the individual concerned, continuing education is sound, desirable, and necessary to his full development. For society, continuing education is essential for an informed and intelligent citizenry. Consequently, the development of a zest for continuing education is certainly a must for the practitioner of adult education.

It is therefore especially important for a graduate program for adult educators to stimulate this zest for continued learning. In addition, however, it is essential that graduate education equip the members of the profession with skills necessary to put this zest into practice, such as those of independent study, research methods, and reading skills.

5.   Enough competence in conducting or interpreting research to enable the practitioner to add to human knowledge through either discovery or the application of new truths.

All professions demand that their graduates continue some kind of learning, and require them to possess at least a minimum understanding of relevant research. Aims vary from "the objective of developing and entrenching the spirit of scientific inquiry," as the Social Work profession expresses it, to the suggestion in the teaching profession that "The competent teacher ... is intellectually curious ..., continues to grow professionally throughout his teaching career,"and "does simple classroom research," to the statement of the medical profession that "By the time a student has completed his undergraduate medical program, he should have developed a genuine spirit of curiosity and be in possession of methods of study which foster the accumulation of facts that lead to new knowledge and the wisdom to utilize it."

Because adult education is a new and emerging profession and needs increasingly thoughtful and sophisticated research in the areas of adult learning and teaching, it can hardly settle for less than the research requirements established by the medical profession.

SOME FURTHER IMPLICATIONS FOR GRADUATE EDUCATION

As previously indicated, this is neither the time nor the place to attempt to describe in specific terms exactly what the curriculum of graduate education in the field of adult education should be. It is hoped, however, that the foregoing sections will suggest the content and will provide some guideposts for the organization and development of such a curriculum.

Throughout this chapter we have talked about a graduate program of adult education. The present stage of development in the field, the variety of skills and tasks involved, and especially the varied methods of entry into the field suggest that at this juncture we must rely upon graduate rather than undergraduate education for the further development of a profession of adult education. By the same token, for some years to come we shall have to depend more upon post- than upon pre-employment training. To move at this point into a situation which requires undergraduate specialization in adult education, or which sets up hard and fast requirements for graduate degrees as a condition of employment, might well inhibit or stifle the flux and the dynamic nature of the field which is so important in an emerging profession.

Taking this into account, it is possible to suggest some tentative conclusions and to summarize some implications about graduate education for adult educators.

1. Because of the very broad and varied tasks, backgrounds, prior education, and experience of practitioners in the field, a graduate program should be quite flexible so that it may be geared to the needs of the individual entering the graduate program, taking cognizance of the prior education and experience of the student.

2. Effective systems should be developed for evaluating the extent to which such prior experiences and education have already achieved the aims and objectives, in order that such graduate programs can be geared to the special needs and educational gaps of the individual student.

3. In the light of this need for flexibility, major emphasis should be placed upon a sound and intensive program of counseling for each student. This obligation for counseling should fall primarily on the professor of adult education.

4. Because of the nature of the field of adult education and the emerging nature of the profession, much of the content of a graduate program must at this time be based upon and borrowed from other disciplines. This will highlight the counseling

responsibility of the professor of adult education in terms of guiding his students to appropriate programs and courses in other divisions and departments in the university.

5. A sound and comprehensive program of adult education which will achieve the objectives outlined should include some work in the fields of history, psychology, social psychology, sociology, economics, political science, philosophy, and administration.

6. In addition to courses or seminars in the areas outlined above, sound graduate programs of adult education should increasingly include special courses and seminars concerned with the philosophy, values, and ethics of adult education; with its techniques and methods; with its history and social background. The place of adult education in the community, the adult education learning situation, and research methods in adult education, should all be thoroughly understood.

7. In view of the variety of tasks and responsibilities of practitioners in the field of adult education and the fact that most students for some time to come will be recruited from persons already working in the field, a graduate program is likely to emphasize content and subject matter which concerns itself primarily with broad knowledge and understanding and the development of a sound philosophy and code of ethics rather than with specific skills and a high degree of specialization related to only one task, one kind of agency, or one specific job in a particular agency.

A last word about the implications of adult education as an emerging profession is in order: On the one hand, the adolescent state of the field is responsible for certain doubts, feelings of inferiority, periods of inadequacy, and compensatory periods of aggressiveness. On the other, the concommitant fluidity places persons now in the field in an especially fortunate and challenging position. Patterns are still open and not rigid; future directions are being explored.

In this exploration professors of adult education and other leaders in the field have an opportunity to avoid the rigid formalism which unfortunately characterizes so many older and more established professions. Mr. Houle, in a discussion of this point, makes the following comment:

The chief safeguard against a rigid formalism results from the fact that adults undertake adult education voluntarily for the most part. When we are sick we have to see a doctor, and when we are poor we cannot get relief unless we see the social worker - but nobody needs to attend adult education activities unless he wants to do so. Not all forms of adult education, of course, are voluntary, but most of them are. Is it not possible that, because we in adult education must always please and attract our clients, we may hope to escape the rigors and rigidities which have characterized other professions?*

Whether we escape these rigors or not, and whether adult education emerges as a pale reflection of the general field of education or as a vibrant, experimental, sentient, and new profession will be determined by the professors, the students, and the practitioners presently involved in the field.

REFERENCES

1. Ralph W. Tyler, "Distinctive Attributes of Education for Professions," Social Work Journal, Vol. 33, No. 2, (April 1952) p. 55

2. Everett C. Hughes, "Professions in Society," Canadian Journal of Economics and Political Science, Vol. 26, (February-November, 1960) p.54

3. Byron J. Horton, Scientific Monthly, Vol. 58, 1944, p.164.

4. Everett C. Hughes, "The Professions in Transition," in Men and Their Work, The Free Press of Glencoe, 1958, p.133.

5. William J. McGlothlin, Patterns of Professional Education, G.P. Putnam's Sons, 1960, pp. xv-xvi.

6. Gale E. Jensen, "The Nature of 'Education' as a Discipline," in Readings for Educational Research, (Gale E. Jensen, Ed.) Ann Arbor Publishers, 1960.

7. Martin Chamberlain, The Professional Adult Educator, Doctoral Dissertation, Department of Education, University of Chicago, 1960.

8. Cyril O. Houle, "The Education of Adult Education Leaders," Handbook of Adult Education Association of the U.S.A., 1960, p. 119.

9. Commission of Professors of Adult Education, Adult Education: A New Imperative for Our Times, Adult Education Association of the USA, 1961.

10. Revised Standards and Policies for Accrediting Colleges for Teacher Education, American Association of Colleges for Teacher Education, 1951.

11. Charlotte Towle, The Learner in Education for the Professions, University of Chicago Press, 1954, p.46.

---

* From a letter to the author of this chapter.

Chapter Five

A CONCEPTUAL FRAMEWORK FOR ANALYZING THE
TRAINING OF TRAINERS AND ADULT EDUCATORS

Roger Boshier (1985)

In many parts of the world the adult education movement is
experiencing an unprecedented boom as people grapple with
new technology, social turbulence and uncertainty about the
future. In other places adult education is in a hiatus induced
by government cutbacks. Despite setbacks, the conceptual
and operational boundaries are expanding and encompassing
people from allied fields who have not hitherto seen themselves as adult educators. Today, there is a profound need to
train new and existing personnel in a manner congruent with
the ethos of the field.

Indeed, the plea for properly trained personnel has
become a full-fledged chorus in most parts of the world. Even
recalcitrant governments are coming to see that an educated
citizenry is an essential corollary of economic development,
national unity, and cultural well-being. Societies that compete
successfully in international markets, satisfy the cultural
yearnings of different groups and harness new technologies,
all place high priority on the education of adults and, as a
result, need trained personnel.

ASSUMPTIONS AND MISGIVINGS

It has generally been assumed that trained adult educators
are better than untrained ones and that a profession with
clearly defined career paths, rewards, and a coherent
knowledge base is better than the marginal circumstances that
still encompass too many practitioners in most parts of the
world. At the World Assembly of Adult Education held by the
International Council for Adult Education, in Buenos Aires,
November 1985, the training workshop was by far the largest
at the conference. But the most clearly articulated call for
'action on training' stems from the Fourth Unesco International Conference on Adult Education, held in Paris, March
1985. One background paper on 'aspects and trends' (Unesco,
1985a) summarized the results of regional consulations. It

devotes four pages to the 'very complex' subject of personnel and training. The roundup of replies to a survey of Unesco national commissions (Unesco, 1985b) discuss problems pertaining to training. However, the most comprehensive and theoretically suggestive analysis is in the report of Commission II in the conference's final report (Unesco, 1985).

Commission II dealt with agenda items related to 'ways and means of extending and improving adult education', including training and status of personnel. It concluded that any discussion concerning the training of adult educators must distinguish between 'teachers and administrators, and between full-time, part-time and voluntary teachers' and between pre-adult education.

Delegates proposed the following: that training is important because it has a 'multiplier' effect; that there should be more regional or sub-regional training activities where cultural or linguistic affinities exist; in times of high unemployment much can be gained from combining adult education training with 'normal university discipline-based' study; diverse modes of training are needed to meet different needs and situations: in-service is often better than pre-service training; relationships between part- and full-time workers need to be carefully nurtured; the 'richness and variety' of experience that part-timers bring should be used; professional workers, such as doctors and engineers, have clear adult education functions and thus are candidates for training; profound dangers are associated with training people along 'specific and rigid' lines; adult educators should learn how to 'identify motivation' and thence 'inspire educational activity' (see Boshier, 1985).

These are worthy exhortations and serious educators will read the three Unesco documents describing conditions that evoked them and reasoning that accompanied them. Delegates clearly ascribed considerable significance to the importance of 'training' and, in this regard, followed a tradition that can be traced to the First World Conference on Adult Education, held in Cambridge, England, in 1929. Moreover, delegates produced two pages of recommendations on training that member states are asked to implement. It appears that those present were convinced that training is a 'good thing' and that the future development of adult education depends on it.

Some Misgivings

Not everyone agrees with such a cheery prognosis. Indeed, in the absence of solid evidence, some people suspect training has little positive impact on the field, especially when linked to credentialling and professionalization. Many workers maintain that no one should be denied an opportunity to practice adult education because of a lack of training. The 'gifted amateur', the mainstay of adult education, should be encouraged. Indeed, some say the best adult educators are those who have never seen the inside of a teachers' training college or university faculty of education.

In North America, Carlson (1972, 1977), Ohliger (1974) and others have bemoaned the attempt to make adult education a profession. According to Carlson (1977), the motives of the professionalizers are partly altruistic but also self-interested. Attempts to professionalize may result in more serious outcomes than leaving adult education as a minor, if somewhat disorganized, profession. Attempts to certificate or credential adult educators threaten the notion of 'friends educating each other.' Carlson, who clearly favours this notion, argues that from 1950 on it was 'supplanted by a view of adult education ... with practitioners defined as properly qualified agents of change certified to practice their leadership upon adults' (1977).

At a European Bureau of Adult Education seminar on the training of adult educators, South (1982) declared his opposition to making adult education a closed shop open only to those holding professional training certificates. In his view, the best form of adult education blurs the distinction between learner and teacher, professional and nonprofessional. Any outstanding writer, artist, musician, actor or other person with something to offer should be able to teach adults and should not be excluded by a 'vast professional apparatus.'

The American Commission of Professors of Adult Education has been under pressure to support the credentialling of trained personnel because of the large number of institutions and persons who have recently discovered adult education. Most members oppose credentialling but some saw this as a way to curtail interlopers and instant experts. What worries many people is that there may be charlatans among the official providers.

Both Carlson (1977) and Ohliger (1974) complicated this discussion by wrongly equating lifelong education with lifelong schooling. Although their warnings about the perils of professionalization were timely, it should be possible to train practitioners without creating a self-serving profession. The adult education movement has to recruit and retain well-qualified personnel and yet resist the urge to encumber itself with ossifying and other undesirable aspects of professionalization. As adult education becomes less marginal and is adopted as an instrument to facilitate attainment of social, economic and cultural goals, it is too important to be left to untrained amateurs, no matter how gifted.

ADULT EDUCATORS

There are many opinions about, but little research pertaining to, the characteristics or training of adult educators. Most attention is on the learner. Adult educators are somehow supposed to look after themselves. Moreover, so many came to adult education through the legendary back door one wonders if there is a front entrance. Unfortunately, many do now realize they are part of the field. Adult education associations are used to discovering people doing similar jobs in different settings barely aware of being part of a large international movement with its own theory and research literature. The planner developing programs for steel mill or shipyard workers has much in common with, and should be resorting to, the same theory as program planners working with indigenous people, pavement dwellers in India, the barrio people of Chile, police officers in New York or white collar workers in industry, government or voluntary organizations all over the world.

There are significantly more adult educators in most countries than primary, secondary or university teachers. The adult sector is by far the largest part of the educational enterprise but, because it lacks conspicuous edifices and largely occurs in nonformal settings, it is difficult for ministers of education and deans of faculties of education to discern. This creates special problems because 'training' has to help practitioners improve their knowledge and skills, but also to bring unity to the field.

Settings and Types of Providers

Another complication is that nearly all adult educators work in settings where adult education is not the primary purpose of the employer: education usually is one of the many instruments used to attain non-educational purposes. In North America, Schroeder (1970) in following the work of Verner and Booth (1964), distinguished between different types of providers.

Type 1: agencies established to serve the educational needs of adults. Adult education is a central function.

Type 2: agencies established to serve the educational needs of youth and have taken on the additional responsibility of at least partially serving the educational needs of adults. Adult education is a secondary function (e.g. university extension.)

Type 3: agencies established to serve both the educational and non-educational needs of the community. Adult education is an allied function used to fulfil only some of the needs that agencies recognize as their responsibility (e.g. libraries, museums, health and welfare agencies.)

Type 4: agencies established to serve special interests (economic, ideological) of particular groups. Adult education is a subordinate function used primarily to further the agency's special interests (e.g. labour unions, governments, churches, and voluntary associations.)

Much adult education occurs in non-institutional settings and is not sponsored by an agency. Remember that the piano teacher or village craftsman is an adult educator; he or she often works from home. Nevertheless, Schroeder's typology had profound implications for the training of adult educators. It is difficult to cite examples of Type 1 agencies which have adult education as the central function. Canada's Frontier College, the English Workers' Education Association, the Nordic study circles, are examples. In general, few agencies have adult education as the central function. In most instances, adult education is a 'secondary', 'allied' or 'subordinate' function juxtaposed against the prime purpose of the agency.

Types 1 and 2 are usually recognized as adult education agencies; Types 3 and 4 agencies, which include museums, hospitals, trade unions and prisons, are rarely seen to be adult education agencies. Adult education occurs within them, but few people looking at a hospital or union hall think of it as an educational institution. Schroeder (1970) also thought agencies of the first three types tend to be oriented to people, while Type 4 ones are preoccupied with the organization. Moreover, none of the four types run comprehensive adult education programs of interest to all adults. A discernible portion of what goes on in Type 2 agencies should be labelled youth education for adults (rather than adult education.) Agencies of one type often related to those of another type to achieve their general or specific educational objectives. Thus libraries (Type 3) provide materials to participants in adult courses at public schools (Type 2.)

Most adult educators do not realize they are part of an international movement and, as noted above, work in settings where the primary purpose is other than adult education. Considered separately or together these two factors create problems for their training. The situation is further compounded by the fact that most adult educators are part-time helpers whose primary affiliation is to some other occupation or social role.

The challenge this situation poses for training can be understood by contrasting it to the education of children. Schools are usually staffed by a principal and teachers who receive pre-service training, have opportunities for in-service education, and generally follow a well-ordered career. Adult education occurs in a bewildering variety of settings where there is no clear career path. Because piano teachers, village craftsmen, the massive operations of the folkschool, university extension or popular education are all part of the adult education enterprise, it is difficult to study career patterns of adult educators in different settings. Moreover, when cultural and national differences are considered, the situation becomes even more complex.

Levels in a Pyramid

Nobody knows exactly how many people work as paid or unpaid adult educators. Houle (1970) said that 'insofar as a pattern may be discerned amid the bewildering variety of forms of leadership in adult education' it takes the general shape of a pyramid. He guessed that the widespread base would be made up of lay leaders - volunteers who work in a variety of community settings. Adult education volunteers 'are legion and their influence enormous' and, in Third World settings, include the many grassroots workers who implement adult education procedures.

At the intermediate level of the pyramid are a smaller but still substantial number of people whose adult education work is part of their regular job or who accept supplemental employment in the field. Examples would be the person who is a government bureaucrat by day but teaches literacy classes at night, or the museum curator who runs an archaeology course in the local folkschool or community centre in addition to his or her normal duties. University extension directors have long suspected that the most enthusiastic lecturers willing to take on extra work have young families and large mortgages. Other reports speak of high levels of enthusiasm and commitment on the part of those doing 'supplemental' work in adult education. Indeed, one suspects that, for many, this is the back door which often leads to a full-time career in adult education.

At the apex of the pyramid is the smaller but still large group for whom adult education is a primary professional concern. This group has grown larger in recent years and includes directors of adult education in universities, schools, hospitals, museums, prisons, voluntary organizations, business and industry. It includes professors of adult education, staff in national, regional and international adult education associations, personnel in the adult or continuing education section of ministries of education and training officers in business, industry, government, and voluntary organizations.

Neither Houle nor anyone else has tried to count how many educators fit into the three levels of the pyramid.

Nevertheless, it has heuristic value and shows that any training given will have to fit the circumstances under which people work. In 1970 the pyramid was thought to have a shape somewhat akin to a classical volcano like Kilimanjaro or Fujiyama. Since then, the nature of voluntarism has changed. For example, women are demanding payment for work that it was assumed they would do at no charge. Moreover, since 1970, more people have committed themselves to a full-time career in adult education.

Although some parts of the world are bedevilled by hard-and-fast distinctions between vocational and non-vocational approaches, discussions impelled by the notion of lifelong education have led to a broadened definition of adult education. In places where adult education used to describe only liberal studies courses, it now encompasses an array of vocational and non-vocational activities found in all types of agencies (Types 1 to 4). As a result, directors of vocational institutes, trade schools, broadcasting establishments, cultural centres, recreational organizations, popular movements and government agencies who would not have seen themselves as 'adult educators' twenty or thirty years ago, now occupy a position in the apex of the pyramid.

Necessity to Unify the Field

Unfortunately, the expansion of numbers at the top of the pyramid has exacerbated rather than diminished the lack of unity in the field. Ironically, those in the middle of the pyramid are probably more inclined to describe themselves as adult educators than those at the apex. Now, it is even more essential for the field to create a sense of unity and awareness of fundamental concepts. If full-time leaders can achieve this there is some chance their enthusiasm and knowledge will be diffused to others, including workers for whom adult education is a secondary, usually part-time, concern.

It is necessary to unify the field by focusing effort on those in the apex without, at the same time, incurring the wrath of the grassroots by adopting excessively rigid rules and practices that emulate other 'professions' but violate assumptions buttressing adult education. For present purposes, the most important aspect of the pyramid is the notion that most practitioners have adult education as a secondary professional concern; they are part-time adult educators and engage in it after discharging other duties. This has immense implications for training.

A MODEL TO CLASSIFY ROLES AND FUNCTIONS

There has been a continuing preoccupation with the training of adult educators but exhortations, statements of need and

even benevolently inspired attempts to mount training programs, often founder because of a reluctance to build theory.
This is not unique to training. Many adult educators are
missionary types who eschew 'theory' in favour of 'applied',
'participatory' or 'problem-solving' research. A major purpose
of this issue of Convergence is to explore the utility of a
model which classifies adult educators according to the following:

- the outcomes engendered by the education they sponsor
  or work with;
- the role they occupy in the field (planner or teacher);
- the extent to which adult education is their 'primary' or
  'secondary' professional concern.

This model may serve as a heuristic device to help
identify the content as well as the process for training for
adult education workers in different parts of the world. The
intent of the model is not to diminish commonalities that
pervade the training of all adult educators, nor to diminish
the extent to which socio-cultural factors shape training
content and processes. It merely provides a framework within
which to consider issues that impinge upon the training of
those in different parts of the field who occupy different
roles.
     The need for a model to classify the purposes and roles
of adult educators has been demonstrated at international
conferences where discussion on training easily becomes
encumbered by a-theoretical exhortations. At the ICAE World
Assembly of Adult Education in Buenos Aires, 200 participants
in the 'training of adult educators' group struggled for a
week to find a frame of reference that could facilitate communication across cultures. Their linguistic differences were
less of a burden than the lack of a theoretical model.
     The accompanying Fig. 5.1 classifies adult educators
according to outcomes engendered by the education they
sponsor or work with, the role they occupy in the field
(planner, teachers) and whether they have adult education as
a primary or secondary professional concern. These variables,
and their interactions, profoundly influence processes used,
and content embodied in training. The model shown here is
embedded in the socio-economic context in which the training
occurs. It can be used to highlight issues and problems
pertaining to the training of adult educators encompassed by
each of the 16 locations. Thus, what distinguishes training
needed by program planners, irrespective of settings in which
they work (top slice) from that needed by teachers (bottom
slice)? Or, what are the distinguishing characteristics of
training needed by planners and teachers involved in education for social integration (front slice) as compared to those
building technical competence (back slice)?

Proponents of lifelong education who envisage a learning society without barriers between different types of education, and/or learners and teachers, might be disturbed by boundaries separating the 16 cubes. It is probable that, in ideal circumstances, commonalities would outweigh differences between the training of adult educators in different parts of the model. In other words, technical educators, and those concerned with social integration, and/or other types of education, would all study the foundations of adult education, and the psychology of the adult learner as well as other 'core' matters. All would be trained with processes reasonably congruent with principles of adult education. It would be desirable to ensure that all adult educators learn about the history of the field in their country and, if possible, the world. It is also necessary to avoid fragmentation that could stem from the existence of idiosyncratic training experiences for educators in each of the 16 cubes.

Unfortunately, such utopian visions are unrealistic. Obvious constraints impinge on the training of adult educators. For example, those for whom it is a secondary professional concern usually cannot be released for extended training in institutional settings. Although it would be good for technical teachers to learn about social integration and change, employers usually demand that their training be directly tied to the attainment of 'technical' goals. In the same vein, administrators and program planners have plenty of theory and research pertaining to their role without immersing themselves in the detail of instructional design, teaching, and the evaluation of learning. Of course, where a person simultaneously occupies the role of planner and teacher he or she must be trained accordingly.

A Common Conceptual Language

Figure 5.1 is presented to highlight issues pertaining to the training of adult educators in the 16 cubes. The model is comparable to a situation where a researcher employs analysis of variance to distinguish main from interaction effects. To what extent would the character of training provided to educators encompassed by cube 1 be shaped by the fact they are program planners? To what extent would it be shaped by their involvement with a setting where the aim is the social integration of learners? To what extent would it be influenced by the fact that adult education is a primary professional concern? Or, more importantly, to what extent would the character of the training be influenced by a two-way interaction (of social integration outcomes and being a planner) or a three-way interaction (social integration + planner + primary professional concern)?

Immense difficulties are associated with systematically classifying or describing a diverse field like adult education.

Figure 5.1

Nevertheless, central to this analysis is the notion that the variables in this model are universal. The language used to describe them may vary, as will the extent to which each is present or absent. But the three variables - 'outcomes', 'role occupied' and 'primacy of role' - are present in all societies to a greater or lesser extent. The model enables us to speak a common conceptual language that, it is hoped, will foster communication. Thus, popular educators employed by the Council for the Education of Adults in Latin America (CEAAL) in Santiago, Chile, are mainly located in cube 3 (those at the head office) and in cube 11 (those in the barrios and with the campesinas) because they are committed to fostering social change and have popular education as their 'primary' professional concern. Planners in technical institutes, polyvalents, polytechnics, whether in Singapore, France or Africa, are usually located in cube 4 if adult education is their 'primary' professional concern.

Some countries have a higher ratio of full- to part-time personnel than others. Adult or popular education in some parts of the world is more oriented to social change (e.g. Latin America) or social integration (e.g. Canada) than others. But irrespective of whether people, agencies, or entire countries manifest 'high' or 'low' scores on each of the variables in Figure 5.1, they still apply. Moreover, none of this means other variables do not impinge on the training of adult educators. Any model is a reified, and thus only one, view of reality. The best way to clarify all this is to consider each variable in turn.

ADULT EDUCATION OUTCOMES

Early this century 'adult education' in Great Britain and her colonies was largely identified with non-vocational, non-credit programs. In North America, the term was habitually used to identify basic education programs and, in Europe, programs designed to satisfy the cultural yearnings of the populace. These caricatures have little utility today because in North America, Europe, Asia and Africa, and other parts of the world, adult education is now broadly defined and, despite exceptions like Latin America, usually the 'umbrella' concept transcends subsidiary operations such as continuing education.

The broadening definition of adult education has been impelled by rapid change and widespread acceptance of adult education as an essential corollary of socio-economic health or social transformation. While most educators welcome the broadening of the field implied by notions derived from lifelong or recurrent education, these developments have complicated discussion concerning the 'aims' or 'outcomes' of adult education. In times past when the English could confidently say that adult education was what went on in the Workers' Educational Association, Scandinavians could point at the folkschool or study circles, and Latinos and Asians at the popular education or literacy centre, it was easy to distinguish 'adult' from other forms of education. Proponents of lifelong education have called for the erosion of barriers between different settings for education, between credit and non-credit programs and between vocational and non-vocational approaches. Most importantly, distinctions between training and education have been blurred.

Despite this, there has never been a single philosophy of adult education or set of aims capable of rallying support in all parts of the field. For example, peace activists are not enamoured by the activities of military educators. Since adult education is now a broad field, the possibility of agreeing on one philosophy or set of outcomes is even more improbable than in times past. The absence of empirical data makes it necessary to resort to philosophical or other literature. The arguments have been particularly lively in recent years with discussion concerning the extent to which adult education should be 'instrumental' or engaged in for its 'own sake.' Another debate concerns the relative merits of 'individualist' and 'collectivist' perspectives.

In some respects the position adopted here was impelled by the same forces that fuel competency-based education (Mitchell & Spady, 1978). There is a widespread belief that education is an expensive business that yields dubious and often invisible benefits. Authorities have become more interested in explicit rather than vague outcomes produced by education. The move to explicit outcomes has made educators more accountable and sensitive to social, technological and other changes that create educational needs. As adult education becomes less marginal, and adopted as an instrument to ameliorate present and future problems, it will need to focus on outcomes rather than only on the processes employed to accomplish them.

A Typology
The outcomes shown in Figure 5.1 arise from broad sets of societal expectations that create a need for adult education. The expectations can be operationalized as 'characteristics' adults should possess if they are to be part of and participate in a society that is orderly, productive and attractive to its members. Adult education is an instrument that helps learners acquire characteristics that help satisfy or change societal expectations. Working through individual learners, there are four major contributions adult education can provide. Adult education can:

1. Evoke and support social integration among individuals, within organizations, cultural groups, nations, and different parts of the world. Social integration outcomes are concerned with acculturation.
2. Nurture each person's sense of social responsibility and awareness of consequences that flow from his or her behaviour whether undertaken as an individual or as part of a group. Social responsibility outcomes are concerned with citizenship.
3. Develop within individuals a critical understanding of problems, and build skills, knowledge and attitudes required to foster social change, particularly where social justice is sought. Social change outcomes are concerned with transformation.
4. Facilitate the building of technical competence so women and men can create, individually or in groups, new material goods. Technical competence outcomes are concerned with intellectual and psychomotor skills.

The extent to which one or more outcome is seen as important depends upon one's views about the nature of an ideal society, the extent to which adult education is perceived to be an instrument for securing it, and socio-economic, cultural or historical circumstances that impel or inhibit the responsiveness of the movement in particular countries. For example, if the social order is threatened, the need to nurture 'social responsibility' will likely be accorded a higher priority than 'technical competence.' If different cultural groups or parts of an organization or country are alienated, social integration may be a priority, as in Canada in the 1970s (when Quebec threatened to separate) and as now in India, Singapore, Nigeria and other places where governments are encouraging different groups to work for national unity. 'Integration' outcomes have been a major priority of former colonies trying to establish a national identity. Where the social order appears to be threatened, 'social responsibility' may be the most sought after outcome.

When one outcome becomes dominant it attracts resources and shapes the character of adult education processes. Education is based on each outcome. Thus, there is 'technical competence-based' adult education, 'social change-based' adult education, and so on. Not all adult educators or providers favour each equally. In some parts of the world, such as Australia, the notion is not readily accepted that programs designed to build technical competence are part of adult education.

Different outcomes draw social and political support from groups inside and outside the adult education movement. Sometimes tension exists where parts of the field are concerned with different outcomes (e.g. 'adult' and 'popular' education in Latin America). For example, during the recent recession in the western world the need for 'technical competence' outcomes was cited by many governments as the excuse for cutting liberal education programs. (Until barriers between formal and nonformal settings and types of education are lowered, it is inevitable that colleagues in different parts of the system will eye each other with some suspicion.)

Learner and Societal-Centredness

The outcome typology shown in the first dimension of Figure 5.1 satisfactorily resolves the long-standing difficulty associated with portraying adult education as 'learner' or 'societal' centred by not including 'individual development' as an outcome. The great tradition of liberal adult education is the mainstay of the movement in many parts of the world. Moreover, the notion of andragogy formulated in Yugoslavia and imported to parts of North America is a radical exemplar of learner-centredness. It is this tradition that Darkenwald and Merriam (1982) label the 'cultivation of the intellect.'

Two assumptions buttress the conspicuous absence of 'individual' or 'personal' development from Figure 5.1. First, individuals learn, and second, when people learn they will also be building one or more of the competencies shown in Figure 5.1 Thus personal or individual development is a general factor that pervades the four outcomes. Even when a participant is enrolled in a program that, on the surface, has little to do with social integration, responsibility, or change, it is inevitable that what is learned will contribute to the attainment of one or more of the outcomes.

The absence of 'personal development' or the 'cultivation of the intellect' from the outcome typology is not an attempt to diminish the importance of the liberal tradition in adult education. On the contrary, there is evidence to show that liberal education, for so long indulged in for its own sake, is a powerful way to engender social integration, responsibility and change. As Patterson (1984) noted, liberal education has social value. Some of the most astonishing evidence suggests it can remediate 'cognitive deficits' in prison inmates (see Boshier, 1983; Duguid, 1981; Morin, 1981) and, as a result, make them more socially responsible and less inclined to show up as a recidivist. Individual or personal development is an inevitable prerequisite to and corollary of attaining social integration, responsibility, change, or technical competence.

The position adopted resembles earlier debates concerning the nature of intelligence. Is there a general intellectual factor that pervades all other abilities? Or is intelligence comprised of separate uncorrelated factors? Spearman and other British psychologists were convinced that a general factor pervades all intellectual functioning; thus, people good at spatial relationships would also be good at numerical reasoning, verbal ability, and so on. In contrast, for Thurstone and other Americans, intelligence consisted of uncorrelated 'primary mental abilities'. People good at spatial relationships are not necessarily good at numerical reasoning. Unfortunately, different factor analytic procedures were used to buttress both positions, and the matter has never been satisfactorily resolved.

In the the present context, the decision to portray 'individual development' as a general factor pervading the three 'social' and one 'technical' outcome shown in Figure 5.1 is an echo of the British position on intelligence. Individual learners are the vehicle through which social integration, social responsibility, social change and technical competence are wrought. Sometimes the relationship between individual and social outcomes is immediate and direct, such as when immigrants learn the language of their new country and quickly become 'integrated.' In other situations the relationship is protracted and indirect. In all situations individual development is a latent though not necessarily a manifest function of adult education.

A CONCEPTUAL FRAMEWORK

ADULT EDUCATOR ROLES OR FUNCTIONS

Adult educators can also be classified according to roles they occupy or functions they perform. Although terminology varies from culture to culture nearly all work as planners or teachers. Since 1960 there has been a worldwide increase in the number of adult education planners (organizers, administrators). In many settings there are insufficient resources to sustain both a planner and a teacher so one person will occupy both sides.

As Planners
Planning is a crucial part of the adult education process that stems from the nature of its clients and its democratic ethos. Whereas pre-adult educators develop 'curriculum' (based on a discipline or subject-matter) adult educators are more inclined to plan 'programs' based on the needs of individuals, organizations and communities. Adults bring considerable experience to educational settings. The planner must also know how to implement a program, facilitate participation, keep people motivated and evaluate outcomes and processes. Many planners do not work directly on programs. They are involved with budgeting, hiring staff, or formulating policy.

As Teachers
Teachers work in a variety of formal and nonformal settings but all are engaged in a direct or indirect relationship with adult learners. They work at the adult education front lines and labour to convince people that old dogs can learn new tricks in a collaborative, enjoyable, and fulfilling way. In some settings the term 'teacher' is avoided because it evokes memories of school. For this and other reasons, the teacher of adults is variously known as an animateur, tutor, facilitator, trainer, advisor, resource manager or counsellor.

Whatever the term used, adult education teachers have to know how to create instructional objectives, analyze them into learning tasks, and employ techniques congruent with the outcomes sought. There is little point in lecturing at people if attitude change is sought; it is pointless to lecture about motor skills or cognitive strategies. The teacher must know how to involve learners in an active way and employ an array of techniques. The teacher must create a climate of equality and reciprocity where learners feel sufficiently confident to reveal their perspectives on the anxieties concerning what is to be learned. According to proponents of andragogy (Knowles, 1970) adult education 'teaching' is a facilitation process; the teacher need not be a master of the content since that will be based on the experience of learners. This is a commendable posture but when technical competence outcomes are sought it is essential that the teacher be both a 'process' and 'content' expert. This has obvious implications for the training of adult educators.

PRIMACY OF ROLE

The extent to which adult education should be run by people for whom it is their primary or secondary professional concern has been the subject of vigorous debate in inter-national forums. For example, delegates at the First International Conference on Adult Education, held at Cambridge in 1929, were an illustrious group committed to adult education as 'the way out' of problems engendered by war, depression and the machine age then transforming industrial Europe and wreaking havoc in impoverished rural areas. Although they had a profound, perhaps exaggerated, faith in the power of adult education to solve problems, few saw it as their primary professional concern.

Today, there is an influential group of North Americans affiliated to Basic Choices who have misgivings about the social commitment of full-time deans, directors and principals of adult education organizations. They fear that North American adult education is being taken over by full-time 'professionals' intent on promoting themselves by foisting 'lifelong schooling' on a hapless populace. Members of this group fear that adult education is becoming a 'business' and want to restore a sense of social purpose. They want adult education to be a 'movement', not a profession'. This kind of feeling led to the formation in 1984 of the International League for Social Commitment in Adult Education.

While there are complaints in the United States about 'control' exercised by full-time adult educators, operations in other parts of the world are inhibited by a shortage of personnel willing to make adult education their primary pro-fessional concern, because of a lack of public funds and a clearly defined and attractive career structure. Public authorities have come to realize that adult education is an essential corollary of or prerequisite to socio-economic and cultural health, but many refuse to establish posts for full-time adult educators. They rely on part-time workers for whom adult education is a secondary professional concern, temporary appointments, or, in many instances, the services of some hard-pressed official already burdened by other responsibilities.

Places that had no full-time adult educators at the time of the 1972 third Unesco world conference now have some. Some Unesco member states that employed only a few full-time adult educators in 1972 now have a cadre three, four or five times greater than 14 years ago. Examples would be directors of university extension units, officials in adult or continuing education divisions of Ministries of Education, senior staff in professional associations and voluntary organizations.

Ideally, senior administrators who plan adult education policy would have some experience as program planners or teachers so they understand what it means to work on the front lines. There is a regrettable tendency to put people with general administrative skills but little specific knowledge of adult education in charge of adult education sub-units or even large university extension operations. The reverse situation is also prevalent, where the adult education administrator leaves to direct other units. Thus, the head of the training department becomes personnel manager or the director of university extension becomes vice-chancellor or vice-president for university development.

Background papers circulated prior to the 1972 and the 1985 Unesco international conferences suggest a worldwide increase in the number of adult education planners after 1960. This trend, which Hely (1962) linked to the 'rise of the professional' has continued to a point where today there are hundreds of thousands of planners who influence the character of adult education in their organizations, societies and nations. More people now have adult education as a primary professional concern than at any other time. But of the total number of adult education workers, they are a small minority. For present purposes, the estimate is that only one-fifth of the teachers and one-quarter of the planners have adult education as a primary professional concern. Figure 5.1 reflects this estimate which is tentative and probably too high. But error is of little consequence because even the most casual observer notices that many adult education planners, and most of the teachers, work part-time. For example, in the United Kingdom the ratio of part- to full-time adult education teachers was 175:1 at the time of the 1972 Unesco conference. At the 1985 conference, a delegate in Commission II, from an unidentified industrialized country, claimed there was only one full-timer for every 20 part-timers. In nearly every part of the world most adult education workers are part-time. For them, adult education is a secondary professional concern.

Part-time adult education teachers constitute a vast army recruited mainly from non-educational settings. As the Kenyan submission to the 1972 Unesco conference noted, 'the extension officer, the local civil servant, the employees of local companies and local government ... are a readily available reservoir of local teachers.' Adult education providers are hard-pressed to find teachers, and usually require knowledge of the course content; it is a rare to require knowledge of adult education processes. Even in affluent countries it is not usual for university extension, ministry of education or other large providers, to worry much about the teacher's knowledge of adult education theory and practice. As Unesco (1985a) observed, many 'training problems' stem from the fact that most adult educators are part-time. But, 'if the right precautions are taken at the time of recruitment, part-time or voluntary teachers can usually be found ...' Their effectiveness 'seems to hinge largely on the existence of a sufficiently large number of fully qualified supervisory personnel.'

Few of the 'primary concern' and virtually none of the 'secondary concern' teachers are formally trained adult educators, though many may be qualified school teachers. Despite the exhortations of the 1972 third Unesco conference, the Unesco (1976) Recommendation on the Development of Adult Education, and the work of Commission II at the 1985 conference, many government and other officials still fail to understand the difference between the schooling of children and the education of adults. A report from Hungary, included in the Unesco (1985b) round-up, said this leads to 'an inability to comprehend the full scope of the problems' and to excessive 'formalism, subjectivism, and bureaucratic attitudes replacing the spirit of initiative and democracy' that ought to be a characteristic of adult education.

TRAINING CONTENT AND PROCESSES

The model presented provides a framework for classifying adult educators and examining questions concerning training content and processes. In the language of multiple regression, to what extent does role occupied, the primacy of professional concern, and the outcomes sought by the adult educator, influence content they should work with and processes to be employed during training? Where does most of the variance (in content and processes) reside - in the nature of the outcomes sought, in the role occupied, or in the primacy of concern?

The model has 16 cubes or locations. Although some training content and processes are common to each, everyone is unique and requires a response tailored to the particularities of its location. Thus, a teacher for whom adult education is a primary professional concern, working in settings where technical competence outcomes are sought, should learn about content and should experience training processes in some respects different to those created for a planner or teacher involved with social change.

The three independent variables (outcomes, role occupied and primacy) have separate and conjoint effects on the dependent variables - training content and training processes. Primacy probably has the greatest impact on training processes as it is difficult to involve people who have adult education as a secondary professional concern in formal courses or degree programs. 'Outcomes' and 'role occupied' also affect the character of training processes but probably have their greatest impact on content.

Some readers may feel it utopian to speculate about training content and processes compatible with the needs of people in each location in Figure 5.1 because, in many parts of the world, the struggle is to secure any training. For such people it may seem churlish or pedantic to match training content and processes with the various locations in the model. Despite this, there has been a plethora of national and international reports of conferences and seminars concerned with training adult educators, (e.g. European Bureau, 1980), but few systematic studies of training concepts and processes.

However, even where no programs exist, as delegates at the 1985 Unesco conference discovered, authorities appear to be contemplating their creation with more than usual vigour. Moreover, many pre-adult education institutions experiencing a decline in enrolment are looking to adult education, and the training of trainers, as a lifeline to the future. In other places, local or national associations have taken the initiative. Many countries are relying on their own resources. It appears that the minimal provision bemoaned at the 1972 Unesco conference is being replaced by more energetic approaches. The apparent readiness of some educational authorities and associations to train adult educators justifies an attempt to analyze content and processes suitable for educators found in different parts of the model.

'Primacy of professional concern' influences processes to be employed during the training of adult educators but has little impact on the content. The entire problem considered in this issue of <u>Convergence</u> is complicated by the fact that most workers have adult education as a secondary professional concern. Just as adult learners have a low margin for participation, educators cannot allocate lavish amounts of time or energy to training. Consequently, most part-time workers receive minimal or no pre-service training. Once on the job they try to learn from experience but, by and large, have little time to participate in formally organized training activities. Indeed, because so many fail to see themselves as part of the education movement, they do not always see the relevance of training even when available.

Despite constraints impinging on workers for whom adult education is a secondary professional concern, and the implications these have for training processes, these people need the same content as colleagues for whom adult education is a primary concern. The content may be covered in a more accelerated or truncated way but will involve the same topics and theory as that used with 'primary concern' people.

The primacy of concern has decisive effects on the amount (or quantity) of training that can be provided, but should not alter the quality of the experience. Those for whom adult education is a secondary concern should thus undergo training which is qualitatively the same as, but quantitatively different from, that given to those for whom it is a primary concern. In an ideal world 'secondary concern' people working in hospitals, trade unions, business, government, prisons, churches, the armed forces, the media, voluntary organizations, statutory boards and other places, would be trained in a way that is quantitatively and qualitatively the same as that provided for those for whom it is a primary concern. But, in the absence of structural innovations, such as paid educational leave, those who have adult education as a secondary concern will continue to get less training than those for whom it is a primary concern.

It is probable that the content used to train those for whom adult education is a primary concern will often be the same as that used with 'secondary' workers. It is the amount (the quantity) that varies, not the character (or quality) of the content. From one perspective it is dubious to speculate about content since it is shaped in accord with local conditions and prevailing needs. Yet, consultations preceding the 1985 Unesco conference and at the ICAE World Assembly of Adult Education, make it apparent that there are 'core' competencies many people think ought to be nurtured in training programs.

The Unesco Institute for Education took a daring step by bringing together people from contrasting cultures to work on a 'content' for lifelong education that could be used for people to learn about global problems (see International Seminar, 1983). Any attempt to speculate about content and processes for the training of adult educators is less daring, but based on the assumptions that buttressed the Unesco Institute's efforts. For instance, one assumes that despite national, cultural and sub-cultural differences, planners need to know how to diagnose needs and translate them into educational programs. They need to know how to distinguish educational from other needs and where to look for theory that broadens their understanding of needs.

QUESTIONS TO ANSWER

Returning to Figure 5.1 and the language of multiple regression, one can now see that the content and processes of training are dependent variables. To what extent is the character (i.e. content and processes) of training shaped by the role occupied (planner, teacher), by the 'primacy' of his or her professional concern, and by the outcomes sought (social integration, social change, technical competence) in setting where the educator works? To fully answer such questions is beyond the scope of this study. Nevertheless, the following articles* contain a tentative and incomplete answer and, in some respects, reinforce the fact that the model can be used to classify adult educators and facilitate discussion about their training, in different parts of the world.

REFERENCES

Boshier, R.W. (1983) 'Education Inside', Motives for participation in prison education programs, University of British Columbia Program for Correctional Education Research and Training, Vancouver.

Boshier, R.W. (1985) 'Adult Education: Motivation of participants', in Husen, T. & Postlethwaite, N. (eds.) The International Encyclopedia of Education, Pergamon Press, Oxford.

Carlson, R.A. (1972) 'Professional leadership vs. the educational service station approach: An historical appraisal', Adult Education, 2.

Carlson, R.A. (1977) 'Professionalization of adult education: An historical-philosophical analysis', Adult Education, 28,1.

Council of Europe (1978) Training and Retraining of Adult Educators, Council of Europe, Strasbourg.

Darkenwald, G. & Merriam, S. (1982) Adult Education: Foundations of Practice, Harper & Row, New York.

Duguid, S. (1981) 'Rehabilitation through education: A Canadian Model', in Morin, L. (ed.) On Prison Education Ministry of Supply and Services, Ottawa.

European Bureau of Adult Education (1980) Newsletter (on the training of adult educators.)

Hely, A.S.M. (1962) New Trends in Adult Education: From Elsinore to Montreal, Unesco, Paris.

Houle, C.O. (1970) 'The Educators of Adults', in Smith, R.M., Aker, G.F. and Kidd, J.R. (eds.) Handbook of Adult Education, Macmillan, New York.

International Seminar on the content of Lifelong Education (1983) (Background papers) Organized by the Unesco Institute of Education, September 12-16.

Knowles, M.S. (1970) The Modern Practice of Adult Education, Association Press, New York.

Mitchell, D.E. & Spady, W.G. (1978) 'Organizational Contexts for Implementing Outcome-based Education', Educational Researcher, 7,7.

Morin, L (1981) On Prison Education, Ministry of Supply and Services, Ottawa.

---

* Refers to the original publication (ed).

Ohliger, J. (1974) Is Lifelong Education a Guarantee of Permanent Inadequacy? Convergence, 12,2.

Patterson, R.W.K. (1984) 'Objectivity as an Educational Imperative', International Journal of Lifelong Education, 3,1.

Schroeder, W.L. (1970) 'Adult Education Defined and Described' in Smith, R.M., Aker, G.F. and Kidd, J.R. (eds.) Handbook of Adult Education, Macmillan, New York.

South, R. (1982) 'Professionalism and Volunteerism' in European Bureau of Adult Education, The Training and Further Training of Adult Educators, Report of a conference, European Bureau of Adult Education, Amersfoort.

Unesco (1972) Third International Conference on Adult Education: Final Report, Unesco, Paris.

Unesco (1976) Recommendation on the Development of Adult Education, Adopted at the 19th general session, Nairobi, October 26 to November 30.

Unesco (1985) Fourth International Conference on Adult Education: Final Report, Unesco, Paris, (ED/CONF 210).

Unesco (1985a) Fourth International Conference on Adult Education: The Development of Adult Education, Aspects and Trends, Unesco, Paris, (ED-85/CONF.210.3).

Unesco (1985b) Fourth International Conference on Adult Education: Adult education since the Third International Conference: Round-up of replies to the survey...among National Commissions. Unesco, Paris, (ED-85/CONF. 210.4).

Verner, C. & Booth, A. (1964) Adult Education, Center for Applied Research in Education, New York.

PART THREE

HISTORICAL PERSPECTIVES

Chapter Six

PREPARING LEADERS IN ADULT EDUCATION

Eduard Lindeman (1938)

If adult educators are to carry conviction supported by valid feelings, sound reasoning, and cultural meaning, they must soon define the goals for which adult education is designed as an instrument. It seems to me inescapably clear that people do not know what we mean by adult education. Their confusion does not derive from lack of awareness that adults are capable of study; what they do not fully and clearly comprehend is why adults should study. As adult educators we have not been clear in our own minds, and consequently the situation with respect to motivation for adult learning is one of muddled confusion.

Perhaps we have all along been using the wrong word. Adult education is a prosiac term which seems to place emphasis upon genetics rather than upon educational aims. In Sweden and Denmark, where adult education has played so important a part in national life, the term "Folk Education" is employed and immediately one begins to sense an important difference. But the word itself cannot possibly be our main difficulty because language, being always responsive to changing meanings, is flexible and we can make the term mean whatever we choose. The real difficulty lies deeper than the mere use of words.

No good can come from avoiding the essential issue. There is a deep-seated conflict in this country concerning adult education and we may as well confront it. The basic question which we are discussing in this conference, namely the training of adult education leaders, cannot be satisfactorily answered until we can speak with greater assurance about the purposes of this new variety of education. There exist at present two schools of thought with respect to adult education and I shall, for convenience sake, give them names or labels. The first, I shall call the "mechanistic" and the second the "organic" school of thought.

1. Those who represent the mechanistic view point seem to believe that adult education is designed to meet the

93

needs of illiterate, unfortunate, or unprivileged persons. To such theorists adult education always means extending something which is already here; that is, extending the existing patterns of education to an older group. The ideas with which they surround adult education are consequently quantitative, if not static, in character. At best, such persons seem to think of adult education in naively instrumental terms; that is, in terms of giving these neglected learners something which other people have acquired in the normal course of experience. Among the mechanistic thinkers in this field one also finds a strong ingredient of philanthropy. They present adult education as a sort of benefit to be given to the under-privileged

2. On the other hand, those who hold the organic point of view assume at the outset that adult education represents a need which is universal. It is, or should be, designed to meet the needs of all citizens. It is not merely "more of the same"; that is, an extension of something which the privileged already enjoy, but rather a new quality and a new dimension in education. Also, such theorists insist that adult education is a right, a normal expectancy, and not charity. Its purpose is to do something for adults which cannot be achieved by conventional education.

With this elementary distinction in mind we may now proceed to discuss the three important questions which confront adult educators in our country. These questions I take to be: (a) What is adult education for? (b) What sort of equipment should an adult educator possess? (c) What is the responsibility for training adult leaders which should be assumed by our teacher training institutions?

(a) The goals of adult education
Unhappily, almost every formulation of an educational goal may be interpreted as propaganda. We live in a period of history in which it is a simple matter to ruin the best of movements merely through the process of labeling them propaganda. In order to make myself entirely clear at this point I wish to resort to a quotation from the recent book of Lancelot T. Hogben named The Retreat from Reason.

Education is only a live social issue when it is frankly tendentious ... Dislike and distrust of education which are the hallmark of the retreat from reason in our own generation are due to the fact that our educational system has ceased to be an instrument to assert the liberties of the country, or indeed to have any intelligible objective except insofar as it helps some people to gain a livelihood.

The key word in this quotation, from my point of view, is "tendentious". It means that education must have a tendency toward some goal. But, it implies also that such a tendency needs to make its way against certain barriers. The difference between tendentiousness and propaganda is this: in propaganda the teacher conceals the true goal, or he indoctrinates the student to the point of being willing to utilize any method or means to achieve the end, or he excludes those facts and truths which tend to weaken his dogma. Tendentiousness, on the other hand, means that the goals proposed are frankly stated, then tested in the light of science, and thereupon made central to the learning process. It seems to me wholly clear that the present function of education is to furnish us with instruments with which we may begin to realize an age of plenty. Or, stated more plainly, the tendency of education for our time is to show us how to use intelligence in meeting the basic needs of human beings. This is a form of tendentiousness which is peculiarly pertinent to adult learners. Experiments may be more readily inaugurated in adult classes: the proper tendency may exert itself without encountering the opposition of those vested interests which make experimentalism so difficult in the vast structure of public school education.

Goal-thinking is always fraught with innumerable difficulties and I must admit hurriedly that my statement of the central purpose of adult education, namely to meet basic human needs, needs considerable clarification. The totalitarian states of Europe promise to meet the basic needs of their people. They ask in return that the people forego their freedom and place all power in the hands of the state and its dictator. I assume that we Americans should prefer, for a time at least, to experiment with methods for meeting human needs which are not in themselves antipathetic to democracy. Hence, our query becomes "How may education become the instrument for meeting basic human needs within the framework of a democratic society?"

I have already said enough, however, to indicate that the goals of adult education are to be social in nature. Adult education, wherever it has become a live issue and wherever it has succeeded in something more that a quantitative sense, has been thought of and pursued as an instrument for social change and not merely as a means for increasing the efficiency or the smartness of a few selected individuals.

(b) What, then, should an adult educator know and how is he to be equipped?

Stated in the briefest terms, an adult educator should firstly know a great deal about motivational psychology. He should be acquainted with the purposes of people and the processes by which purposes come into being. And, the moment one begins the study of motivations one discovers how important is the role played by the intellectual climate of the era, by the social environment, and by the conditions of life. An adult educator should, therefore, know cultural history, and if he is to probe further into the processes of purpose, he must also know logic, ethics, and aesthetics. He must be oriented in the sphere of contemporary social movements. Secondly, the adult educator should be peculiarly aware of the relation between genetics (growth) and learning. An adult educator who neglects the previous crises in learning which have accompanied growth will never become thoroughly sensitized to the needs of his adult students. Thirdly, an adult educator should be capable of understanding the work experience of his students. An appropriate interpretation of the adult student is impossible without an understanding of the way his life is now being conditioned by his work. Fourthly, the adult educator should be equipped to interpret and make use of the inter- and the intra-relationships of the various disciplines of knowledge. The basic needs of people will never be met through specialization alone. Acute human situations arise at those very points of wholeness from which the specialist takes his departure. And finally, the adult educator should be familiar with the techniques of group work and must be himself a person who can participate in group activity.

(c) The training of adult educators

If our thinking is relatively clear with respect to the goals of adult education and the sort of equipment which an adult educator should possess, we should then be able to discuss more meaningfully how the training is to be done. In order to begin this discussion I shall merely state a few of the considerations which must be taken into account.

It is my conviction that all students now studying in teacher training institutions should be offered one unit in adult education. If students are preparing themselves for administrative work in education, they should pursue a full unit in adult education covering one whole academic year. A few of our teacher training institutions should begin to specialize in order to offer facilities for specialized study in adult education. There should be an agreement among these institutions concerning this specialization so that students may select the college which is best equipped to meet their special needs.

Administrators of teacher training institutions should begin to introduce adult education items in their budgets. School administrators should do likewise. Adult education is a necessity for a democracy and we must all do our share in educating the public so that funds are made available. We will never have an effective adult education movement in this country so long as we depend upon private support or philanthropy.

Before adult education can be incorporated as a permanent part of public education and in turn integrated with the plans of our higher institutions of learning, something will need to happen to the cloistered members of our faculties. It is my firm belief that nothing would do more to thrust the colleges and universities out of their academic isolation than to begin exercising a responsibility towards adult education. I am not now concerned about subject matter, although I do recognise that the existing subject matter as taught would not fit the needs of prospective adult educators. In some institutions this defect could be remedied by employing a co-ordinator. But the deeper readjustment remains as a great perplexity; namely how to re-orient our college and university faculties to the concept that the purpose of education is to meet the basic needs of the people. They need to understand what Thomas Huxley saw so plainly, namely that "the great end of life is not knowledge but action."

Chapter Seven

THE MAKING OF THE MAKERS

Harry A. Overstreet and Bonaro W. Overstreet (1941)

At a regional conference we sat in on a section meeting devoted to problems of leader training. As the discussion developed we felt impelled to put a question: How many people in this group had ever been trained to be adult education leaders? The answer was silence, and no hands raised.

Sometimes when in similar groups we have put a similar question a few indecisive hands have faltered into view, a few tentative voices have given carefully qualified affirmative answers: "I had a summer session course in adult education," or "I was trained to be a Y.M.C.A. secretary - I suppose that is adult education," or "Would you say I was trained by a course I took in discussion methods?" Never in any group have the raised hands represented a confident majority.

By putting such a question we have never intended to imply that the group was unqualified to judge training methods or programs. On the contrary, we have put the question only when we have known ourselves to be in the presence of persons qualified by experience to know what to look for in leaders of adults. But, in addition to satisfying our own curiosity, we have wanted to point a peculiar characteristic of adult education: most of the outstanding leaders who are today concerned with the training of future leaders were never themselves trained by any such deliberate process.

We take it for granted that faculty members in teachers colleges have themselves been through the mill, and that professors in charge of the Ph.D. examinations of future professors have themselves at some past time survived similar examinations. Within the academic system we can assume, in short, that the teachers have been trained by a process not entirely unlike that which they recommend to others. But as soon as we step over into adult education we have to change our assumption: most of those who occupy the status of trainers were themselves trained by experience rather than by courses.

Schemes of leadership training, as a result, derive their validity from two curious sources. On the one hand, they represent an effort on the part of experienced people to provide future leaders with insights and skills which they feel they themselves would have profited by having. Thus, many a leader feels that his own trial-and-error learning might have been less wasteful in time and effort if he had enjoyed some initial training in sociology, and this feeling shows itself in the increasingly frequent inclusion of courses in sociology within training programs. On the other hand, training programs represent an effort to stimulate deliberately attitudes and points of view which are seen to characterize outstandingly successful leaders but to which these leaders were stimulated by haphazard experience. While such programs may lack the on-going tradition of learning which characterizes academic education, they do have a validity peculiarly their own: they are based upon a constant down-to-earth study of the types of experiences that have already made leaders.

Before we go on, therefore, to a detailed analysis of the methods common in training programs, it seems worth while to put together some of the stories that have come to us from those whose names are spoken whenever the leaders in adult education are being listed. Again and again we have put to such leaders some such question as this: "You were not trained to be an adult educator. By what series of experiences did you turn into one?" The varied answers make a suggestive picture of the experiences we can wisely try to invoke by deliberately planned training courses.

FROM CLASSROOM TO LABOR STAGE

Psychology may be peculiarly fitted to turn a man's attention from what goes on inside the classroom to what goes on outside. When once a person is absorbed with the behaviors of people and sensitized to the ways in which hidden states of mind are externalized in action, that person cannot very well confine his interest to those members of the human race who happen to sit in front of him in class. At lease, such would seem to be the logic of the psychological pursuit. In actual practice, however, many an academic psychologist has turned his subject into one that keeps him so absorbed with meticulous details that he never sees even one human being as a whole.

The story, then, of one psychologist's emergence from his academic chrysalis is as good as any story with which to begin this record of the making of adult educators. This man has a certain flair for classroom teaching and a certain vividness of phrase that made students say to one another, "Get into so-and-so's class. He's swell." He liked his students. He liked his subject matter. He liked the teaching experience. He seemed to be making a perfectly adequate use of his knowledge.

Then he was invited to teach a psychology class sponsored by a labor group. Suddenly he was up against an entirely new sort of student body. His audience was made up of people who had a passionately practical interest in what he could teach them about human behavior - the how and why of it. The questions they put to the teacher stemmed from actual experience, and they expected answers applicable to experience. The points of view they expressed opened to their college-made instructor a new world, a world of the hopes and perplexities and fears generated by the working conditions of modern society. He found himself learning by trial and error new methods of presentation. He found himself, finally, applying to his own field of expertness entirely new tests of significance.

By the time the course was finished, this man himself had undergone so many mental and emotional experiences that he could no longer be satisfied to work solely with adolescents in the prepared atmosphere of a classroom. He had discovered how intensely interesting grown-ups are - grown-ups who could talk to him as an equal, who could put his knowledge to the test of experiences quite outside his own range, who could force him to be interesting by the simple device of staying away if he bored them. He welcomed a second chance to teach an adult class. Before he had completed this second course, the damage was irrevocably done, or the salvation irrevocably wrought. He had become an adult educator. That is, he had reached the stage where he regarded as a necessary habitual part of his life an opportunity to gear his material to adult groups and have him check its usefulness and interest by their attitude toward it. Having, in short, stepped down from the status of well-trained college professor, he stepped up to the status of searching human being. Today he is still at the job of learning from adult classes how to teach adult classes.

STORY AFTER STORY

What happened to this man differs in detail rather than in principle from what has happened to scores of others to bring them within the unconfining confines of adult education.

We recall the story of one man distinguished both for the position he holds in a national organization and for experiments he has carried on in vocational rehabilitation. As a young man, newly out of college, he did not care what kind of work he found, just so long as it would provide an income sufficient for marriage. He was offered, finally, the principalship of a diminutive Mid-western high school, a position for which he had no special training or special inclination.

When he had had time to savor the new situation in which he found himself, he became acutely aware of the fact that his students had parents and that many of these parents, themselves innocent of any save the most rudimentary schooling, regarded high school education with an almost pathetic awe. Never before had this young man encountered people who hoped so much from a type of education which he himself took for granted. Was there any reason, he began asking himself, why these men and women should have to be satisfied in the best American tradition with admiring their educated children and declaring that these would have a better life than they themselves had had? More and more he found his interest shifting from students to parents, from those to whom schooling was an expected routine to those to whom it was a mysterious and wonderful open-sesame.

Not at all thinking that he was changing his status from ordinary schoolman to adult educator, but rather merely responding to the logic of a local situation, this man set up evening classes for grown-ups and by working with these grown-ups began to learn how they learned and what they wanted to learn. From that time to the present in one organization after another this man has been resourcefully at the job of studying adult needs and how they can be satisfied.

Then there is the story told us by a distinguished librarian, one of the women responsible for the extent to which other librarians are beginning to think of themselves as adult educators. When she first became a member of a library staff in a Mid-western city, she was perfectly satisfied to look upon librarianship as an orderly job that had to do with checking out books and keeping card catalogues in proper shape. But she had the good fortune to have as her superior a man of rare social insight who saw that no library has a right to exist in splendid isolation from the community it pretends to serve. She was shocked to discover that this man did not regard her as already qualified for her work. Instead he told her to spend the first several months becoming acquainted with the city. He laid down no rules by which she was to achieve such acquaintanceship. He simply told her to go and find out what kind of place it was, what kinds of people were in it, what chief problems these people faced in their American pursuit of life, liberty, and happiness, and in what possible ways books could be of use to them if presented so temptingly that they could feel free to use them. Hers was the kind of search in which tentative step led to step, tentative insight to insight. By the time her odd training period was over she was committed to the belief that the library has to justify its existence by its power to render help to adult Americans on a far broader front than it has traditionally claimed as its own.

101

Now when this woman sets up classes for future librarians, she in turn sends these young men and women out to become familiar with their communities. They, in turn, are shocked. They go as she herself went, with a reluctant backward glance at the neat world of shelves and card catalogues. But most of them gradually learn why she sent them out - and the army of adult educators gains new recruits thereby.

Another story is of the successful businessman who wanted to take a course in public speaking. He did not know where to look for such a course nor how he thought such a course should be conducted. But it seemed to him reasonable that an intelligent adult who found himself handicapped by platform shyness should have a chance to gain the skill he needed. No doubt he could have found some serviceable course in the city where he worked. But he lived in a suburb. He did not want to have to spend an evening a week in the city with all the attendant dreariness of waiting around after dinner for the class hour to arrive. The suburb he lived in was a full-fledged city in itself and seemed small only by contrast with an overshadowing metropolis. Certainly it was big enough to provide for its adult population such educational opportunities as they might wish. Or so this man argued. Like A.A. Milne's king who asked nothing more than a little butter for his bread, this man might well have insisted plaintively:

"I'm not a fussy man,
No one can say I am a fussy man ...

but I do want a little public speaking class." The more he thought about what he wanted the more he wondered about the unsatisfied wants of his neighbours and was inclined to look askance at a beautiful local high school that stood dark at night. This man is still the successful businessman. But his avocation, that of director of one of the most successful adult schools in America, would be enough in itself to keep any ordinary man busy.

Such stories multiplied many times over can be summed up perhaps in the thoughtful, mulling words of one leader, a distinguished scientist, who was telling us how he became an adult educator: "It was mostly a matter of happy accident. I didn't wake up one day seeing a great light. I wasn't a crusader for a new world. I was just earning my living and caring about my science - and then because new adult needs were emerging in society, new ways of teaching science were opened up to me. Teaching in these new ways to new audiences, I myself began to see educational problems and opportunities I had not thought about. I began, also, to find myself in a new educational fellowship that meant a lot to me. That's all there is to it. Accident made me an adult educator

- and it is probably what has made most adult educators: some accident that has thrust new experiences upon them and has made them like those experiences."

This word "accident" loomed large also in the talk of a woman who found that she had become an adult educator by the simple process of adding certain elements to the orthodox program of her women's club. "We stumbled upon our program by accident," she declared. "We were just going along doing the things all women's clubs do. Then, for a certain reason, it became imperative for us to know more about what the other organized groups in our community were doing. By the time we had carried through a simple scheme of having these other groups report at our meetings, we began to see things we'd never dreamed of before about the need for some co-ordination of community activities. That is, some of us did - and we just got together and set about doing what there was to be done." When this woman made a report at a regional adult education conference, she still seemed a bit surprised to find that one becomes a member of the adult education body simply by taking part in some enterprise that adds to the individual or social insight of adults; and that one becomes a leader simply by doing one's part well enough so that other people, similarly engaged, begin to ask questions and to study one's methods.

WHAT THE STORIES SEEM TO TELL

Whenever adult educators sit around pooling their experiences, one can pick up stories that illustrate the way in which circumstance rather than deliberate will or specific training has turned potential leaders into actual leaders.

Out of such stories, we believe, certain meanings emerge: meanings highly relevant to the training of future leaders. We can grant that all these people - and the many others with similar stories - had latent in them peculiar sensitivities that made them respond with feeling and insight to experiences that would have made no dent upon the consciousness of the incorrigibly obtuse.

But granting such sensitivity, the fact still remains that they might have gone on for the rest of their lives doing above-average work in their special fields but never tackling the problem, so important to the health of modern society, of how adult minds are to be made and kept flexible. When we study the circumstances that brought about in them significant shifts of interest, we cannot help noticing certain facts.

First, not one of these people had his initial interest in adult education stimulated by any course he took in college. In every instance, the significance of this subject matter to the life of adults was something he had to discover for himself. This would seem to suggest that college professors are not yet, as a rule, indicating to their students the broad social implications of what they are learning.

Second, not one of them was persuaded to become an adult educator by some other adult educator, already at work in the field, who undertook to explain to him in words the vital importance of the new movement. Each of them, instead, through one circumstance or another, was persuaded to turn his attention to the habits and problems of adults. Each, as a result, undertook some new enterprise or varied some old one. And each, somewhere along the line, discovered to his own surprise that he had become a member of an emerging group of people called adult educators.

Third, each was already at work before he became an adult educator. No one of these people made his first vocational approach to the world as a conscious reshaper of adult ways of thinking and acting.

Fourth, each one acquired the skills necessary to him as an adult educator by a trial-and-error, on-the-job process. No one of them, having glimpsed the possibilities of the new field, thereupon took time off to return to academic walls and prepare himself for adult education.

We notice, moreover, that the formative experiences these people underwent, various as they were, exhibited certain repetitive elements. The things that occurred forced them to widen their customary circle of associates and their customary field of interest. The things that occurred to them, again, forced them to look with measuring eyes at community provisions for satisfying the mental and social needs of grown-up men and women. Finally, the things that occurred forced them to look at their own fields of expertness from a new angle and adapt their knowledge to a new audience.

Perhaps the principle of laissez faire is as obsolete in adult education as in economics. We have now reached a stage of growth in the movement where a deliberate fostering of points of view and social skills has to be substituted for an accidental fostering. Happy accidents do not take place often enough. Besides, while such happy accidents in the past may have netted us our best adult educators, we have no way of knowing how many potentially excellent members have been lost because the accidents did not happen to them.

But what we can learn from the stories of the early and accidental crop of adult educators is something like this: Such training as is deliberately set up should be based more closely upon such experiences as have already proved their power to make adult educators than upon the training courses traditionally employed to staff our public school systems. Methods courses can effectively supplement but must not crowd out field work. Courses in history and philosophy of the movement can supplement but must never crowd out firsthand contacts with adults who have problems to solve and with communities that have various social agencies as part of their make-up.

One of the tragedies of religious history is that no method has ever been devised for passing on in undiluted form the insights of prophet and saint. As soon as a movement becomes institutionalized, leaders have to be multiplied in number. Their training tends to be patterned by institutional demands rather than by the original insight that parented the institution. More and more, accordingly, their training goes on within the walls of training schools. Less and less it goes on in the outside world. Very few religious bodies - and those only briefly - have trusted life enough to believe that young men and women who were urged to a vigorous, many-sided contact with it would become wise and sensitive to the spiritual needs of human beings. The tendency, rather, has been to gather potential leaders into a place where they could be exposed to a carefully selected set of impressions, and the long-range result has been almost invariably unfortunate. The leaders have become people who have felt at home in only a limited range of situations, who have accordingly distrusted other situations, and who have tended to translate their own feeling of unease into a conviction that their own limited range of experience is somehow finer than that which lies outside it.

In many respects, adult education resembles a religious movement more than it resembles our regular school system, and the training programs it sets up are subject to the same hazards. If the hazards are less acute in the case of adult education, that is because the movement stems not from one leader but from a whole flock of leaders, no one of whom claims to be the bringer of the Word. Also, happily, the movement remains so many-sided that the chances of its becoming organized along lines too highly selective are perhaps slight. There is safety of a sort in the very vagueness of the term "adult education."

Nonetheless, there is danger that the movement will develop its own "patter"; that the wish for neatness will threaten the down-to-earth ruggedness of such haphazard training as the original leaders were blessed with; that adult educators will be more comfortable talking with other adult educators than with other adults. As an antidote to our own wish to define and catalogue and measure results, we need to remind ourselves every so often that the best leaders of the future will probably be made by processes not unlike those that have made the best leaders of the past and present: processes that have had a minimum to do with academic routines and curricular niceties and a maximum to do with the handling of concrete situations in a world of living men and women.

Chapter Eight

TRAINING ADULT EDUCATORS

Wilbur C. Hallenbeck (1948)

Many thousands of adult educators are constantly at work in regular jobs throughout the United States and Canada. The majority of these, however, have either been pushed into their jobs by circumstances or been pulled into work with adults by their own concerns and interests, without previous training. Many of them have received in-service training, and some have acquired professional training after they have had considerable experience. Others have obtained their positions after they have had professional training. Such a situation as this is inevitable in a profession which is in the process of developing.

OPPORTUNITIES FOR TRAINED ADULT EDUCATORS

As the fields of operation of adult education have increased, and experience has accumulated, the need for professionals has grown. And yet opportunities for trained adult educators are still equivocal. The need is there, and in some quarters the demand is turning to pressure, but the support is still inadequate and unsteady. It is still true in most situations that adult education gets done by a bootlegging process on the part time of persons employed primarily for other functions.

There are three areas where positions in adult education are steadier. The first is the teaching of English and citizenship to foreign-born residents and the elementary phases of education to the functionally illiterate in the larger cities. This type of teaching, however, is a part-time job with hourly pay for a short term, and it must consequently be done on the margin of time of people otherwise employed. Standards and requirements have been set up which, for the most part, are inadequate, especially with regard to methods and materials useful in dealing with adults. There are also some part-time jobs in evening high schools, where requirements are the same as those for teaching in day high schools, without regard to the fact that most of the evening students are adults. It is scarcely possible to have adequate requirements for part-time, poor-pay jobs.

The second area of steady employment in adult education is the Cooperative Extension Service in agriculture and homemaking, where a large proportion of the professional adult educators are to be found. The basic training for this work is done in the land-grant colleges. Home demonstration agents major in general home economics, county agents in general agriculture, and state specialists in their various special fields. Under the leadership of the federal extension service office in the Department of Agriculture and the state extension offices, a program of leaves-with-pay has been worked out so that extension service employees may take up graduate study in adult education. Programs in several universities have been approved for this purpose.

The third area is group work. Since positions in this area are in large measure with agencies and institutions which consider themselves social-work agencies, group work has been looked upon as social work. The basic training for it has therefore been in social work, with specialization in the techniques of group work and in community organization and community planning. The question inevitably arises: Is group work social work or education? In actual practice, it is more nearly adult education. Group workers find a need for training in adult education and adult educators find a need for group-work training. In fact, adult education training is heavily loaded with group-work concepts and techniques. The answer to the question above is, of course, that group work is both social work and adult education; that it involves some training in both fields; and that the major emphasis in each individual case should depend on the circumstances, agencies, and problems involved.

ADULT EDUCATION AS A PROFESSION

The three essential elements that make a profession a body of knowledge, specific training, and jobs must be considered in the preparation of adult educators.

Jobs have already been discussed in general. Among the many adult education jobs, there is a great variety. Compare, for example, such diverse tasks as teaching those who have been deprived of formal education and leading discussions on the current social, economic, and political issues; teaching handicrafts and teaching psychology; developing music appreciation and carrying on parent education. The diversity of these tasks indicates the need for a common denominator of training and shows the types of specialization which are practical. A partial list of these types includes: (1) work with a particular group of people - parents, workers, recent immigrants, etc; (2) various subject-matter fields, broadly rather than narrowly conceived; for example, social sciences rather than history or economics, development of personality and human relationships rather that psychology, communication rather than English and the like; (3) types of adult education, such as leading forums, or discussions, or developing skills, or recreation leadership; (4) community organization and community planning, involving group-work techniques and methods, stimulating indigenous organizations and democratic processes; and (5) organization and administration of adult activities.

Training has two points of reference: on the one hand, the jobs to be done, already referred to, and on the other hand, the body of knowledge. The latter is the determining factor for training. There are still many issues and differences of opinion with regard to training, but the main problem is the concept around which the training is built. Two things must be borne in mind: first, adult education is a function and a process, not an end, and consequently it becomes valid with reference to definite objectives; second, education cannot be accomplished, as such, in a vacuum. We speak of an educated person, but he is educated by virtue of the definite knowledge, skills, attitudes, etc. which he has acquired. Consequently, while a teacher teaches people he must teach them something.

THE BODY OF KNOWLEDGE

With reference to the body of knowledge, there are four possible positions. First is the traditional position held by most universities: All that good teaching requires is mastery of a subject-matter field. This position assumes that the main objective is a systematic coverage of an organized field of knowledge per se. The method which is implicit in this view is the lecture; the materials are textbooks or readings organized by the instructor.

Second is the position that methods are the "tools of the trade" of teachers, and that, consequently, the training of teachers is primarily a matter of their acquiring knowledge about and experience with methods. Many teacher training institutions hold this position. The assumption is that the subject matter to be taught is available, but that, only as tested methods of teaching are used, can subject matter be effectively transmitted to students, in terms of objectives set by teachers. Methods are laid down, and materials are a matter of the best possible selection.

Third is an essentially different position. It holds that adults have peculiar problems of learning and that the conditions imposed by these peculiarities make the teaching of adults unique. Consequently, an understanding of the psychology of the adult and how to obtain knowledge about adults as individuals is basic in training adult educators. This point of view has gained increasing recognition as the knowledge of adult psychology has grown. The assumption here is that adults "call the tune" through their interests and needs, and that the conditions of learning dictate methods and materials. Because of the wide range of individual differences in any group of adults, each situation is unique. Methods involve experience in how to apply principles in real situations; materials must be created, because there is a dearth of satisfactory ones.

Fourth is an eclectic position taking those things from each of the other positions which are applicable and useful. It is necessarily built around the psychology of the adult and is gaining increasing acceptance.

This fourth position is essentially the one that we are taking here, with the following additional emphases growing out of the sociology of adults.

1. The community is the setting of any adult education situation and determines the kind of adults who will participate, the problems they will have, the character of activities involved in the solution of these problems, and the adult education possibilities.
2. The motivation on the part of adults for educational experience is closely related to the problems which they encounter in daily living. Their educational opportunities should therefore take account of these problems.
3. Since it is the pressure for action which is the focus of experience motivation, the completion of the educational experience for adults involves action.
4. The aim of adult education must be the satisfaction of the adult participants, not the completion of a course of study or a term of classes.
5. Since the world of experience of the majority of adults is very limited, in our present day with its great opportunities for the enrichment of living, adult education has the obligation of "expanding the horizons" of adults.
6. Growth into effective democratic citizenship is an adult education process.

CONTENT OF TRAINING FOR ADULT EDUCATORS

The content of training for adult educators grows out of the philosophy of training and the concept of the body of knowledge. There follows a general descriptive outline of the major areas of studies for those in training under the philosophy which has been stated.

General Introduction to and Knowledge about Adult Education

History of adult education, not as such, but rather to discover the place it has held in various times and in various cultures, the objectives and purposes under which it has operated, the forms it has taken, and its accomplishments; the precipitate of history in the adult education of the present day; the factors which have made adult education effective in the past and their relevance today.

Philosophy of adult education: the character of purposes and objectives and how they are determined, both ultimate and immediate; the ideas with which to work; principles derived from experience; the necessity for and the process of developing a "working philosophy."

Functions of adult education deduced from an analysis of the social scene, involving a knowledge of the chief characteristics of American culture and an understanding of the place of adult education in that culture, the conditions imposed on adult education by democracy, the relation of the cultural function to community functions.

Administration of adult education including the organizational structure of American adult education, the roles of various institutions, practical problems of organizing and operating a program, the community approach, problem of integration.

Emotional requisites for adult educators; belief in people and a better world, sense of mission, genuine interest in adults, broad interests, and experience in rich living.

Community and Community Organization

This area of study would include a basic knowledge of sociology and the techniques of community study; an acquaintance with sources of data about communities; the theory and facts about community organization and community planning; a practical understanding of the relation of adult education to community organization and community planning and of group life and cooperative activity.

Psychology of Adults

Factual data about adult learning; deductions regarding the peculiarities of education of adults; implications for methods in adult education.

Methods and Materials

How to meet the conditions of adult learning: individual attention and group experience; informality; attitude toward and character of methods. Methods found useful by experience: cooperative participation; discussion of various types; workshops; psychodrama, etc. Problems of materials: readability; printed matter, use of mimeograph, radio, films, discussion out-lines, etc.

Problems of Experience
Some of the best material available for use in training adult educators grows out of the problems, which have been, or are being, encountered in experience. Provision should be made for the use of this material as a basis for criticism, analysis, and evaluation.

PROGRAMS AND AGENCIES

The program of training adult educators assumes a liberal arts education as a background. It is professional training on a graduate level in graduate schools of education. Teachers' colleges and education departments in liberal arts colleges can and occasionally do offer introductory courses. Only one or two institutions have so far attempted comprehensive training, and their programs follow in general the outline above. Specialized courses in subject matter, skills, etc. are not special to adult education and are obtained through work in other deparments. In-service training through summer courses, institutes, conferences, and workshops is offered by many universities. Frequently organizations with extensive programs and large staffs provide training for their own people. Among such organizations are federal agencies, public schools, young people's organizations, churches, workers' education organizations, women's clubs, etc., etc. A listing of institutions where training is to be offered during the summer, together with their programs, is published annually in the April number of the Adult Education Bulletin of the National Education Association.

METHODS IN TRAINING ADULT EDUCATORS

It would seem quite unnecessary to say that adult educators should be trained as they are taught to train others, and yet all too often they are lectured about the disadvantages of lectures as compared with other methods. Methods must be a matter of experience, and instructors who cannot demonstrate methods are not able to do the job of teaching methods. There is as much art as knowledge in the use of methods, which means that field-work experience is an essential part of the training of adult educators. Actual working with adults, during, or in preparation for, the training period, should be supervised. The supervisor should be sympathetic and cooperative, and capable of giving constructive suggestions and helpful criticism.

TRAINING ADULT EDUCATORS

The whole process of training should be informal. Since the focus is upon the use rather than the possession of knowledge, most of the material can be handled more effectively through discussions and conference processes. The training will likely be climaxed in a seminar on problems in which not only the problems and plans of the participants, but also the general and common problems of adult education are cooperatively explored by instructors and students together.

TRAINING OF LAY LEADERS

The increasing use of lay leaders is inherent in the very character of adult education; a cooperative learning experience related in one way or another to group action. The most successful adult education enterprise in the United States, both quantitatively and qualitatively - the Cooperative Extension Service in Agriculture and Homemaking - depends almost entirely on lay leadership in its group activities; its success would not have been possible otherwise. Money will never be available to do the necessary job of adult education by professional leadership. All adult educators, consequently, will be responsible, sooner or later in some way, for training lay leaders.

The training of lay leaders is not essentially different from the training of professionals. It will, however, be more limited in scope and more specifically related to the job in hand. It will necessarily involve less time and so be more selective in content.

SOME ISSUES IN THE TRAINING OF ADULT EDUCATORS

Adult educators are born and not made. The issue suggested in this statement always appears in the early stages of the development of any profession. The question here really is whether the spirit of the teacher is not more important than his knowledge. The answer is that in adult education both are essential. When rules and techniques take ascendancy over personal qualities and dedication to a job one believes in, then adult education loses its vitality.

Trained adult educators can handle any adult education situation. The sweeping positiveness of this statement makes it impressive, but not true. It should be obvious that the tremendous variety of situations, objectives, types of study and kinds of people involved in adult education precludes the possibility of anyone's being equal to all occasions. Even a trained adult educator is illiterate in some areas of living and in many areas of knowledge. One is sometimes teacher and at other times learner.

In the last analysis, the competence of a teacher lies in his mastery of his field of knowledge. One cannot interest students in a subject of which he knows little. The eager response to the fascination and challenge of knowledge is contagious; it is passed on from those who have it to others. The context of the training of adult educators is a professional body of knowledge for the edification of those being trained. This is not the knowledge, engendering the love of knowledge, which the teachers in training are later to pass on to their students. That is something else, something so important that, without it, an adult educator will be a sterile worker in a world which needs his fruitful labors greatly.

Chapter Nine

THE EDUCATION OF ADULT EDUCATIONAL LEADERS[1]

Cyril O. Houle (1960)

At the heart of the educative process is the student, but he cannot go far in his quest for knowledge without some kind of teacher. This fact has always been as true of the education of adults as of children. The conscious effort of individuals to improve themselves, the sense of mission which causes leaders to take their message to others, and the collaborative effort of groups to increase their understanding are familiar themes throughout recorded history. But in the present century, the effort to provide adult education has grown into a much more highly organized movement, and the location and training of capable and inspiring leaders has emerged as a central problem which has had to be solved in countless ways.

Most adult learning takes place spontaneously and naturally, as men and women decide they want to learn something and proceed to do so by their own efforts. Wherever adult education takes on social form, however, two groups of people are differentiated: those who accept responsibility for providing focus and direction and those whose activities are thereby shaped and led. This duality has many patterns: the teacher and the student; the leader and the participant; the counselor and the person counseled; the administrator and the staff; and the planner and the person who is guided by plans. A certain awkwardness of phraseology grows out of this diversity, but, in an arbitrary fashion, we may give to the first party in each of these pairs the generic term "leader" or "educator of adults." It is in preparing such a person for his role that the need for adequate training arises.

THE PRESENT STATUS OF TRAINING

Most leadership training, like most adult education, is self-directed. An individual confronted with the responsibility of becoming an educator of adults learns partly by the process of participation and partly by his own examination of that process. He studies books or pamphlets or manuals, he talks with others in a similar situation, he goes to meetings, he asks for supervisory assistance, he visits other programs, or he analyzes his own performance in terms of a standard which he has developed himself or adopted from some source. The quality of his learning depends in essence upon his capacity to teach himself.

The largest volume of organized (as distinguished from self-directed) training of adult educational leaders occurs within the institutions which sponsor programs, such as the public schools, the Cooperative Extension Service, and the voluntary associations. Some of these agencies have clear cut patterns of advancement up the ladder of professional responsibility, and training is a prerequisite for taking each step. Among the techniques used are: constructive and continuing assistance by supervisors; internship; regular or occasional short courses, conferences, and workshops; continuing staff seminars; collaborative training with other agencies; and the deliberate use of decision-making processes in such a way as to broaden the horizons of staff members (as when program-planning is done by a group rather than by the head of the agency acting alone.)

Since organized adult education is still in a relatively primitive state, it does not have such complete systems as have been developed for the preparation of teachers or administrators of childhood education or for such established professions as law, medicine, or the ministry. Any comprehensive plan calls for the use of certain major procedural steps: 1. The definition of the traits of the successful practitioner. 2. The recruitment and selection of promising candidates. 3. The training of these people in such a way that they will gain competence in the duties they are expected to perform. (This is usually called "pre-service training.") 4. The adjustment of the new worker to his first position. ("Induction training.") 5. The continuing education of the worker to keep his capacities at a high level, to equip him with new knowledge, or to enable him to meet new responsibilities. ("In-service training.") While individual institutions of adult education have developed excellent special approaches to one or more of these tasks, no large-scale adult educational program, with the possible exception of the Cooperative Extension Service, has yet worked out and put into effect a comprehensive plan for training its leaders. A number of ambitious efforts are now being made, however.

The most important single influence on the training of educators of adults since the end of World War II has been the study of group behavior. Some of the psychologists and sociologists who have pioneered in this field have been interested only in theoretical studies, but others have been concerned with the development of techniques which would permit groups to work more intelligently and flexibly and to analyze their own processes. The most notable example of what might be called "pure" group relations training has been the annual summer program operated by the National Training Laboratory at Gould Academy in Bethel, Maine, but other activities of like nature are now conducted throughout the country. Even more important, perhaps, has been the gradual incorporation of group concepts or group techniques into virtually all training practice in adult education. While most programs are not centrally group-oriented, and perhaps never will be, it would be hard to find any training program which had not been influenced, however subtly, by the group dynamics movement.

THE PYRAMID OF LEADERSHIP

Insofar as a pattern may be discerned amid the bewildering variety of forms of leadership in adult education, it takes the general shape of a pyramid. This pyramid is divided horizontally into three levels which are essentially different, although at their edges they blend into one another, so that no sharp lines can be drawn to differentiate them. Let us look first at the whole pyramid and then turn back to examine each of its three levels.

At the base of the pyramid is the largest group of people, those who serve as volunteers. Their number is legion and their influence is enormous. There is no brief way to indicate the scope and diversity of volunteer leadership but its nature can at least be suggested by listing the groups which Liveright studied in his comparative analysis of voluntary adult leadership: the county educational program of the Montana Farmers Union; the educational program of the St. Louis Mental Health Association; the home demonstration program of the Cooperative Extension Service; the program of training for supervisors in human relations and problem solving sponsored by the Elgin National Watch Company; the parent education program of a branch of the P.T.A.; the discussion programs of a state League of Women Voters; the steward training program of a local union; the program of training in basic economics provided for the supervisors of the American Viscose Company; the Great Books Program; the World Politics Program; the Presbyterian Bible School Program; the Lutheran Bible School Program; the discussion program of the Henry George School of Social Studies; and the first-aid program of the American Red Cross.[2]

At the intermediate level of the pyramid is a smaller group of persons who, as part of their paid employment, combine adult educational functions with the other duties which they perform. They include: general staff members in public libraries, museums, and settlement houses; school, college, and university faculty members who teach both young people and adults; educational officers in the armed services; personnel workers in government and industry; and persons employed in mass media of communication.

At the apex of the pyramid is the smallest group. It is composed of specialists who have a primary concern for adult education and basic career expectations in that field. They include: those who direct the adult educational activities of public schools, universities, libraries, museums, social settlements, prisons, and other institutions; professors of adult education and others who provide training; those who concentrate on adult education and others who provide training; those who concentrate on adult education on the staffs of voluntary associations or agencies concerned with health, safety, or other special interests; directors of training in government, industry, or labor unions; and most of the staff of the cooperative Extension Service.

These three groups of leaders are intimately inter-related. A strong program of lay leadership requires the leadership of specialists or part-time workers. These latter groups, in turn, may be isolated or ineffective if lay leaders do not help them carry knowledge to the community. Some volunteer and part-time leaders become intrigued with their adult educational responsibilities and extend their range of knowledge and competence, thereby moving up in the pyramid. Also, while the content of the training program must be pitched at the appropriate level of each of the three groups, there are at least some common elements; certain fumdamental principles must be drawn, for example, from the intensive training of the specialist to be included in the briefer training of the lay leader. Certain skills (such as the nature of group processes and the technique of leading a discussion) may also be common to all three.

THE TRAINING OF LAY LEADERS

Lay leaders for the most part require specialized, brief, and clear-cut training to give them the immediate skills they need to carry out their responsibilities. They learn to lead a series of discussions, to demonstrate a technique, to plan a program, to discharge an elective or appointive office, or to conduct a campaign. Their concern is with the task at hand and how to perform it well.

A great deal of thoughtful work has been done in lay leadership development. The large-scale organizations which rely heavily on volunteer assistance - such as the American Red Cross and the various youth-serving organizations - usually employ training specialists and publish extensive libraries of manuals and special aids. Most of these national programs concentrate their efforts on the pre-service aspects of leadership training.

The central task in training lay leaders is to help them understand the appropriate principles of action which seem significant in the light of their experience. This result cannot be brought about by experience alone. As Cardinal Newman pointed out, "If experience were all that is significant in this world, you would expect sailors to be the wisest of men, for they travel around and see everything. But the multiplicity of external objects which they have encountered forms no symmetrical and consistent pattern upon their imagination."[3] And so it is with potential lay leaders. They have had much experience with groups but lack sufficient insight to be able to lead them.

The leadership of a group is a complex process which can never be analyzed and understood in a simple and uncomplicated way. But a training program which sets out to teach a potential leader something about the whole range and complexity of the interpenetration of adult minds will usually end by frightening him and destroying his confidence in himself. He needs, instead, the assurance which comes from understanding the central rules for effective group behavior, the core principles which will cover most of the situations with which he must deal. Given these, he will ordinarily succeed reasonably well. Later, as he gains experience, he will realize that these rules are not enough and that he must move beyond them. He will begin to understand the subtleties of the group process and, in his constant re-examination of his own experience, he will move toward deeper levels of understanding thereby increasing his competence as a leader.

The in-service growth of leaders should not, however, be left to chance or self-direction. One weakness of many programs of lay leadership development is that they are based on the assumption that an initial training period is enough. Ways must be found to encourage potential leaders to realize that, while they are having the experience of leadership, they must also think about it and try to discover ways of improving their own performance. Machinery must be set up to assist that process: advanced courses, friendly supervision, visitation of other groups, guided reading, and meetings with other leaders to talk about the group process.

Inherent within the very idea of lay leadership is the concept that the leader will not want to continue the same task forever. One who leads a specific course several times will gradually discover that it is losing its interest and appeal for him. He will want to go on to some other course - or, indeed, to some other form of leadership. This desire is normal and natural, and anyone who is concerned with the establishment of training programs must realize that he will have a continuing responsibility to replenish the supply of new leaders.

The other aspects of a comprehensive training - identification of leader traits, recruitment, and entrance training - should receive more attention than they normally do. Unfortunately, the directors of many programs find that they cannot secure an adequate supply of prospective leaders and therefore must accept those who are available. Also those who operate leadership training programs are often so hard-pressed for time that they feel they can provide nothing more than pre-service education. As more adequate resources become available for adult education, the breadth and caliber of training plans will improve.

The use of lay leaders for adult education has always been a matter of controversy. There are two major areas of disagreement.

The first has to do with the suitability of using lay people to lead discussions which have to do with highly complex subject matter. To a professor who has made a lifelong study of Plato, international relations, economics, or literature, it may seem preposterous that someone with no specialized subject-matter competence should be allowed to lead a discussion of the "Apology," sovereignty, the gross national product, or "The Wasteland." The dangers are even greater if the subject matter deals with such emotion-laden topics as parent-child relationships, marital adjustment, or mental health. To specialists in these fields, it sometimes seems perilous to trust the handling of such matters to "blundering amateurs."

The advocates of lay leadership make a number of responses which may be summarized as follows: (1) It is the function of lay leaders to help many people gain a few central concepts; if these concepts are carefully chosen and presented in pamphlets, films, recordings, or other media prepared by specialists, the lay leader can be an indispensable means of reaching large numbers of people. (2) There are not enough specialists to handle the mass job which is required. (3) Even if there were enough experts, there is not an adequate public interest in the lengthy and detailed study, which requires expert teaching, whereas, in most fields, a fairly large number of people can be interested in a briefer and more general approach. (4) The role of a lay leader is carefully defined so that he acts not as a specialist but as first among equals in the exploration of the work of specialists. The study materials provided are the teachers and he is merely the leader of a discussion about them. (5) A lay leader deals only with normal situations; part of his training should equip him to know when he is dealing with some problem which goes beyond his own capacity to handle it.

Such arguments as these, and others which might be added, have been advanced for many years, but the debate still rages, partly because lay leadership training is still not as effective as it should be.

The other major area of controversy has to do with the nature of the training provided to lay leaders. Here there are many points of disagreement. Is it possible to have generalized leadership training or must training always be specific to each program? Or can there be general elements which apply to all programs but which can be supplemented by the special requirements of each program? Should the training of leaders concentrate on the materials they are to teach or the methods they are to use? If the latter, should the potential leaders be taught careful rules for performing such functions as discussion leadership or is it better to try to focus directly on the group process? Such questions as these have been discussed for a good many years but little agreement has yet been produced, perhaps because the proponents for any given point of view tend to insist that their own solutions are universally applicable.

Actually, no solution is universally applicable. Adult education is so richly diversified that no single approach to lay leadership is possible. Liveright[4] has performed a service in analyzing a number of groups and developing a typology. He analyzes programs in terms of two different factors. The first has to do with whether a program is basically concerned with changing attitudes, understandings, or skills. The second factor has to do with whether it is appropriate for the group to have high, intermediate, or low group cohesion. The comparison of these elements thus produces a typology in terms of which it is possible to define appropriate leadership styles and to establish training programs for them.

PART-TIME LEADERS

There is a rapid increase in the number of people who earn part of their total compensation by teaching adults. Many school teachers, librarians, group workers, health educators, personnel directors, labor union officials, and others find that they are drawn in some fashion into adult educational activities. Usually they make such adjustment to the situation as seems to them appropriate, and do their work without any formal training for it.

As the number of such people increases, the need for some kind of systematic pre-service instruction in how to teach or lead adults becomes more apparent. Teachers' colleges have begun to introduce courses or units on adult instruction. In the fields in which adult classes are frequently found (such as vocational agriculture or home economics) special courses on the teaching of adults are now being initiated on a number of campuses. Methods courses for those who may go into the Cooperative Extension Service are also becoming common in colleges of agriculture and home economics. Librarians (particularly those who expect to serve in public libraries) are sometimes given a special introduction to adult services. Similar activities have been initiated in other professional fields.

The theory of what might be done, however, has far outrun practice. In many fields of adult education, there has been much committee and conference work, often at a national level, and a number of useful books and pamphlets have been published, pointing the way to a better understanding of adult education by its part-time workers. It is doubtful, however, whether actual practice during pre-service training programs has yet been widely influenced.

Nor is the situation very much better so far as the in-service education of part-time workers is concerned. University professors and high school teachers, for example, usually do not believe that they need special assistance when they turn from adolescent to mature audiences. A few extension deans and evening school principals have ingeniously met this situation by developing such special techniques as invitational week-end conferences, manuals, or workshops. These activities are not widespread, however, even in universities and schools, and in many of the other situations in which adult education occurs little or nothing is done to provide in-service training for the part-time leader.

SPECIALISTS IN ADULT EDUCATION

The specialists in adult education, as has already been pointed out, are chiefly identified by the crude test that they earn their living and expect to continue earning their living by teaching adults or by administering such instruction. Often the word "professional" is used instead of "specialist" but such usage probably obscures the situation more than it clarifies it. Certainly the group of present practitioners of adult education cannot yet meet such accepted canons of a profession as: universal social recognition; a highly complex body of verified and widely accepted knowledge; and the existence of a corps of persons trained in a rigorous discipline and organized in such a way as to enforce conformity to its standards of behavior.

Even more important, the traditional pattern of professional training has little relevance to present practices in preparing specialists in adult education. In the ministry, in law, in medicine, and in all the other occupations whose practitioners are educated at universities, patterns of selection, pre-service, induction, and in-service training are followed in a reasonably clear-cut fashion from the time the boy or girl is selected for the professional school until the accomplished professional returns for his last refresher course. Most educators of adults do not prepare for their responsibilities in the field during their youth, but acquire an interest in it only after they have become mature. The young man who wrote to George Bernard Shaw for advice on how to become a drama critic got the answer: "There is no way of becoming a drama critic. It happens by accident." When the educators of adults talk about their own entry into the field, it is clear that in their case, too, accident has played a large part. They came in, they usually say, "by the back door"; the comment is made so often as to raise the speculation that there is no front door.

University Training in Adult Education

But there are, at any rate, some people who have prepared initially for another occupation, have then found their way into some form of adult education, and who have then decided to undertake organized study in that field. To meet this need, a number of universities have developed courses of various sorts and a few have gone beyond the provision of special offerings to develop complete programs leading to the master's and doctor's degrees. The 1936 Handbook of Adult Education identified forty-nine institutions which had offered courses in adult education during the previous year; Teachers' College at Columbia University had already developed degree sequences. Since that time various authors have examined and appraised the extent of training opportunities for specialists. Beginning in 1941, for example, the present writer wrote ten annual articles in the Adult Education Bulletin identifying the institutions which were then offering work in adult education and describing various aspects of their work. The latest comprehensive study is that of Svenson, who found that in 1952-53 twelve institutions offered advanced degree programs in adult education and fifty-three institutions offered some kind of professional study in adult education.[5]

Each such institution has its own conception and pattern of instruction but the scope and nature of graduate study in this field are becoming more clear-cut. In large measure this result has been achieved by a series of annual conferences sponsored by the Commission of Professors of Adult Education of the Adult Education Association, with financial assistance provided by the W.K. Kellogg Foundation. At these gatherings, of which there have now been four (including one conference held prior to the receipt of the Kellogg grant), the full-time professors of adult education have been able to examine their own work carefully, decide on common themes, and project desirable courses of action. As of July, 1958, there were twenty-two such full-time professors representing fourteen institutions, one of them in Canada. The report of the commission, which will probably be issued in 1962, should provide much information to those interested in the advanced training of specialists in adult education.

Fund for Adult Education Grants

The intensive education of specialists has also been greatly aided by the Study-Grant Program of the Fund for Adult Education. Acting on the recommendations of a Development Committee of eleven educators, The Fund for Adult Education began, in 1952, to make study and training awards to individuals. These grants had four objectives: (1) to enhance the skills and increase the knowledge of those already in leadership positions in adult education; (2) to recruit and develop persons capable of administering and guiding the operation and growth of programs of liberal adult education; (3) to help strengthen university graduate programs in adult education; and (4) to utilize operating liberal adult education programs as training situations. These interrelated aims remain unchanged.

By January, 1960, nearly three hundred awards had been made to individuals in adult education and the total amount spent was more than one and one-half million dollars. In the main, the FAE Fellowships have gone to persons pursuing careers in the major divisions of the adult education complex: general and agricultural extension; evening colleges; public schools; libraries; and national and local organizations and agencies. Fellowships have also gone to adult educators working in labor unions, government industry, and the clergy.

Objectives of Specialist Training

All educators of adults believe in lifelong learning. Therefore, neither the student who comes to the university to learn how to be a specialist nor the professor who teaches him can assume that the graduate program will provide final and complete achievement of the qualities which characterize the outstanding leader of adult education. The objectives of the graduate program may serve, equally as well, for lifelong professional aims. Universities vary in the way in which they define the basic attributes of the outstanding educator of adults and in the emphasis which they place upon each one. Most of them, however, try to help potential specialists work toward the achievement of the following general objectives:

1. A sound philosophic conception of adult education based on a consideration of its major aims and issues and embodying convictions concerning the basic values which it would seek to achieve. Since those who became educators of adults usually have no background of study or investigation in the field, they often tend to accept each new plausible suggestion as a

fundamental principle of the universe. Experience and inquiry produces a broader viewpoint. The leader of adult education comes to understand the breadth and variety of his field and accept the fact that it includes countless aims and approaches. He also develops his own set of values which enables him to select the activities he wishes to undertake and guides him in building the program for which he is responsible. His philosophic conceptions cannot be imposed by someone else but must grow naturally within him; they are nurtured by reading, study, discussion, reflection, and the analysis of experience.

2. An understanding of the psychological and social foundations on which all education (and particularly adult education) rests. Adulthood is not merely one stage or level of life but a general term covering the successive phases of development through which the individual passes from the time he leaves adolescence until he dies. Moreover, his education during maturity is based on the kind and quality of the education which he experienced during childhood. The educator of adults must, therefore, examine closely what is known about the psychological development of the individual in order to understand both the fundamental laws of learning which apply throughout life and the distinctive aspects or principles which are most significant during maturity.

The individual lives in a society which ranges in scope from intimate groups to the world community of nations. Both the goals he seeks and the methods he uses are powerfully conditioned by his immediate social environment. This fact is true throughout life but is particularly significant in maturity, because men and women play a more active part in society than children ever can. The educator of adults must, therefore, study the social sciences in order to understand the ways in which group life influences and is influenced by education.

3. An understanding of the development, scope, and complexity of the specific agency or program in which he works and the broad field of adult education of which it is a part. Because most people enter adult education by accident, their initial impressions are largely circumscribed by the specific jobs they undertake. Usually they are not even aware that it is a part of a broader field. Like Moliere's would-be gentleman who was surprised to learn that he had been speaking prose for forty ,years, they are amazed to discover that their activities could be called "adult education." Many workers in the field have only a limited knowledge even of the history and scope of the very agencies in which they work, but are aware only of local policies and immediate routines.

One of the essential tasks of educating a specialist, therefore, must be to broaden his horizons to reveal the full range of the field. Invariably he finds far more possibilities for growth in his work than he had ever expected. He discovers that others in his own field of service have developed programs which are new and interesting to him. He learns that the basic problems of education are everywhere the same and that those who work in other kinds of agencies have developed principles which have significance for him. He learns, too, something of the historical and current perspectives of the whole field and sees the place of his own work in its larger setting.

4. An ability to undertake and direct the basic processes of education: the refinement of objectives; the selection and use of methods and content; the training of leaders; the provision of guidance and counseling; the promotion of program; the co-ordination and supervision of activities; and the evaluation of results. The effective operation of an adult educational program depends on the capacity of those who direct it to understand and use these central processes in a constructive and creative fashion and to realize how each is related to the other. At the graduate level, the student should not be concerned with the mere techniques or with specific procedures. Naturally it is important for him to have such skills and, if he does not, he must take the responsibility to remedy his deficiencies. His advanced instruction, however, must give him the competence to discharge more basic capacities and to supervise and train those whose levels of knowledge and skill are not equal to his own.

5. Personal effectiveness and leadership in working with other individuals, with groups, and with the general public. Personal effectiveness is so much a matter of basic personality, as tempered and developed by previous experience, that advanced training can merely reinforce and supplement patterns which were previously established. Within this broad limitation, however, potential specialists can be helped to gain confidence in themselves, to participate in activities which give them increased competence, and to survey their own capacities and learn how to remedy deficiencies in them.

6. A constant concern with the continuance of his own education throughout life. Nobody would deny the importance of lifelong learning but there is a great difference between understanding its significance and putting it into practice. The lawyer is not above the law, the doctor must conform to the rules of health, the priest lives by the laws of his faith, and the educator of adults must continue to learn. More than other men, he should plan and execute a continuous program of self-education. It he fails to do so, the consequences are serious. He limits his own growth, he becomes a sham, his work grows mechanical and perfunctory, and he ceases to

have the personal insight he needs into the rewards and the difficulties inherent in the educative process. His professional education must instill in him an awareness of his own need to continue to learn and it should aid him to understand how to do so.

THE FUTURE

Those who occupy positions of responsibility in adult education must operate in a far more complicated pattern than do those who practice a traditional profession. The educators of adults belong potentially not to a single profession but to a family of professions. Moreover, the future is probably one of increased diversification rather than greater simplification.

As the broad field of adult education grows, however, the education of leaders can increasingly be built around a common core of tested knowledge and belief. While the general shape of the field is no longer as obscure as it used to be, it still has many dark corners. Many of the fundamental principles which underlie successful theory and practice have yet to be discovered. It may be hoped, however, that as knowledge grows the future will bring clearer and firmer - as well as more co-ordinated - ways of educating adult educational leaders for their important responsibilities.

FOOTNOTES

1. Most of the material in this chapter was adapted from two earlier publications of the present author: "Professional Education for Educators of Adults," Adult Education, VI (Spring, 1956), 131-141; and "The Development of Leadership," Liberal Adult Education (White Plains: The Fund for Adult Education, 1956), pp.53-67

2. A.A. Liveright, Strategies of Leadership (New York: Harper & Brothers, 1959), pp. xix-xx.

3. J.H. Newman, On the Scope and Nature of University Education (New York: Dutton, 1933.)

4. Liveright, op. cit., pp. 37-46.

5. Elwin V. Svenson, "A Review of Professional Preparation Programs," Adult Education VI (Spring, 1956), 162-66.

Chapter Ten

THE EMERGENCE OF GRADUATE STUDY
IN ADULT EDUCATION*

Cyril O. Houle (1964)

American universities respond rapidly to social pressures. As
soon as a new movement or association or cause or crusade is
founded, its sponsors often begin to demand that institutions
of higher learning should establish programs to educate its
present or prospective leadership. The universities themselves
may be eager to comply; in fact they often hasten the growth
of the new movement by providing training programs for it
even in advance of any highly organized demand. The history
of higher education in this century has largely been one of
the addition of new professional curricula, of which education, social work, journalism, pharmacy, engineering,
veterinary medicine, public health, and nursing are prominent
examples. Grayson Kirk may have been correct in pointing
out that a "presumption of illegitimacy....often is attached to
the birth of a new academic subject, particularly in the field
of the social studies (1)," but oftener than not the new
subject matter fairly rapidly acquires acceptance which, in
academic circles at least, may be as good as legitimacy.

THE SPREAD OF UNIVERSITY COURSES

So it has been with adult education. Soon after the American-
ization movement achieved its first powerful thrust during
World War I, universities began to offer special courses
designed to train teachers and administrators for the work.
In 1917 Columbia, for example, offered a course entitled
"Educational Problems of the Immigrant." Other early
university offerings were built around vocational education,
particularly after the passage of the Smith-Hughes Act in

---

* Unless otherwise indicated, the data used in this chapter
were secured from the professors of adult education at the
universities now offering this work.

1917, and were designed to aid those who taught or administered evening classes in agriculture, home economics, and industrial subjects.

With the expansion of various kinds of adult education in the 'twenties and 'thirties, and particularly with the establishment of a more coordinated movement, the scope of university graduate offerings was both extended and broadened. Courses for teachers in various specialized occupations were presented on many campuses, but also there began to be more general approaches. The term "adult education" as part of a course title first appeared at Columbia in 1922; in the next twenty years more and more universities followed its example. A canvass of colleges and universities made in 1941 revealed that at least forty-four had such courses at that time, and thirty-two others had recently offered them (2). The number declined during World War II, but rose again immediately thereafter: where only 26 such courses were offered in the summer of 1945, the following year there were 52, and the year after that 70 (3). Although there has been no recent comparable survey to discover how many institutions now offer one or more graduate courses in the field, the number has probably continued to rise, although more slowly than in the years immediately following World War II.

THE GROWTH OF INSTITUTIONAL PROGRAMS*

Fairly soon after the emergence of the adult educational movement in 1923-1926 there appeared the first intensive effort to provide a coordinated program of graduate offerings. Dean James E. Russell of Teachers College, Columbia, was active in the creation of the American Association of Adult Education, and Edward L. Thorndike, also of Columbia, carried on basic studies of adult learning and adult interest which established the psychological foundations of the field. Building on this strong faculty interest, Columbia created a new department of adult education in the summer of 1930, and in 1931-1932 established curricula leading to advanced degrees in that field. John D. Willard, formerly Director of Co-operative Extension in Michigan and in Massachusetts, was made head of the department and was thus the first full-time professor of adult education in the country. In 1933-1934, Edmund de S. Brunner became head of the department, with F.E. Johnson, Frank W. Cyr, and Elizabeth C. Morriss on the staff. In the summer of 1934 Lyman Bryson was added,

---

* Information about the status of graduate programs is current as of June 30, 1962.

and in 1935-1936 Irving Lorge first began giving his course entitled "Psychology of the Adult."

In 1935 Wilbur C. Hallenbeck and William Stacy were the first graduates with Ph.D's. in adult education and Dr. Hallenbeck was added to the Teachers College Staff in adult education, becoming administrator of the program in 1936. Dorothy Helverson Novotny followed Mrs. Morriss in elementary education for adults, which was subsequently dropped but picked up later for a couple of years with Carol Stensland. Per Stensland was an instructor for several years and Andrew Hendrickson taught classes on several occasions.

By this time the department had established the basic pattern of its instructional program that has been maintained, with minor variations, to the present. In 1941 the Institute of Adult Education was established at Teachers College, under a grant from the Carnegie Corporation, to carry on research, field service, and publication, as well as instruction, and Morse Cartwright was appointed director. He and his associate, Glenn Burch, were in the teaching group. Paul L. Essert was appointed to the faculty in 1947, took over the administration of the program in 1948, and became director of the Institute in 1949. Ralph Spence began teaching in the field in 1949; the last two named, with Jacob Tuckman taking over the course in "Psychology of the Adult" after the death of Professor Lorge in 1961, constitute the instructional personnel at this time. In addition, Ernest G. Osborne carries on closely related work in parent education, and Floride Moor, Frank W. Cyr, and Sloan R. Wayland are advisors for an interdepartmental program in Cooperative Extension Services, which is functionally integrated with the program in adult education.

In 1931 Ohio State University followed Columbia's example and created a Department of Adult Education, the courses being taught by Jessie Allen Charters. In 1935 the department was combined with the Bureau of Special Education. The adult education courses were taught by Charles Berry until 1936-1937, when Herschel W. Nisonger was added to the staff of the Bureau as Assistant Director and professor of Adult Education. Andrew Hendrickson joined the staff in 1947; since 1960 he has served as director of the Center for Adult Education created that year.

The University of Chicago established its full-fledged program in 1935. Floyd W, Reeves had been professor of Higher Education at the institution for some years but his period of service as Director of Personnel of the Tennessee Valley Authority had led him to become interested in adult education. On his return to the University, therefore, he established a graduate program which he taught until 1939. He was succeeded by Cyril O. Houle, who has directed the graduate program ever since.

The pattern at all three universities was essentially the same: each moved directly into a major graduate program.

The next institution to use this method of entering the field was Florida State University. In 1945 a Citizen's Committee on Education appointed by the governor laid the groundwork for a state system of school finance which included support for adult education. The State Department of Education suggested to the administration of the University the need for a graduate program to develop competent administrators for such work and in 1953 Coolie Verner was appointed to guide and direct such a program. He was succeeded in 1961 by George Aker.

The fifth institution to follow this pattern was Boston University, where the program was established as a result of recommendations of a faculty-administrative committee charged to study "the role and responsibility of the University in adult education." The graduate program called for by this committee was duly established in 1960, under the direction of Malcolm Knowles.

The more customary way of developing a graduate specialty in adult education, however, has been gradual growth out of an earlier offering of one or more courses. In some cases, in fact, it is difficult to identify the precise point at which a graduate program came into being, a fact which should be kept in mind in reading the following accounts.

At New York University courses in adult education were offered prior to 1935, but an adult education department with a graduate degree program was established only in that year. The faculty involved at that time included Thomas Fansler, John Herring, and Sidney Hook. This department alternately enjoyed growth and suffered shrinkage. Administered for a number of years by the chairman of the Department of Higher Education, Alonzo F, Myers, it was reorganized in 1948 when John Carr Duff took over its administration. In 1958 the courses were absorbed into the Department of Administration and Supervision, and in 1960 Ronald Shilen was appointed to direct the program.

At the University of Michigan an introductory course in adult education was first taught as early as 1935, but the program itself was not established until 1938 when Howard Y. McClusky was placed in charge. In the early years work centered mainly on research and the development of new extramural activities, but in 1947 the program was expanded and given a more formal organizational pattern within the School of Education. Watson Dickerman served from 1952 to 1956; Gale Jensen has been on the faculty since 1955, and William Cave since 1957.

Early offerings at the University of Wisconsin began in 1939, when Paul H. Sheats was appointed to the faculty. He served until 1942, after which Leslie Brown taught the basic courses until Shirley Cooper filled the position in 1948-1949. In 1949 Burton Kreitlow was appointed to the faculty and the adult education program was officially established in the School of Education in 1950. In 1951 a curriculum in extension education was begun in the Department of Agricultural and Extension Education within the College of Agriculture, although the courses in adult education were those provided by the School of Education. A National Agricultural Extension Center for Advanced Study created in 1956, also within the College of Agriculture, has since then offered a graduate program. whose students take their courses in adult education in the School of Education. Wilson Thiede was appointed in the latter unit in 1958 and has served ever since. Robert Boyd was added to the staff in 1961.

At the University of California (Berkeley) courses in adult education were offered from the 'thirties onward, but the graduate program was not fully established until 1946, when Watson Dickerman was appointed to direct the work, serving in this position until 1952. He was succeeded in 1953 by Jack London, who remains in charge of the program.

At the University of California (Los Angeles) instruction in adult education was initiated about 1935, but the program was not formally established until the appointment of Paul Sheats in 1946. Abbott Kaplan was appointed to the staff in 1952 and has since been actively engaged in the program; Watson Dickerman has been on the faculty since 1956.

In 1947 a Bureau of Studies in Adult Education was established at Indiana University under the direction of Paul Bergevin and a program of graduate instruction began the following year. The Bureau is part of the Extension Division of the University, although its program of graduate instruction is conducted in the School of Education. Four graduate degrees in adult education are conferred by Indiana University: Master of Science in Education and Doctor of Education, both in the Graduate Division of the School of Education, and Master of Arts and Doctor of Philosophy in the Graduate School. The major purposes of the Bureau are to train adult educators, both lay and professional, and to study the field of adult education. The following additional faculty members, appointed on the dates indicated, serve on the faculty of the Bureau of Studies in Adult Education: Dwight H. Morris (1949), John McKinley (1952), Robert M. Smith (1953), II Mason Atwood (1957), and Roye M. Frye (1961).

Cornell University offered special courses for agricultural and home economics extension workers as early as 1930. These were followed in subsequent years by other offerings increasingly focused on adult education and designed for teachers as well as extension workers. In 1946 courses including the words "adult education" in their titles were started in the College of Home Economics. A full-fledged graduate program, established in 1949, leads to both master's and doctor's degrees in extension and adult education. J. Paul Leagans was appointed to direct this program and has continued actively in charge. While it has been focused on the needs of workers in extension education, its students have been drawn from many fields of employment and the curriculum has been based on content in the general field of adult education. The following additional faculty members have also served on the staff: Irene Patterson from 1946 to present, A.T. Mosher from September 1956 to July 1958, John M. Fenley from September 1957 to July 1961, and Robert L. Bruce and Arthur E. Durfee from September 1961 to the present.

Graduate study in adult education began in the School of Education at Syracuse University in 1936, but a full-scale program leading to advanced degrees was not initiated until 1951, under the direction of Alexander Charters. Clifford L. Winters, Jr., was appointed in 1959 and both he and Dr. Charters remain actively in charge of the program.

At the University of Buffalo graduate courses in adult education were begun in 1947. Four years later Carl E. Minich was appointed to carry forward such courses and to develop a program of graduate studies. Related courses in parent education have been taught by Mary B. Parke over the same period.

At Michigan State University many early course offerings were provided. In 1955 Harold Dillon was appointed to organize and direct a program of graduate study in adult education within the College of Education. Michigan State University also supports a special program in agricultural extension education, which, however, operates on a separate basis.

By 1962, therefore, fifteen universities in the United States had active programs leading to master's and doctor's degrees.

The development in Canada has somewhat paralleled that in this country, with a number of special offerings at the graduate level being offered from time to time by various universities. The only university offering a full-scale program, however, is the University of British Columbia. The graduate program at the University of British Columbia began in 1957 with the introduction of courses in adult education and communications under the direction of Alan Thomas. During the 1959-1960 session Coolie Verner from Florida State University was visiting professor of adult education to get the program under way; the first graduate degree was granted in 1960. Since that time the program has expanded to include graduate work on the master's level in the Faculty of Education, and also in the Faculty of Agriculture to meet the needs of those interested in extension education. In 1961 Professor Verner joined the faculty full time in charge of the graduate program of adult education in both faculties. The program has been expanded to include graduate work on the doctoral level, although at the moment most of the students are working at the master's level.

NUMBER AND KINDS OF STUDENTS

Some idea of the total services being provided at these sixteen institutions is suggested by Table 10.1, which shows the number of students of various categories formally registered at some time during the period from summer 1961 to spring 1962. These figures are substantially comparable, though there are minor variations in interpretation from institution to institution. The "special" category includes nondegree students as well as those taking one or more courses in adult education as part of a degree program in another field.

Most of the students now concentrating on advanced degrees in adult education secured their bachelor's degrees some time previously in a variety of fields. In the course of their early careers, however, they found themselves engaged in adult education or strongly drawn to it. As a natural consequence, they returned to a university on either a full-time or a part-time basis to prepare themselves adequately for careers in the field.

Probably most such students are drawn from and return to service in public school adult education, general university extension, or the Cooperative Extension Service, since these three kinds of services have the largest programs now being offered. Many other kinds of employment are also found: in libraries, voluntary associations, industry, labor unions, churches, settlement houses, community centers, and elsewhere. A substantial number of students are educators in foreign countries who have come to the United States in order to learn how to improve the programs of their own countries.

Professors of adult education do not, of course, concentrate all of their attention on teaching. Like their colleagues in other departments they also engage in research, in community service, and in consultation. In the latter capacity they are often called upon to assist other parts of the university in designing and conducting their own adult educational programs.

ADDITIONAL PROGRAMS IN ADULT EDUCATION

The foregoing observations have been concerned solely with the sixteen universities which have complete graduate curricula. In rounding thirty years it has become widely recognized both in the field and on the campus as a suitable

Table 10.1: Students of Various Categories Registered in Graduate Courses in Adult Education at Universities which have Master's Degree Programs in that Field, 1961–62

Institution	Doctoral candidates		Master's candidates		Special	Unknown	Total
	Full-time	Part-time	Full-time	Part-time			
Boston University	3	12	3	16	70	0	104
University of British Columbia	0	0	5	4	27	0	36
University of Buffalo	1	0	0	6	1	0	8
University of California (Berkeley)	13	11	2	2	20	0	48
University of California (Los Angeles)	3	7	0	2	9	0	21
University of Chicago	16	8	2	4	6	0	36
Columbia University	11	5	4	4	44	0	68
Cornell University	21	0	26	0	10	0	57
Florida State University	7	6	1	2	27	0	43
Indiana University	41	12	8	0	38	0	99
University of Michigan	4	8	5	6	169	2	194
Michigan State University	5	20	2	19	100	0	146
New York University	2	9	0	2	23	0	36
Ohio State University	5	1	3	0	76	0	85
Syracuse University	0	0	0	0	7	0	7
University of Wisconsin	42	15	130	29	140	4	360
Total	114	174	191	96	767	6	1,348

area of specialization, but several persistent problems still stand in the way of its universal acceptance.

To begin with, there is the question as to whether the field has, as yet, an adequate content based on research. This familiar problem is encountered by every discipline in its early years in a university. For example, when the colleges of agriculture were first created, in the middle of the last century, their professors had to fill the curriculum with courses requiring the students to memorize the Latin names of the various classifications of plants and animals or to study the references to agriculture in the Bible. Four hours a day of manual labor on the college farm was defended on the ground of its great educational value-waved aside as irrelevant was the fact that the young men concerned had been working on farms since their early childhood. Today, as everyone knows, there is a vast science and technology of agriculture, of such size and complexity as to create serious problems of curriculum-building. What has happened in agriculture has happened almost everywhere on the university campus.

It might seem appropriate that a field should first build its content and then be accepted as a discipline. The reason why this does not happen is because the university itself is the chief pioneer of knowledge. It develops fields after it admits them. Some institutions are naturally more enterprising than others and press on ahead into new fields, earning praise as pioneers if they succeed and criticism as rash opportunists if they fail. Some institutions, on the other hand, are remarkably conservative. In 1954, for example, the retired vice-chancellor of Oxford defended the exclusion of sociology from his institution on the ground that its very name was an etymological barbarism. "It's not a proper word at all!" he protested.

Those who have had the task of building graduate departments of adult education have had to take their content where they could find it, chiefly from psychology, sociology, history, the study of foreign and domestic institutions, and the education of children. Somehow they have woven these subjects into a pattern which has more or less coherence. Slowly-far too slowly-that pattern is now being enriched by studies focused more directly than before on the education of mature people. This present volume is a first effort to assess and help establish the present status of the adult education curriculum.

Another difficulty which stands in the way of a widespread acceptance of this field is the fact that it is designed to turn out practitioners of adult education who have not first gone through a preservice curriculum designed to prepare them for such work. In an ideal situation the modern university would doubtless provide a number of separate undergraduate curricula or courses of this type. The college of

Table 10.2: Doctorates in Adult Education, by Institution, January 1, 1962*

Institution	Year of first doctorate	Total number of doctorates
Columbia University	1935	78
University of Chicago	1940	32
University of Pittsburgh	1942	1
Ohio State University	1945	9
University of California (Los Angeles)	1947	21
University of Illinois	1948	1
University of Michigan	1948	15
Cornell University	1949	32
University of Buffalo	1953	3
Northwestern University	1953	1
University of Wisconsin	1953	66
Indiana University	1954	8
State University of Iowa	1954	2
Stanford University	1955	1
University of Tennessee	1955	1
University of California (Berkeley)	1956	12
University of Denver	1956	2
Florida State University	1956	6
University of Kansas	1956	1
Michigan State University	1956	12
University of Nebraska	1956	1
New York University	1956	8
Texas Technological College	1956	2
Harvard University	1958	1
Iowa State University	1958	1
University of Missouri	1958	1
Syracuse University	1958	2
University of Texas	1959	1
George Washington University	1959	1
Pennsylvania State University	1960	1
Total		323

* Adult Education, XII (Spring, 1962), p. 132.

education would train its students to teach either children or adults. The library school would prepare librarians for adult educational services. Comparable curricula or courses might be found in schools, colleges, or departments of theology, agriculture, home economics, business, public health, and social work. Each major university would also have a graduate curriculum of adult education designed for those desiring larger responsibilities or deeper study. Such a department would provide a focus for campus-wide efforts and would continuously enrich the curricula of the various professional schools by providing basic research and training for faculty members who teach the undergraduate courses.

Dim outlines of this design are now appearing on a few campuses, but as yet the field is not far advanced; no university has as yet worked out a satisfactory pattern to serve as a guide to others. As was pointed out earlier, graduate students in adult education today are for the most part people who were trained in some other discipline, who just happened to enter the field, who were educated in its essentials by the school of hard knocks, or who decided to build a career for themselves, and who returned (usually between the ages of 35 and 45) to embark on a graduate program. This pattern will doubtless prevail for some years to come; on a few campuses, however, there is already apparent an effort to try to recruit people earlier and thereby shorten the long delay before they are fully prepared for their careers. We may safely predict that gradually over the years the average age of those securing degrees will decline somewhat. More important is the fact that graduate training programs will gave to be designed on new bases, particularly with respect to providing more direct experience and internship for students.

One special problem at the present time is the fact that inadequate funds for fellowships prevent a large number of able people from entering graduate programs. Since the people who wish advanced study in this field are usually in their 30's, they are usually married and have children, which makes it difficult, if not impossible, to cease earning for a year or more. Even when they can subsidize part of this graduate education from savings or by greatly lowering their standard of living, these measures are usually far from adequate. As a result, the few meager scholarship programs now in existence are inundated with applicants, only a small fraction of whom can receive grants. The only other alternative for those who cannot finance full-time study is to work on a degree part time; such a procedure takes a long time, often makes it impossible to meet residence requirements, and is available only to those who can commute to the few graduate programs available.

As noted earlier, almost all graduate programs in adult education are located within schools, colleges, or departments of education. While this placement can be defended on the grounds of logic (for education is a basic process even though its application varies with the age of the individual), the student of adult education often encounters real hardships. Most of his fellow-students are preparing for careers in the schools, and almost all of the research on education has been carried out with children as subjects. In order to fill out a graduate program, therefore, the student may have to take courses which have little or no connection with his interests or concerns-such as high school guidance, problems of the school principalship, teaching arithmetic in the elementary school, or the junior high school curriculum. Much more serious is the fact that general required courses (for example, history of education, educational psychology, educational sociology, or comparative education) are taught as though such subjects had application only to children in formal school situations.

Even the formal organization of work in adult education within the department or school or college presents a problem, to which there are about as many answers as there are institutions involved. On some campuses adult education is a clearly recognized field of specialization; on others it is virtually submerged within some larger concentration, such as administration or curriculum; on still others, it is divided up among several such fields.

The situation with respect to these last two problems will almost certainly change as the content of adult education is strengthened and particularly as the number and caliber of students increase. A professor of educational psychology who has one student in adult education in a class of thirty is likely to ignore the concerns of that student or at least slight them; but if there are ten such students, he is likely to restudy his course to see how he may meet their needs more adequately. He may even be encouraged to undertake some research in adult education himself. Similarly, when there are only a few students in adult education in a large college, or when the courses are organized and taught as though the field were an adjunct of administration, of psychology, or of sociology, adult education can safely be viewed as a subspecialization. But as the content or the student enrollment is enlarged, the faculty usually finds it expedient to re-examine the fundamental structuring of the college, giving the work in adult education a more distinctive place. A similar change occurs in the total education curriculum, for, as adult education grows and research in the field is carried forward, the basic courses in education must change to reflect that fact.

Perhaps the most perplexing problem of all is: How many universities should provide graduate curricula in adult education? As yet the only answer by advocates of the field has been "more than at present!" This answer may be quite true, but the matter is too complicated to be dismissed so easily. Once again a parallel may be useful. It is widely agreed, for example that too many universities now offer graduate curricula in educational administration, and active steps are being taken to establish such high standards of quality that many institutions will abandon that field. Adult education as a field of graduate study has not reached a comparable saturation as yet and perhaps, since the career opportunities it could eventually offer are probably far larger than those in educational administration, it never will. Still, the fact remains that most of the universities whose programs have been mentioned in this chapter have fewer students than they would like to have and new universities seem to be entering the field each year.

Should they be encouraged to do so? The cautious person would say: "No, let all present programs reach an adequate size and only then let there be an enlargement." But can the field really grow if this practice is followed, even if the new universities could be persuaded to abandon their plans? Some of them would open up new geographic areas of service: until Boston University began its program, for example, residents of New England had to leave the region if they wished to study in the field; in the whole South there is still only one program.

More fundamentally, however, growth in number of programs will help to establish the field, make graduate study more essential to practitioners, enlarge the content, and demonstrate new curricular approaches which may later be widely adopted.

CONCLUSION

All of the foregoing discussion assumes, of course, that graduate study in adult education is a good idea and deserves further development. Actually the proof of the pudding must be in the eating. Most practitioners of adult education, including some of the most eminent, received their early training for their present positions by apprenticeship or trial and error. Can graduate curricula (now in existence or to be developed in the future) provide a group of leaders in the field who are so significantly better than those trained by apprenticeship that the cost of such curricula can be justified? Can those who are recruited for graduate training measure up to those who have been chosen by the crude but effective self-selection which is now the rule? Can the great lore of the creative but untrained pioneers of adult education be studied so that it can be passed on in a more systematic fashion? These questions confront the professors of adult education and their colleagues, and they will be answered, one way or another, in the next quarter-century.

REFERENCES

1. The study of International Relations, on Foreign Relations, 1947, p.5.
2. Cyril O. Houle, "Opportunities for the Professional

Study of Adult Education-1941," Adult Education Bulletin, Vol. 5, (April, 1941) pp. 81-85.

3. Cyril O. Houle, "Opportunities for the Professional Study of Adult Education," Adult Education Bulletin, Vol. 12, (April, 1948), pp. 111-117.

PART FOUR

PROFICIENCIES OF ADULT EDUCATORS

Chapter Eleven

THE COMPETENCIES OF ADULT EDUCATORS

Martin N. Chamberlain (1961)

What should an adult educator know, what should his attitudes be, what should he be able to do to be considered professionally competent? This decision was rendered by ninety leaders in our field who responded to a study-instrument in which they rated forty-five different concepts, skills and values.

The profile which emerged from these responses described an administrator in adult education who believes in the potentiality of growth for most people, who has a strong commitment to adult education, and who practices this by carrying on a continuing learning project for himself. He has an open mind and can accept others' ideas. He believes in freedom of thought and expression and prefers a dynamic to a static concept of the field of adult education. He has thought out and accepted a system of values - a philosophy of adult education. His skills include the ability to speak and write well, to lead groups effectively, to organize and direct complex administrative activities, and to be imaginative in the development of his programming. He understands the conditions under which adults learn and the motivations which bring them to his programs. He knows his community, its structure and its organization, and he knows his own strengths, weaknesses, and personal philosophy. He is not specially trained in a particular discipline nor is he particularly conversant with the organization or history of adult education. He is not an enthusiast for group techniques, nor of the use of mass media as educational means. He does not see himself as a professional consultant or counselor. In short, he is a successful administrator who is devoted to his work and finds personal security and satisfaction in it. He is more concerned with knowing things that work than in knowing why they work, although he recognizes some inadequacies in this view.

THE COMPETENCIES OF ADULT EDUCATORS

THE CONCEPTUAL FRAMEWORK

The first step in determining what competencies should constitute an inclusive list was an examination of the literature of
adult education and associated fields. Not much was available,
but helpful sources proved to be Harry and Bonaro
Overstreet's Leaders for Adult Education, Thurman White's
Ph.D. dissertation on "Similarity of Training Interests Among
Adult Education Leaders," Cy Houle's article in Adult Education on "Professional Education for Educators of Adults,"
and John Walker Powell's book, Learning Comes of Age. Other
sources were interviews of adult education leaders and
surveys mailed to a similar group including deans and
directors of university evening colleges and extension
divisions, graduate students in adult education, leaders in
agricultural and cooperative extension, and professors of
adult education.

Several problems were posed in the development of a list
of competencies. One of these, a semantic problem, was the
need of wording the statements describing each competency in
a way that provided the same meanings to each person
reading the statement. This problem was dealt with by several
group interviews of adult educators, undertaken with the
purpose of securing clarification of thought and expression in
the statements of competency. Statements were read to a
group, and, if agreement as to meaning was lacking, the
wording was changed until a reasonable agreement was
reached. The statements were refined in this manner through
several reviews.

A second problem was the need to select a statistical
technique which would provide definitive information about the
elements which make up successful adult education practice.
There was a further need to enable an observer to make
critical decisions about the relative importance of those elements. The selection of a forced choice design, known as a
Q-sort, was the solution to this problem. This design makes
possible the analysis of factors within the data, the collecting
of data by group or sub-group, and the weighting of the
various categories into which the items of the Q-sort were to
be divided.

A third problem was that of assuring adequate coverage
(within the statements of competency) of the range of social
situations in which an adult educator functions. It was
necessary to anticipate the adult educator's needs to deal with
individuals, groups, and with the larger social setting which
may be described as society. This problem was dealt with by
use of a grid which served as a framework for developing
statements of competency. The grid contained nine squares,
with one axis consisting of the three criteria of concepts,
skills, and values and on the other axis, the criteria of
individual, group, and society. By relating five statements

was obtained which gave equal emphasis to all of the criteria of the grid.

TESTING AND MAILING THE STUDY INSTRUMENT

The tentative list of competencies, prepared from the sources previously mentioned, was tested by asking respondents to sort the cards listing the statements of competency. Acceptable agreement was found on most of the cards. Some statements were reworded and others rejected. The final instrument consisted of forty five statements of competency, each on a single card, together with directions for sorting.

Respondents were asked to sort the cards into nine piles ranging from those favored most to those favored least. The top and bottom piles each had three cards, the next piles four, the next five and the middle three piles each required seven cards. In sorting the cards into the nine piles, they were asked to keep in mind the following definition of an adult educator:

A full-time administrator of a program of adult education, for example an evening college dean or assistant, the educational director of a labor union, the director of adult education of a public school, the training director of an industrial organization, the head of an adult education department of a library, a senior staff member of a cooperative extension division. The administrator may also be a teacher or act as a consultant, but we are primarily interested in his role as an administrator.

The study instruments containing the cards and directions were sent to 125 leaders of adult education. Ninety usable responses, or seventy-two per cent of the total mailing, were received by the established deadline. Comments upon the design of the instrument varied considerably, ranging from praise to scorn. Many respondents wrote of the pleasure they derived from their attempts to sort the cards containing the statements of competency. It was apparent from their comments that few of the respondents had previously encountered an experimental design using a forced choice technique in which the sorting of cards was the method of making their choices.

THE POPULATION SAMPLE

The rationale for the selection of the sample of the population of adult educators was to try to get the best thinking available in the field rather than to select a representative sample of a cross section of the field. This was possible because of the writer's acquaintance with many of the leaders in the field, and because of the availability of expert opinion as to the leaders in each of the categories desired. The selection of names for the sample was made by the writer with the help of several authorities. These included the executive secretary of the Adult Education Association of the United States of America, the director of the Center for the Study of Liberal Education for Adults, and officers of the National University Extension Association, the Association of University Evening Colleges, and of the Adult Education Association.

In order to get several viewpoints, three general categories of respondents were established. These were: (1) the persons who were teaching in the present graduate programs of adult education - the professors of adult education, (2) the students who were taking part in these programs or who had been recently engaged in them, and (3) the persons who typically would employ the graduates of adult education programs - the heads of the agencies of adult education. In the latter group were deans and directors of university evening colleges and extension divisions, public school adult education administrators, leaders of voluntary organizations in adult education, training directors in labor and industry, librarians, observers of adult education, and college and university presidents. The graduate students in adult education were selected from the list of those persons receiving study grants from the Fund for Adult Education for the year 1956-1957. The group of presidents or vice-presidents of college or universities was selected on the basis of the individual's previous experience in adult education or because he had recently appointed a dean or director of extension. Some libraries have developed strong programs of adult education. Such libraries often employ adult educators as staff members. Librarians were selected on the basis of their association with such institutions. The group which was labelled observers of adult education included staff members of the major associations in adult education and of foundations which had recently made contributions to agencies of adult education. Most of these persons are themselves adult educators. Through their positions of influence, they have a marked effect upon the field and the workers in it.

RATING THE COMPETENCIES

One of the major interests of respondents who returned the competed study instrument was the order of preference shown for the forty-five statements of competency. The order was established by listing the statements on the basis of the mean score given each statement by the ninety respondents. The statements which were rated at the top and at the bottom of the list are thought to be most accurate in terms of relative position. This difference in value stems from a comment made by several respondents. They were sure of their top and bottom categories, but we weren't so sure that, were they to sort the statements again, the middle categories would have been scored in just the same way. For this reason, emphasis in the analysis has been placed on the fifteen most highly and most lowly rated statements.

The actual rating of the forty-five statements of competency is as follows:

1. Believes that there is potentiality for growth in most people
2. Is imaginative in program development.
3. Can communicate effectively - speaks and writes well.
4. Has an understanding of the conditions under which adults are most likely to learn.
5. Is himself learning.
6. Is an effective group leader.
7. Knows himself-his values, his strengths and weaknesses.
8. Has an open mind-is willing to accept others' ideas.
9. Has an understanding of what motivates adults to participate in programs.
10. Has a strong commitment to adult education.
11. Can organize and direct complex administrative activities.
12. Has developed a system of values about adult education.
13. Has an understanding of the structure of the community, its organization and groupings.
14. Believes that innovation and experiment are necessary to the development of the field.
15. Believes in freedom of thought and expression.
16. Has an understanding of the problems and principles of administration.
17. Can carry through procedures of evaluation of his programs.
18. Can organize learning situations.
19. Is capable of formulating the criteria for selecting teachers and lay leaders.
20. Believes he should develop and learn throughout life.
21. Believes that participants should help make program decisions.
22. Has an understanding of the process involved in group or community change.
23. Is effective as a member of a group.
24. Believes in a responsive and responsible citizenry.
25. Can effectively deal with differences in people who come from a variety of backgrounds.
26. Can use the techniques of promotion and publicity effectively.
27. Has an understanding of the theories which relate to the method of adult education.
28. Has an understanding of the process involved in attitudinal change.
29. Can apply democratic principles to everyday life.

30. Has confidence in his ability as an adult educator.
31. Has an understanding of the democratic process as applied to daily living.
32. Can apply generalizations to specific situations.
33. Desires to be a responsible leader of his profession.
34. Understands the changes in physiological, mental and social development throughout the life span.
35. Has an understanding of the group process-the dynamics of group behavior.
36. Recognizes the existence of the developmental tasks of adulthood such as marriage, raising a family, preparation for retirement.
37. Believes in the effectiveness of group energy and group action.
38. Can plan and conduct research in matters relating to his field.
39. Can carry on self-directed study.
40. Understands the history and organization of adult education.
41. Can perform as a professional consultant and counselor.
42. Believes group methods of instruction have special relavance for adults.
43. Can use the mass media as an educational means.
44. Is competent in a particular discipline or field of study.
45. Believes that tested and accepted methods of carrying on programs of adult education are best.

The top rated five competencies suggest that the successful adult educator realizes the potential for learning of his likely customers and understands how to provide the necessary conditions for the learning to take place. He is imaginative, an effective communicator, and believes in his mission to the extent of practicing it himself. This is not an unusual finding; it would apply to almost any top educational administrator. Perhaps more significant are some of the lowest rated items. Some of the "sacred" beliefs of a segment of adult educators, such as that of group methods of instruction, have been rated as relatively unimportant by this group of leaders in the field. Some skills, such as consultant and counseling abilities and the use of the mass media as an educational means (i.e. television), are similarly lowly rated, possibly, in the latter case, through a misunderstanding of the intent of the question. Most academicians, it would seem, would rate competency in a particular discipline or field of study at the very top, particularly for university adult educators. This opinion is shared by Harry and Bonaro Overstreet in Leaders for Adult Education, who stress the importance of having command of a discipline upon which to build a knowledge of general education. Yet the group of ninety leading adult educators rated this competency next to the lowest of the whole list.

OTHER FINDINGS

The data obtained from the responses to the study instrument were factor-analyzed to determine the underlying structure of opinion in the responses. From this analysis came nine models of the adult educator, seven of which represent significant groupings of opinion that cut across the lines of institutional affiliation - the traditional manner of classifying adult educators. This finding suggests that there may be other ways of classifying our field, a development that deserves further investigation.

The responses of the eleven groups of adult educators, which made up the total sample, have been tabulated to indicate the differences in responses by institutional grouping. A summary of these positions shows that the group of professors tends to place a higher value on concepts - the intellectual aspects - as do the directors of adult education in voluntary organizations and the observers of adult education. However, the directors also highly regard relationships to the group, while the observers emphasize relationships to society. On the other hand, the directors of evening colleges downgrade concepts while emphasizing skills - the practical approach - and the deans of general extension divisions follow a similar pattern but also give positive emphasis to values.

College presidents and librarians have given no emphasis in the overall tabulation, although an examination of the grid boxes shows a slight preference for societal relationships a global view-in both cases.

The training directors in labor and industry, somewhat surprisingly, stress values and downgrade relationships. There is no describable pattern to the preferences of the graduate students in adult education. They show a lack of enthusiasm for skills and group relationships, with some emphasis on societal relationships. The directors of public school adult education are similarly unclassifiable. They downgrade values and have a slight prejudice favoring group relationships.

Chapter Twelve

KNOWLEDGE AND SKILLS FOR THE ADULT EDUCATOR:
A DELPHI STUDY

Mark H. Rossman and Richard L. Bunning (1978)

INTRODUCTION

Since the advent of the industrial revolution, education has
been forced to play an ever increasing role in answering
human needs and demands. Scientific and technological progress requires continual updating of skills. Our society's
institutions - families, schools, and churches - are in a
constant state of flux. Continuing education has become a
necessity for the adult members of our society.

It is obvious that the adult educator must now play a
variety of roles and possess many skills to meet effectively
the ever changing needs of the adult constituency. The
university has traditionally offered training for professionals
in most fields and currently does so for adult educators.
However, in a changing world, training for the adult educator
may also have to change.

The field of adult education as an area of study has
emerged only in this century. The American Association for
Adult Education, founded in 1926 (13:23), issued its first
periodical, Adult Education Journal, in 1929. Only one year
later, in January of 1930, the publication carried an article
describing an early experiment in California which dealt with
the preparation of adult educators through a summer school
program. The author described the instructional staff as
employing "independent methods," and the curriculum consisted of topics such as problems of human adjustment,
parental education, aesthetics in everyday life, economics as
the determining factor in social institutions, and public
opinion and adult education. The article concluded with the
thought that perhaps what was an experiment, "...may have
been but the beginning of what will eventually become an
indispensable part of the training of teachers of adults."
(19:67-74).

Most early authors used the term "adult educator"
synonymously with "teacher of adults." In 1931, MacKaye
(14:290-294) noted that a mass of literature had been devoted

150

to the justification of adult education but that little had been devoted to how to teach adults. He added that adult education was "essentially an act of war" and that the adult education instructor had to have the skills and knowledge or "tactical training" which would prepare him for the "trenches." In 1938 a colloquy of 15 adult education experts addressed themselves to a number of questions concerning their profession. One of the questions was, "Who are our leaders and how are they trained?" Of the 15 panel members, only two felt that much could be done to improve instructional methodology. A spokesman for the majority said, "... the leader who is full of his subject will find that method takes care of itself." (3:59-64). An opposing view came four years later, however, when Hill said that the most urgent need of adult educators was for teaching methods. (11:106-108).

One of the first particularly comprehensive writings concerning the preparation of adult educators was published by Hallenbeck in 1948. He proposed an eclectic training program that included not only a knowledge of the specific subject matter to be presented, but also instructional methodology and materials, adult psychology, sociology of the adult, the history and philosophy of adult education, the functions and administration of adult education, community organization, programs and agencies, and, finally, the emotional requisites for adult educators (10:4-10). Professional training opportunities expanded quickly and by 1956 twelve universities had full-time faculty members in the field of adult education. That same year, Cyril Houle of the University of Chicago suggested to his fellow adult education professors that they try to help the student achieve the following "general objectives":

1. A sound philosophical conception of Adult Education based on a consideration of its major aims and issues and embodying convictions concerning the basic values which it should seek to achieve.
2. An understanding of the psychological and sociological foundation on which all of education (and particularly Adult Education) rests.
3. An understanding of the development, scope, and complexity of the specific agency or program in which he works and the broad field of adult education of which it is a part.
4. An ability to undertake and direct the basic processes of education: the refinement of objectives, the selection and use of methods and content, the training of leaders, the provision of guidance and counseling, the promotion of programs, the coordination and supervision of activities, and the evaluation of results.
5. Personal effectiveness and leadership in working with

other individuals, with groups, and with the general
public.
6. A constant concern with the continuance of his own
education throughout life. (12:137-139).

In addition, Houle listed a variety of learning experiences, methods, and techniques which would be of value to
the adult educator in his development. This listing included
traditional college classes, continuing education seminars,
special tutorial work, the writing of a major report, written
or oral comprehension exams, assisting faculty members with
selected projects, informal discussions and work with colleagues, individual conferences with faculty members, the
visitation of adult education programs, participation in adult
education conferences, and supervised work in adult education agencies. Houle ended his article with a look into the
future. He stated that much was to be discovered about the
field of adult education and that the universities should take
a large responsibility in educating the emerging leaders
(12:140-141).

Chamberlain conducted a rather intensive study of the
competencies (knowledge, skills, and attitudes) which adult
educators should have to be considered professionally competent. Forty-five statements were submitted to 90 study
participants, including adult education professors, students
enrolled in or recently enrolled in graduate adult education
programs, and institutional administrators who would typically
employ the graduates of adult education programs. The top
rated 15 statements according to mean scores were found to
be:

1. Believes that there is potentiality for growth in most
   people.
2. Is imaginative in program development.
3. Can communicate effectively - speaks and writes well.
4. Has an understanding of the conditions under which
   adults are most likely to learn.
5. Is himself learning.
6. Is an effective group leader.
7. Knows himself - his values, his strengths, and weaknesses.
8. Has an open mind - is willing to accept others' ideas.
9. Has an understanding of what motivates adults to participate in programs.
10. Has a strong commitment to adult education.
11. Can organize and direct complex administrative activities.
12. Has developed a system of values about adult education.
13. Has an understanding of the structure of the community,
    its organization and groupings.
14. Believes that innovation and experiment are necessary to
    develop the field.

15. Believes in freedom of thought and expression. (6: 78-82).

The 1960's showed a number of authors addressing themselves to the same topic, including Robinson (16:243-245), Aker (1:12-13), and Butcher and Le Tarte (4:81-82). However, as late as 1971, Fuller was concerned not with how adult educators would be prepared but more fundamentally if they were obtaining preparation. As the result of a search of the literature he concluded, "... in over 100 years of adult education, an adult educator had never thought of providing an in-service education program for adult education faculty. And if it had ever been thought of before, it had not been implemented. And if it had been implemented, it had not been recorded for posterity." (8:20).

A summary of the literature, then, revealed that (1) many authors had suggested various skills, knowledge, attitudes, and attributes which were desirable for adult educators to possess in order to enhance their effectiveness; (2) a few studies had been conducted to assess current needs or recommendations for adult education staff development; and (3) no study addressed itself specifically to the needs of the future adult educator.

PURPOSE

In view of the above summary, the purposes of this study were (1) to determine a core of common skills and knowledge which adult educators of the future would need to gain in order to perform their jobs adequately, and (2) to determine the learning experiences most appropriate in obtaining the more important skills and knowledge. Both purposes were determined by administering four rounds of Delphi question-naires to a panel of experts consisting of adult education professors from throughout the United States and Canada.

METHODOLOGY

The Delphi Technique was chosen as appropriate for this type of "futuristic" study. Developed by Helmer and several of his associates at the RAND Corporation (9:41) in the early 1950's, the Delphi Technique was designed to obtain group opinions about urgent national defense problems. Named "Delphi" in honor of the oracle of Apollo, "... the method provides for an impersonal anonymous setting in which opinions can be voiced without bringing the 'experts' together in any kind of face-to-face confrontation." (15:155). The technique is basically a method of collecting and organizing data comprised of expert opinion. An effort to produce a

A DELPHI STUDY

convergence of group consensus is accomplished through a series of three or four questionnaires dealing with future-oriented questions. A setting is provided in which ideas can be modified on the basis of reason rather than the bandwagon effect of majority opinion. Contact is usually made with the respondents through a set of mailed questionnaires with feedback from each round of questions being used to produce more carefully considered opinions in succeeding rounds. The exact procedure may vary depending on the type of study and the anticipated results. (17:248)

The present study utilized a series of four questionnaires. The first solicited open-ended responses to the question, "What knowledge (and what skills) will be needed by the adult educator of the coming decade?" The second asked respondents to prioritize the statements generated by Questionnaire I on a five-point rating scale. The third fed back the modal consensus of respondents in Questionnaire II and asked them to either join the consensus or to defend their dissent with individual statements. The final questionnaire asked respondents to choose learning experiences which would be most appropriate for the adult educator to acquire the knowledge and skills which were rated as "highest priority" on Questionnaire III.

Any study which attempts to deal with future events tends to raise concerns over the credibility of the technique. The Delphi is no different. The Delphi did, however, have unique merits built into its special techniques and various modifications:

1. It avoids specious persuasion, leadership influences, hidden agendas, personality conflicts, and other problems encountered in group decision making.
2. It allows a variety of individuals, perhaps widely separated geographically, to participate equally.
3. Several studies showed the Delphi to have remarkable accuracy. (9:21), (18:111)
4. It provided documentation of a precise nature, including minority opinions.

However, there are critical problems with any attempt at predicting the future through this type of methodology:

The only thing certain in dealing with the future is that forecasts will seldom prove entirely correct or complete. Inevitably, there will be discoveries and events which cannot be anticipated: new scientific understanding for which no paradigm exists, political traumas, natural catastrophies ... (9:5).

Another disadvantage can be in the selection of a panel of experts as the respondents for a Delphi study, particularly when no ready-made criteria are available for determining expertise:

> It is very tempting to include in this group all who are influenced substantially or who can make a significant and/or unique contribution to the resolution of the problem. (2:8)

A final disadvantage of the technique can be the heavy expenditure of time in completing the series of questionnaires.

THE STUDY POPULATION

The population for this study consisted of professors of adult education in college and university graduate programs throughout the United States and Canada. In selecting the participants to be involved in the study, two reference sources were utilized: (1) a list of members of the Commission of Professors and Adult Education of the Adult Education Association of the U.S.A.; and (2) a list of chairmen of graduate programs in adult education throughout the United States and Canada as listed in The National Association of Public Continuing Adult Education 1974 Almanac. Letters of solicitation were sent to June, 1975 to 197 persons compiled from these two sources. Of the contact population, 141 professors agreed to participate in the study.

DATA COLLECTION

Table 12.1 displays for each round of questioning the number of questionnaires sent, the number of questionnaires returned, the percentage of questionnaires returned, and the percentage of the original sample of 141 who returned questionnaires. The number of questionnaires mailed diminished with each round of questioning; but the overall percentage of returns when computed by comparing for the four rounds of questioning (total questionnaires sent with the total questionnaires returned) resulted in a rate of 94.7 per cent. The percentage of responses when compared with the initial contact population of 197 adult education professors ranged from 67 per cent for Questionnaire I to 54.3 per cent for Questionnaire IV. This return rate was reasonably high when consideration is given to the following:

1. Mailed questionnaires normally result in a low percentage of returns.

Table 12.1: Summary of Questionnaire Returns

Questionnaire	Total number sent	Total number returned	Percent returned each round	Percent returned of original sample
I	141	132	93.6	93.6
II	132	126	95.5	89.4
III	126	113	89.6	80.1
IV	113	107	94.7	75.9

2. Four separate mailings were administered to the participants over a five-month period of time (September 1975 through January 1976).
3. A majority of Delphi studies shows a sizable drop in returns after the second or third round of questioning.
4. The questionnaires, particularly Questionnaire III, were very time consuming.

RESULTS

Questionnaire I solicited open-ended responses to the questions, "What skills will be needed to fulfill the role of the Adult Educator in the next decade?" and "What knowledge will be needed to fulfill the role of the Adult Educator of the next decade?"

Many duplications were evident among the statements which were submitted on Questionnaire I. These statements were edited to form 48 "knowledge" statements and 53 "skills" statements. They show that participants pictured the adult educator of the future as needing skills and knowledge in many areas.

The second questionnaire was then formed from the initial "knowledge" and "skills" statements. It was submitted to respondents with instructions to rank each statement as to its importance to the adult educator of the coming decade according to the following scale.

1. Highest priority.
2. Above average priority.
3. Average priority.
4. Below average priority
5. Lowest priority.

Tables 12.2, 12.3 and 12.4 show the statements which were rated as "highest priority" and "second highest priority"

Table 12.2: Highest Priority Knowledge and Skill Statements Ranked by Mean Score

Statement	Mean	S.D.
KNOWLEDGE:		
1. of the psychology of the adult: intellectual development, adjustment, personality theory, the effects of aging, the psychology of dying, etc.	1.1	.50
2. of the ever-changing nature of the adult and his needs	1.2	.52
3. of himself	1.2	.91
4. of the process of change	1.2	.67
5. of contemporary society: its subgroupings, needs, trends	1.2	.83
6. of the functions of the adult educator	1.3	.79
7. of the principles of adult education	1.4	.88
8. of the broad field of adult education as it relates to the individual, the community, and/or society	1.4	.96
9. of learning theories in practice	1.4	.96
SKILLS:		
1. in communicating (including listening skills)	1.1	.51
2. in continuous self-improvement	1.1	.58
3. in systematic inquiry, critical assessment, and problem solving	1.1	.68
4. in diagnosing education needs of the individual	1.1	.72
5. in designing learning experiences based on need	1.1	.71
6. in initiating the self-actualization process in the adult	1.1	.61
7. in encouraging creativity	1.1	.61
8. in conducting learning experiences based on need	1.2	.82
9. as a change agent for himself, individuals, organizations, and/or the community	1.2	.90
10. in creating non-traditional learning opportunities	1.3	.77
11. as a competent instructor	1.3	.78

Table 12.3: Second Highest Priority Knowledge and Skill Statements Ranked by Mean Score

Statement	Mean	S.D.
KNOWLEDGE:		
1. of the evaluation of methods, techniques, and devices as to appropriateness	1.9	.56
2. of the community: its organization and power structure as well as methods of development	1.9	.51
3. of organization, group, and/or individual behaviour	1.9	.60
4. of the broad spectrum of changing adult characteristics	1.9	.60
5. of the implementation of innovative programs	1.9	.56
6. of educational planning techniques	1.9	.41
7. of educational institutions: their functions, their interrelationships with society, and how they may be changed	1.9	.76
8. of the designing of innovative programs	1.9	.59
9. of community resources	2.0	.65
10. of societal trends as they affect adult education	2.0	.57
11. of the decision-making process	2.0	.56
12. of the implications of updated research	2.0	.68
13. of group dynamics	2.0	.71
14. of current events and their relevancy to adult education	2.1	.59
15. of human resource development theory	2.1	.66
16. of the proper use of various educational methods, techniques, and/or devices	2.1	.83
17. of trends of higher and continuing education	2.2	.79
18. of use of mass media as it relates to adult education	2.2	.71
19. of professionalization: a sense of mission and purpose and how the professional functions	2.2	.84
20. of other ways to define knowledge beside the dominant scientific one	2.3	.97
21. of philosophy	2.4	1.07

as compiled from Questionnaire II data, and the mean and standard deviation of each statement as compiled from Questionnaire III returns. Priority was determined by modal consensus; that is a statement was categorized as "highest priority" when the frequency of responses was greatest in that particular priority. A total of 20 statements received "highest priority" ranking, while 47 statements were rated as "above average priority." The rating scale showed little discrimination since only one statement received a rating of "4" and two statements received a rating of "5". The modal consensus was returned to participants in Questionnaire III along with their individual responses to each item. They were then asked to either join consensus or to write minority opinions explaining their lack of agreement.

A major convergence of opinion occurred after the participants were informed of the first consensus reached by the sample. The "average standard deviation" for knowledge statements decreased from .98 in Questionnaire II to .76 in Questionnaire III, while a similar decrease occurred in the skills statements, that is from .97 to .71. The overall rate of consensus found for statements on Questionnaire III was 80.4 per cent.

Most respondents to Questionnaire III joined consensus on most of their non-consensus responses, writing minority opinions for approximately 20 of the 101 statements. Somewhat of a trend was generally found in writing minority opinions in that an "adjacency" or minority ranking that was immediately next to consensus was changed to a consensus ranking while minority opinions were written most often for rankings which were two or more priority rankings away from modal consensus.

CATEGORIZATION OF HIGHER RATED STATEMENTS

In order to elucidate statements rated as "highest" or "above average" priority, a categorization process was employed by the researchers after consultation with adult education faculty at Arizona State University. Similar statements were grouped together and a six-category system was created. These six categories were created by a "gestalt polarization" process developed by the researchers in conjunction with organizational development activities. Gestalt polarization is a technique used to classify raw data into various categories based on the similarities (or dissimilarities) among individual concepts. Each datum is written on an individual piece of paper, discussed, and then placed in a particular category through inductive reasoning. New categories can be created as needed and individual statements can be placed into several categories if appropriate.

Table 12.4: Second Highest Priority Knowledge and Skill Statements Ranked by Mean Score

Statement	Mean	S.D.
SKILLS:		
1. in implementing strategies for adults to self-diagnose learning needs	1.8	.50
2. in evaluating the effectiveness of the educational product	1.8	.48
3. in gaining the cooperation of community agencies and/or groups in education endeavors	1.9	.62
4. in human motivation	1.9	.66
5. in providing for the individual within group learning situations	1.9	.56
6. in helping groups engage in problem solving	1.9	.58
7. in finding and/or creating educational resources	1.9	.49
8. in leadership; group, academic, and/or community	2.0	.55
9. in counseling adults	2.0	.52
10. in utilizing educational resources	2.0	.51
11. in helping others idenify life goals	2.0	.55
12. in utilizing research findings to improve instruction	2.0	.61
13. in promoting teamwork as a member of the total educational team	2.0	.58
14. as an educational consultant	2.1	.72
15. in organization maintenance, development and/or renewal	2.1	.61
16. in diagnosing the educational needs of society	2.1	.91
17. in administration or management of adult programs	2.1	.66
18. in being accountable to the public	2.1	.69
19. in the proper utilization of advisory committees	2.1	.76
20. in identifying alternative futures for current issues	2.1	.76
21. as a teacher trainer	2.1	.72
22. in balancing individual and social needs when different	2.1	.69

Table 12.4: (continued)

---

23. in creating and enhancing interpersonal   2.2   .51
relationships

24. in fiscal aspects of the educational process   2.2   .80

25. in objectively merging personal perceptions   2.3   .82
with those of the adult clientele

26. in the use of educational technology   2.3   .85

Through this process, it was found that all of the selected statements fit into at least one category while several statements fit into more than one category. The statements falling within each category were then described and analyzed.

The six general categorization areas, a brief definition of each, and the numbers of the skills and knowledge statements (see Tables 12.2, 12.3 and 12.4) attributed to each category follow:

1. The Adult Educator
   Statements included in this category were those which related to the adult educator's personal development, attitudes, and, ultimately, effectiveness as a person. Knowledge: Highest priority, 3,4; second highest priority, 3,11,13,21; Skills: Highest priority, 1,2,3,9; second highest priority, 23,25.

2. The Field of Adult Education
   This category included statements which were directed toward knowledge and skills which would be of value to the field of adult education itself, including an understanding of and influence on its scope, goals, functions, and trends. Knowledge: Highest priority, 6,7,8; second highest priority, 7,10,14,15,17,21. Skills: Second highest priority, 14, 20.

3. The Adult Learner
   Skills and knowledge placed in this category were those dealing with an understanding of the adult learner including making and maintaining contact and the providing of guidance and leadership. Knowledge: Highest priority, 1, 2, 4; second highest priority, 3, 4. Skills; Highest priority, 6, 7, 9; second highest priority, 4, 9, 11, 22, 23, 25.

4. The Adult Education Environment.
   Categorized here were statements which were aimed at providing the adult educator with the skills and knowledge necessary to deal effectively with groups, forces, and other environmental factors that interact with the process of adult education.
   Knowledge: Highest priority, 4, 5, 6; second highest priority, 2, 3, 7, 10, 13, 14.
   Skills: Highest priority, 1,3,9; second highest priority, 3, 4, 6, 8, 13, 14, 15, 16, 18, 22.

5. Adult Education Programming.
   Skills and knowledge included in this category dealt with the planning, designing, and implementation of educational experiences. Also included were certain aspects of programming such as staffing, resource development, and administrative functions.
   Knowledge: Second highest priority, 5, 6, 8, 9, 11, 15, 18, 20.
   Skills: Highest priority, 1, 3, 4, 5, 10; second highest priority, 3, 7, 10, 12, 15, 17, 19, 20, 21, 24.

6. The Adult Education Process
   Statements of skills and knowledge listed in this category were those that dealt with the process of adult education as it directly interacts with the learner. These included effective use of methods, techniques, and devices; how adults learn and change; and of process evaluation.
   Knowledge: Highest priority, 4, 9; second highest priority, 1, 2, 11, 12, 13, 16, 18.
   Skills: Highest priority, 1, 4, 6, 7, 8, 9, 11; second highest priority, 1, 2, 4, 5, 6, 7, 10, 12, 23, 26.

These six categories, then, represent various aspects of the future adult educator's functions: personal attributes, knowledge of the field, and skills in doing the job.

LEARNING EXPERIENCES

Questionnaire IV consisted of the 20 statements (9 "knowledge" and 11 "skills") which were rated as "highest priority" by participants on previous questionnaires. (See Table 12.2.) The purpose was to identify appropriate learning experiences which the adult educator of the future could undertake to acquire the knowledge or skill represented by each item. A list of 17 learning experiences was attached to the questionnaire and respondents were asked to choose two experiences which they felt were more appropriate for learning the particular skills or knowledge.

Table 12.5: Learning Experiences and Percentage of Responses from Questionnaire IV

Learning experience	Percentage of responses
1. Internship (on-the-job work experience)	15.9
2. Traditional class (lecture, tests, written assignments, discussion, etc.)	11.3
3. Seminar	10.8
4. Sensitivity, human relations, or similar group training	8.3
5. Practicum (on-the-job research experience)	7.9
6. Simulated materials and/or experiences	6.7
7. Independent study	5.9
8. Informal discussions with students, professors and practioners	5.9
9. Participation in professional groups/organizations	4.1
10. Independent research project	4.1
11. Non-credit conferences (i.e. continuing education workshops	3.4
12. Student teaching	3.1
13. Observation	3.0
14. Completing a thesis, dissertation, or similar work	2.6
15. Self-contained instructional modules	2.5
16. Modular course offerings	2.0
17. Correspondence courses	0.3
18. Other	2.2
Total	100.0

Table 12.5 shows the learning experiences and the percentage of responses accrued to each particular experience for all 20 statements. This percentage was obtained by comparing the actual number of responses by participants to each learning experience with the total number of responses for all learning experiences.

The general theme of responses to Questionnaire IV was that the most appropriate learning experiences were practical "on-the-job" situations integrated with university-based experiences, such as classes and seminars. Sensitivity-type training was also highly rated, particularly in relationship to personal development statements such as "knowledge of himself" and "skill in communicating."

The overall response rate for the four questionnaires was 93.4 per cent. The range was 95.5 per cent on Questionnaire I to 89.6 per cent on Questionnaire III.

DISCUSSION

This study was designed to secure information which would lead to the skills and knowledge needed by the adult educator of the coming decade. The utilization of the Delphi Technique as the methodology in the study and the findings of the study led the investigators to the following conclusions:

1. The minority opinions generated by the study participants were relatively insignificant when compared with an overall consensus rate of more than 80 per cent. In keeping with the above, there is major agreement among adult education professors as to future adult educator knowledge and skill needs. Many minority opinions were due to a lack of semantical precision in certain statements. This imprecision was due both to a lack of generally understood definitions for certain terms and phrases as well as to the editorializing limitations of the investigator.

2. The adult educator of the coming decade was viewed by study participants as possessing an increasing variety of roles and sub-specialties. Common skills and knowledge required to fulfill these varying roles can be grouped into six general categories of learning. These categories are the adult educator himself, the field of adult education, the adult learner, the adult education environment, adult education programming, and the adult education learning process.

3. The best method for the future adult educator to learn the recommended skills and knowledge may be practical "on-the-job" work experience integrated with selected university based experiences such as classes and seminars. An important additional experience is sensitivity or similar group training for personal development.

4. The least desirable learning experiences for the future adult educator to undergo in learning the recommended highest priority skills and knowledge are correspondence

courses, modular course offerings, and the undertaking of major research projects such as a thesis or dissertation.

RECOMMENDATIONS

The recommendations based upon the conclusions are findings of this study are presented in two areas: (1) those relating to practical application of the study findings, and (2) those relating to future studies.

Recommendations for Practical Application of Study Findings

1. Adult educators and those involved in the education of adult educators could begin preparing for a rapidly changing future requiring an increasing number of multi-faceted roles and sub-specialties.

2. Criteria could be developed based upon the knowledge and skill statement ratings of this study so that individual competencies (and lack thereof) may be identified. These criteria could, in conjunction with identified needs, then form the basis of graduate training programs, adult educator continuing education programs, and individual courses of professional development. The categorization process generated from this study could form the foundation for basic areas of competence. In addition, professors and students of adult education could use these findings to compare their own programs with the considered judgment of the study participants.

3. Future adult educators could be seen as falling into one of two categories: (1) those who are professional educators who control, direct, evaluate, provide leadership, and enhance the adult education process, and (2) those who are facilitators of the process because of expertise in any given area. Appropriate individualized learning experiences could be provided accordingly.

4. Learning experiences designed to teach knowledge and skills generated by the study could be oriented toward practical on-the-job learning activities. Supporting integrated programs could include university-based classes and seminars while personal development could be enhanced through sensitivity training or similar group training. The utility of theses, dissertations, and similar topics could be questioned in the professional preparation of most adult educators as could other least selected learning experiences as shown in this study's findings.

5.　Those interested in the certification of adult educators could use the findings of this study as a basis for appropriate certification standards.

Recommendations for Additional Studies

1.　An in-depth study of the mechanics of the Delphi Technique could be considered as a possibility for future study. The utilization of several questionnaires, a study of the questionnaire administration and return process, and the validity of the present predictions as compared with future realities should all be examined. Such studies should be valuable in improving methodology for forecasting educational futures.

2.　A study correlating the professional competency of a variety of adult educators with their mastery of the knowledge and skills rated as most important in the present study would be an area of potential research. Such a study would be important in ascertaining the validity of the experts' ratings in the present study.

3.　A Delphi study of the ratings given the baseline data of the present study by adult education practitioners could be conducted. Comparisons could be drawn with data generated by the present study. Any inconsistencies found could be of concern to adult education professors and practitioners alike.

4.　A study could be conducted verifying the validity of the knowledge and skills generated by this study. Conducted at the end of the coming decade, such a study could give valuable insight into other future trends in adult education.

REFERENCES

1.　George F. Aker, Criteria for Evaluating Graduate Programs in Adult Education, Findings of a Study Conducted for the Commission of Professors of Adult Education, University of Chicago, (March 11, 1963).

2.　Donald P. Anderson, Exploring the Potential of the Delphi Technique by Analyzing the Applications, An AERA Symposium, Ohio State University, (March, 1970.)

3.　Ralph A. Beals and Morse A. Cartwright, editors. Partial Inventory, Journal of Adult Education, 10 259-264, (1938.)

4.　Donald G. Butcher and Clyde Le Tarte, Teacher Training for Adult Basic Education. Perceptions of a State Director of Adult Education. Adult Leadership, 17, 81-82, (1968).

5. Robert M. Campbell, A Methodological Study of the Utilization of Experts in Business Forecasting, Doctoral dissertation, University of California at Los Angeles, (1966).

6. Martin N. Chamberlain, The Competencies of Adult Educators, Adult Education, 11, 78-82, (1961).

7. Norman C. Dalkey, and Olaf Helmer, An Experimental Application of the Delphi Method to the Use of Experts, Management Science, 9, 458-467, (1963).

8. Jack W. Fuller, An in-Service Program for Adult Education Faculty, Adult Leadership, 20, 205-206, (1971).

9. Theodore J. Gordon and Robert H. Ament, Forecasts of Some Technological and Scientific Developments and Their Societal Consequences, Institute for the Future, (September, 1969).

10. Wilbur C. Hallenbeck, Training Adult Educators, Adult Education Journal, 7, 4-10.

11. F.E. Hill, Training Volunteers for Adult Education, Adult Education Journal, 1, 106-108, (1942).

12. C.O. Houle, Professional Education for Educators of Adults, Adult Education, 6, 137-139, (1956).

13. Malcolm S. Knowles, ed. Handbook of Adult Education in the United States, Adult Education Association of the United States, Washington, D.C., (1960).

14. David L. Mackaye, Tactical Training for Teachers of Adults, Journal of Adult Education, 3, 290-294, (1931).

15. John Pfeiffer, New Look at Education, Western Publishing Company, Princeton, New Jersey, (1968).

16. C.O. Robinson, Criteria for the Education of Adult Educators, Adult Education, 12, 243-245, (1962).

17. Mark H. Rossman and Dennis M. Carey, Adult Education and the Delphi Technique, International Journal of Continuing Education and Training, 2, 247-252, (1973).

18. Alvin Toffler, Future Shock, Random House, New York, (1971).

19. Norman Uhl, Encouraging Convergence of Opinions Through the Use of the Delphi Technique in the Process of Identifying an Institutions's Goals, Educational Testing Service, (1971).

20. Bonaro Wilkinson, Teaching Teachers in a New Way, Journal of Adult Education, 2, 67-74, (1930).

Chapter Thirteen

COMPARATIVE STUDY OF ADULT EDUCATION
PRACTITIONERS AND PROFESSORS ON FUTURE KNOWLEDGE
AND SKILLS NEEDED BY ADULT EDUCATORS

Richard Daniel and Harold Rose (1982)

Planning a graduate program in adult education is a complex
process made more difficult by the tremendous variation in
the educational and occupational backgrounds of the participants. The use of such descriptors as an "emerging field
of study," a "marginal education program" and other related
terminology, reflects an awareness and concern for the development of adult education.

Liveright (10:85), in analyzing the variation among
practitioners and a lack of shared common goals, indicated
that the field of adult education was not at the point where
the desirable content and organization of a program of
graduate study for adult educators could be specified.
Others, such as Aker (1) and Chamberlain (3), have moved
ahead in an effort to identify competencies in adult education.
In addition, several models for graduate programs have been
developed.

Knowles (7:137) argued that doctoral programs in adult
education must produce graduates with common competencies.
In addition to these competencies, each graduate must possess
specialized skills in the role he or she plans to assume upon
graduation. Knowles suggested that graduate curricula be
developed by following a five step diagnostic procedure. The
steps are:

1. analyze the functions required by the student in performing as an adult educator,
2. determine the competencies required to perform each
   function,
3. diagnose the knowledge, understanding, skills,
   attitudes, values and interests that make up each competency,
4. formulate objectives in terms of behavior changes to be
   sought in these, and
5. plan a program of activities that will achieve these
   objectives.

Boone (5:47) maintains that one should think of adult education as a field of professional practice with each student required to master certain core competencies before branching out into a speciality. "The graduate will be first and foremost a generalist; second, a specialist." It is through the development of specialized tracks that an adult education department will be able to tailor its program more closely to the needs of specific target groups. The implementation of specialized tracks is dependent on:

1. the level of knowledge developed in each track,
2. the identification of competencies for each track,
3. the availability of faculty and learning experiences appropriate for students specializing in each area,
4. the establishment of internship opportunities.

Additional models for graduate programs which included reference to both the core curriculum and an area of specialization were developed by Essert (4) and Veri (13). The acceptance of the concept of a core curriculum and an area of specialization does not indicate an agreement on what should be included in each area. Knox (8:24a), in a study of adult education graduate programs, found that professors reported more problems related to the issue of what specialized continuing education courses should be included in the graduate program than any other issue.

While there appears to be agreement that the identification of knowledge and skills is a primary requirement in the development of effective graduate preparation programs in adult education, there is some question about the awareness level of people who develop training programs. Mocker states that:

> Persons responsible for developing individual courses and total degree programs have little basis for making decisions concerning content. Colleges and universities concerned with the training of professionals who will assume leadership positions in adult education must have some base other than tradition to make curriculum selection decisions. (11:vi)

Griffin made the following observations about graduate program development.

> The planners of a program do not have or do not make explicit their rationale for the courses they offer, or the rationale they use is not visibly linked to the beliefs they have about adult education as a field. Too often, a graduate program is a repeat version of the one at the chairman's alma mater. Or it is an eclectic collection of

courses that the existing or available faculty want to teach. (6:1)

The competencies of the adult education faculty have to be considered in any graduate department. It should be noted that the lack of competence in a specific area does not indicate incompetence; it is simply a reflection of the diversity within the field. Often professors, by attempting to meet the needs of adults in specialized areas, create serious problems of credibility.

Kozoll was also concerned about the extent of expertise of professors of adult education who were trying to meet the needs of adult basic education teachers.

In most cases, the initial experience in an adult education graduate course was positive for ABE teachers ... but after the first introduction, past the theory and generalization, dissatisfaction becomes apparent when the professor couldn't give answers to specific everyday problems. What the ABE teachers wanted was what most faculty couldn't provide (curriculum construction, material selection, teaching of reading, testing and counseling)unless they brought in specialized assistance from other parts of the faculty. (9:28,29)

Without question, those working in the field of continuing education are practical people. Every day they deal with such practical problems as working with inadequate budgets and inadequate facilities, defending the legitimacy of their programs, dealing with instructional methods that fail to work, and improving participation.

According to Apps (2:19), continuing educators tend to spend their time putting out brush fires as they erupt. By expending all of their energy on practical problems, they are left without sufficient time, energy or resources to attack the basic problems. Included in the basic problems are those dealing with "the adult as a learner, the field of adult education and what it is, the purposes of continuing education, the content and curriculum of continuing education and research." Only by developing an understanding of basic problems in the field of continuing education can we be successful in working with everyday problems.

PURPOSE

The concern of this study was not to rehash the argument of theory versus practice. Basic problems and theoretical problems are interrelated and should not be viewed in an either/or argument. The purpose was to examine the extent of agreement between practitioners and professors of adult education on the skills and knowledge needed by adult educators.

This study was initiated as the result of a recent publication by Rossman and Bunning (12) in which they assessed the knowledge and skills areas of future adult educators as perceived by the professors of adult education. A question immediately arises as to similarity which might exist between professors and practitioners on their perception of knowledge and skills needed by future adult educators. In order to make this analysis, a group of specialized adult education practitioners were surveyed to obtain comparative information between adult education professors and practitioners on needed knowledge and skills of future adult educators.

POPULATION AND METHODOLOGY

Deans and directors of Region III of the National University Continuing Education Association (NUCEA), formerly the National University Extension Association, were selected from among the possible adult education practitioner groups as the study population. This population included members from 12 states in the southeastern U.S. plus Puerto Rico and the Dominican Republic. A directory containing the names of deans and directors was obtained from the NUCEA Region III Chairman. Eighty deans and directors were listed in the directory; however, at the time of the initial questionnaire mailing, the directory was purged of four individuals who had left their respective positions.

The original study by Rossman and Bunning (12) identified the knowledge and skills being investigated in the current study. Therefore, a modified Delphi Technique was employed since it was not necessary to perform the usual first round process of generating forecast statements. The initial questionnaire contained knowledge and skill statements in random order within the appropriate category. Respondents were requested to rank each statement as to its importance to the adult educator of the coming decade according to the following scale:

1. Highest Priority.
2. Above Average Priority.
3. Average Priority.
4. Below Average Priority.
5. Lowest Priority.

The second questionnaire provided the respondents with the mean as well as mode responses for each item from the initial mailing, and statements were priority ranked. Respondents were requested to indicate agreement with these rankings using the above scale.

COMPARATIVE STUDY

The first mailing went out in March 1980. Fifty-eight returns were obtained, a 73 percent return rate. The second mailing, to the 58 respondents, was administered in May 1980; responses were received from 46 persons for a 79 percent return rate. The second mailing resulted in a return rate of 60 percent of the initial population of 76 deans or directors.

In analyzing the data, the mean was used to rank the statements in priority order. Mode and standard deviation were utilized as indicators of agreement among respondents on priority rankings. To examine agreement between the practitioners' ranking of the statements and those of professors of adult education, the Kendall Tau Coefficient at .05 probability level was employed. In addition, the "difference in rank" of individual items between the two groups was examined. For example, a statement ranked as second by practitioners which was ranked fifteenth in the Rossman and Bunning Study would have a difference in rank of plus thirteen. For the reverse situation, the difference in rank would be minus thirteen. No test was employed to determine the statistical significance of the "difference in rank" values. For discussion purposes, the difference of one-half the ranked items within the respective category was used to identify statements showing major differences. Employing this criterion, only knowledge statements which showed a difference as great as 15 and skill statements with differences of, or greater than, 18 were discussed as being ranked differently by the two groups.

RESULTS

Tables 13.1 and 13.2 show the 30 knowledge and 37 skill statements employed in the questionnaire. Knowledge statement items 1-6 (Table 13.1) were ranked as "highest priority" with modes of one. Skill statement items 1-8 (Table 13.2) were similarly ranked. Knowledge statement modes for items 26-30 were "average priority" or 3. Skill statement items 35, 36 and 37 also had modes of 3. The balance of all skill and knowledge statements had modes of 2 or "above average priority."

"Average standard deviations" for knowledge and skill statements on the initial returns were 83 and 86, respectively. The second round produced greater convergence of opinion as illustrated by reduced average standard deviations of .65 and .58, respectively.

The Kendall Tau Coefficients computed between practitioners' and professors' rankings were .13 for knowledge and .48 for skill statements. The z score for the tau coefficient for knowledge was 1.02 and was not significant at the .05 level. Therefore, the rankings between the two groups were not significantly related. For skill statements,

Table 13.1: Practitioner Priority Ranking of Knowledge Statements by Mean and Difference in Rank Between Practitioners and Professors of Adult Education

Priority ranking of statements by practitioners					
Rank	Knowledge statement	$\bar{X}$	S.D.	Mode	Diff. in Rank with Professors
1	of the ever changing nature of the adult and his needs	1.24	.48	1	+1
2	of professionalization: a sense of mission and purpose and how the professional functions	1.39	.61	1	+26
3	of community resources	1.39	.61	1	+15
4	of the designing of innovative programs	1.44	.72	1	+13
5	of the functions of the adult educator	1.47	.69	1	+1
6.	of the community: its organization and power structure as well as methods of development	1.59	.72	1	+5
7.	of societal trends as they affect adult education	1.87	.54	2	+12
8.	of the decision making process	1.92	.58	2	+12
9.	of the proper use of various educational methods, techniques and/or devices	1.94	.53	2	+16
10.	of trends of higher and continuing education	1.94	.65	2	+16
11.	of the process of change	1.96	.51	2	-7
12.	of the psychology of the adult: intellectual development, adjustment, personality, theory, the effects of dying, etc.	1.96	.63	2	-11
13.	of current events and their relevancy to adult education	2.00	.63	2	+10
14.	of the implementation of innovative programs	2.02	.45	2	0

Table 13.1: (continued)

Rank	Knowledge statement	X̄	S.D.	Mode	Diff. in Rank with Professors
15.	of the evaluation of methods, techniques and devices as to appropriateness	2.02	.63	2	-5
16.	of the broad spectrum of changing adult characteristics	2.04	.63	2	-3
17.	of educational planning technique	2.04	.66	2	-2
18.	of educational institutions: their functions, their inter-relationships with society, and how they may be changed	2.11	.74	2	-2
19.	of himself	2.13	.65	2	-16
20.	of contemporary society: its subgrouping, needs, trends	2.15	.62	2	-15
21.	of use of mass media as it relates to adult education	2.17	.74	2	+6
22.	of the broad field of adult education as it relates to the individual, the community and/or society	2.17	.74	2	-14
23.	of organization, group and/or individual behavior	2.17	.83	2	-11
24.	of the principles of adult education	2.20	.79	2	-17
25.	of the implications of up-dated research	2.28	.62	2	-4
26.	of group dynamics	2.67	.70	3	-4
27.	of learning theories in practice	2.70	.66	3	-18
28.	of other ways to define knowledge besides the dominant scientific one	2.83	.68	3	+1
29.	of philosophy	2.87	.83	3	+1
30.	of human resource development	3.00	.70	3	-6

Table 13.2: Practitioner Priority Ranking of Skill Statements by Mean and Difference in Rank Between Practitioners and Professors of Adult Education

Rank	Knowledge statement	$\bar{X}$	S.D.	Mode	Diff. in Rank with Professors
1.	in communicating (including listening skills)	1.11	.32	1	0
2.	in administration or management of adult programs	1.11	.38	1	+26
3.	in leadership: group, academic and/or community	1.13	.45	1	+16
4.	in continuous self-improvement	1.17	.44	1	-2
5.	in designing learning experiences based on need	1.22	.51	1	0
6.	in being accountable to the public	1.26	.56	1	+23
7.	in fiscal aspects of the education process	1.37	.57	1	+28
8.	as a change agent for himself, individuals, organizations and/or the community	1.50	.62	1	+1
9.	in finding and/or creating educational resources	1.72	.50	2	+9
10.	in conducting learing experiences based on need	1.78	.59	2	-2
11.	in human motivation	1.83	.64	2	+4
12.	in evaluating the effectiveness of the educational product	1.85	.47	2	+1
13.	in gaining the cooperation of community agencies and/or groups in education endeavors	1.87	.53	2	+1
14.	in diagnosing the educational needs of society	1.89	.67	2	+13

Table 13.2: (continued)

Priority ranking of statements by practitioners				Diff. in Rank with Professors
Rank	Knowledge statement	$\bar{X}$	S.D.	Mode	
15.	in systematic inquiry, critical assessment and problem solving	1.91	.63	2	-12
16.	in diagnosing education needs of the individual	1.94	.53	2	-12
17.	in helping groups engage in problem solving	1.94	.56	2	0
18.	in encouraging creativity	1.94	.49	2	-11
19.	in promoting teamwork as a member of the total educational team	1.94	.68	2	+5
20.	in utilizing educational resources	1.96	.63	2	+1
21.	in creating non-traditional learning opportunities	1.98	.45	2	-11
22.	to utilize research findings to improve instruction	1.98	.61	2	+1
23.	in objectively merging personal perceptions with those of the adult clientele	2.04	.52	2	+13
24.	in providing for the individual within group learning situations	2.04	.52	2	-8
25.	in organization maintenance development and/or renewal	2.04	.59	2	+1
26.	in identifying alternative futures for current issues	2.13	.58	2	+5
27.	in initiating the self actualization process in the adult	2.13	.72	2	-21
28.	in counseling adults	2.13	.72	2	-8
29.	as a competent instructor	2.13	.78	2	-18
30.	in the proper utilization of advisory committees	2.17	.68	2	0
31.	as a teacher trainer	2.17	.68	3	+1

Table 13.2: (continued)

Priority ranking of statements by practitioners				Diff. in Rank with Professors
Rank	Knowledge statement	$\bar{X}$	S.D.	Mode	
32.	in implementing strategies for adults to self-diagnose learning needs	2.23	.57	2	−20
33.	in balancing individual and societal needs when different	2.26	.61	2	0
34.	in helping others identify life goals	2.28	.72	2	−12
35.	in creating enhancing interpersonal relationships	2.58	.65	3	−1
36.	in the use of educational technology	2.60	.68	3	+1
37.	as an educational consultant	2.82	.90	3	−12

the obtained tau coefficients of .48 was statistically significant at the .05 level with a z value of 3.80; therefore, the ranking of skill statements appeared to be related in that the probability of practitioners and professors ranking any given item in the same relative order was .48 more than the probability that they would rank them differently.

Examinations of difference in rank between the Rossman and Bunning results and the current study show both agreement and lack of agreement on priority rankings of knowledge and skill statements. As previously indicated, items which differed by more than one-half within the respective categories were classified as areas showing lack of agreement. For knowledge statements (Table 13.1,) eight of the 30 statements showed a difference in rank of 15 or more. For skill statements (Table 13.2), six of the 37 statements showed differences in rank of 18 or more.

Rossman and Bunning categorized the statements into the six general areas presented below. Only those statements which exhibited lack of agreement in rank between the two populations are presented within each category.

1. The Adult Educator
   Statements included in this category were those which related to the adult educator's personal development, attitudes and, ultimately, effectiveness as a person. (12:150)

177

Knowledge of professionalization: a sense of mission and purpose and how the professional functions (+26)
Knowledge of himself (-16)

2. The Field of Adult Education
This category included statements which were directed toward knowledge and skills which would be of value to the field of adult education itself, including an understanding of and influence on its scope, goals, functions and trends. (12:150)
Knowledge of trends of higher and continuing education (+16)
Knowledge of the principles of adult education (-17)
Skill in initiating the self-actualization process in the adult (-21)

3. The Adult Learner
Skills and knowledge placed in this category were those dealing with an understanding of the adult learner including making and maintaining contact and the providing of guidance and leadership. (12:150)
Skill in initiating the self-actualization process in the adult (-21)

4. The Adult Education Environment
Categorized here were statements which were aimed at providing the adult educator with the skills and knowledge necessary to deal effectively with groups, forces, and other environmental factors that interact with the process of adult education. (12:150)
Knowledge of contemporary society: its subgrouping, needs, trends(-15)
Skill in being accountable to the public (+23)

5. Adult Education Programming
Skills and knowledge included in this category dealt with the planning, designing, and implementing of educational experiences. Also included were certain aspects of programming such as staffing, resource development, and administrative functions. (12:150)
Knowledge of community resources (+15)
Skill in administration or management of adult programs (+28)
Skill in fiscal aspects of the educational process (+28)

6. The Adult Education Process
Statements of skills and knowledge listed in this category were those that dealt with the process of adult education as it directly interacts with the learner. These included effective use of methods, techniques and devices; how adults learn and change; and of process evaluation.

(12:150-151)

Knowledge of the proper use of various educational methods, techniques and/or devices (+16)

Knowledge of learning theories in practice (-18)

Skill in initiating the self actualization process in the adult (-21)

Skill as a competent instructor (-18)

Skill in implementing strategies for adults to self-diagnose learnings needs (-20)

DISCUSSION

The practitioners surveyed, on the second administration, appeared to move toward consensus regarding priority ranking on both knowledge and skill statements, as indicated by standard deviation and mode.

Agreement on rankings between the two groups showed, according to tau coefficients, dissimilar results for knowledge and skills statements. For knowledge statements, there appeared to be no relation between practitioners and professors of adult education in priority ranking. For skill statements, the agreement between practitioners and professors to rank items in the same relative order was statistically significant. Therefore, the two groups tended to agree more on skill statement priority than on knowledge statement priority. However, examination of the data indicated that for both types of statements, several items showed major differences in rank.

Practitioners ranked higher than professors the knowledge statements of professional function (item 2); community resources (item 3); educational methods, techniques and/or devices (item 9); and higher and continuing education trends (item 10). Practitioners ranked lower than professors knowledge statements relating to self (item 19); society (item 20); principles of adult education (item 24); and learning theories (item 27). Skill statements ranked higher by practitioners than professors were administration (item 2); accountability (item 6); and fiscal aspects (item7). Those ranked lower by practitioners were statements concerned with the self-actualization process (item 27); competence as an instructor (item 29); and adult self-diagnosis of learning needs (item 32).

The items ranked higher by practitioners appear to relate to pragmatic areas of administrative concern. The lower ranked items seem to relate to philosophical and/or theoretical as well as instructional considerations. Deans and directors of continuing education are program administrators and accordingly rank high knowledge and skills related to administration. Professors might view the field of adult education in more general terms and priority rank knowledge and skills needed by educators in general. The professors' rankings might be in response to those skills needed as a generalist in the field of adult education, while the administrative rankings tend to support the need for specialized curriculum to develop the particular competencies and understanding needed by the individual to perform the tasks associated with the professional role one plans to assume in working with adults.

The discussion of this study has emphasized differences between this particular practitioner group and professors. However, it should also be emphasized that more consensus of ranking existed than lack of consensus. Therefore, professors of adult education are addressing any needs perceived to be of importance to practitioners.

IMPLICATIONS AND RECOMMENDATIONS

Professors of adult education might be expected to provide future adult educators with knowledge and skills consistent with their own opinions regarding needed knowledge and skills. Should this preparation of adult educators happen without input from practitioners, future educators may not be provided the opportunity to gain expertise in some areas viewed to be of high priority by current practitioners. Therefore, decision makers within programs that prepare adult educators need to recognize the specialized knowledge and skills required by adult education administrators, as well as other specialty area populations, in order that appropriate learning objectives be identified and pursued. A procedure for assessing knowledge and skills needed by these populations should be developed and utilized in order to gain input from practitioners for curriculum decisions regarding programs preparing adult educators.

Additional studies could be conducted to assess knowledge and skills required by other specialty area adult education populations. Literature within the field of adult education has addressed the idea that graduate preparation programs should respond directly to the professional needs of graduates. The current study has indicated a discrepancy between one group of practitioners and professors regarding priority of some identified needs. Additional studies could be conducted to determine if this discrepancy manifests itself in professional adult educators being ill prepared to function in some areas within the field.

REFERENCES

1. George G. Aker, The Identification of Criteria for Evaluating Graduate Programs in Adult Education, Doctoral Dissertation, The University of Wisconsin, Madison, (1962).

2. Jerald W. Apps, Problems in Continuing Education, McGraw-Hill, New York, (1979).

3. Martin N. Chamberlain, The Competencies of Adult Educators, Adult Education 11, 78-82, (1961),

4. Paul L. Essert, A Proposed New Program in Adult Education, Adult Education, 10, 131-140, (1960).

5. Bertie Edwards Fearing, The Department of Adult and Community College Education at North Carolina State University, 1963-1978, A Need, A Response, and a Model, North Carolina State University, Raleigh, N.C., (1979).

6. Virginia R. Griffin, Thinking About a Graduate Program in Adult Education (No. 2): Alternate Starting Points for Organizing the Program into Courses, Department of Adult Education, The Ontario Institute for Studies in Education, Toronto, Ontario, (1971).

7. Malcolm S. Knowles, A General Theory of the Doctorate in Education, Adult Education, 12, 136-141, (1962).

8. Alan B. Knox, Development of Adult Education Graduate Programs, Adult Education Association of the U.S.A., Washington, D.C., (1973).

9. Charles E. Kozoll, Response to need: A Case STudy of Adult Education Graduate Program Development in the Southeast, Occasional Paper No. 28. Syracuse University, Syracuse, New York, (1972).

10. A.A. Liveright, The Nature and Aims of Adult Education as a Field of Graduate Study, in "Adult Education: Outlines of an Emerging Field of University Study" edited by Gale Jensen, A.A. Liveright and Wilbur Hallenbeck, Adult Education Association of the U.S.A., Washington, D.C., (1964).

11. Donald W. Mocker, Report on the Identification, Classification, and Ranking of Competencies Appropriate for Adult Basic Education Teachers, Center for Resource Development in Adult Education, University of Missouri, Kansas City, (1974).

12. Mark H. Rossman, and Richard L. Bunning. Knowledge and Skills for the Adult Educator, A Delphi Study, Adult Education 28, 139-155, (1978).

13. Clive C. Veri, Building a Model Doctoral Degree Program in Adult Education, Paper presented at the annual meeting of the Adult Education Association of the U.S.A., Atlanta, Georgia, (October 29, 1970).

PART FIVE

CHARACTERISTICS AND ORIENTATIONS OF ADULT EDUCATORS

sheep have
vertebrations ?

Chapter Fourteen

LIFE CRISES AND CAREER CHANGE IN
ADULT EDUCATORS

Lynn E. Davie (1979)

In recent years, many investigators have documented the
existence of a series of life crises or major life stages during
adulthood (Erikson, 1959; Lowenthal and Chiriboga, 1973;
Gould, 1972; and Sheehy, 1974). Though each study varies
somewhat in the names and positions of the various life
stages, the studies taken together provide impressive evidence for the existence of major periods of change for the
adults in the early thirties and early forties. These periods
in life are posited as major branching points in people's lives.
    Very little is known about the educators of adults,
though the field has been growing explosively in the past
decade. There are a few descriptive studies such as Susan
Wilson's 1973 study of the status of women in the Adult
Education Association of the United States (Wilson, 1973), and
collections of biographical material. Yet, for the size of the
adult education activity, and the complexity of the required
job skills, few studies have focussed on the kinds of decisions and changes which occur in the lives of adult education practioners. This study was part of a larger study
which examined a variety of questions related to the career of
an adult education professional. (Abbey et al., 1978)
    The present study focussed on the following questions;

(1)   What kinds of life crises or major changes have the
      individuals experienced?
(2)   What kinds of emotions predominated during these
      changes?
(3)   When did the most recent life stage begin?
(4)   How are career changes related to life cycle con-
      cerns?
(5)   Are there differences in life cycles patterns among
      educators who identify themselves as administrators,
      teachers or counsellors of adults? and
(6)   Are there sex differences in the relationship bet-
      ween career changes and life cycle concerns?

METHOD

Population and Sample

The population was comprised of full-time, adult educators residing within approximately 300 miles of Toronto. Adult educators were broadly defined as persons whose primary occupational role involved them in teaching, counselling or administering in education programmes for adults. Based on a preliminary screening of approximately 500 adult educators randomly selected from lists of relevant professional associations, a sample of 90 individuals were selected, equally distributed in two age panels representing presumed differences in a career stage (young adult educators aged 35 and less and mid-career adult educators aged 40 and more). Due to funding restrictions, the sample had to be reduced to 69 individuals living in and around Toronto.

Interview Instrument

Each participant was asked to engage in a collaborative exploration of the relationship between the person's career and his or her life concerns.

The participant was asked to describe the change that led to his or her present stage of life. In addition, he or she was asked to indicate the age at which the change began, whether other significant individuals were involved, whether it was a time of high emotion, and what the predominant emotions were. After the description was complete the individual was shown the interviewer's notes and asked if they were complete, and if they accurately reflected the individual's memories of the time of change. Next, the participant was asked to think about the time before the beginning of the present stage of life.

The participant was asked to identify changes in the following:

(1) Changes in career or job;
(2) Changes in where you lived;
(3) Changes in your values;
(4) Major changes in income;
(5) Changes in the size or composition of family;
(6) Changes in relationships with other people;
(7) Changes in health;
(8) Changes in marital relationship; and
(9) Other important changes.

Finally, the participant was asked to think of the time after the beginning of the present stage of life and to indicate changes which resulted from the life stage change.

Most interviews required approximately 45 minutes to complete and the participants reacted favourably to the process. No one refused to participate and several commented positively about the experience.

Coding the Results
The first step in coding the results was to compare the data recorded on the forms with the tape recordings of the interview. A sample of the interviews were selected and 30 of the forms were checked against the tape recordings of the interviews by the principal investigator. The results were remarkably consistent. Although the tape occasionally clarified the notes, the forms proved to be complete and accurate. Second, the description of the beginning of the present stage of life was examined and a set of categories was developed which described these major life changes. The emotions reported by the participant at the time of the major life change were also classified into a set of descriptive categories.

RESULTS

Type of Major Changes
Ten descriptive categories were developed for the analysis of the changes marking the beginning of the present stage of life. The number of life changes in each category are reported in Table 14.1 by job category.

The major finding of interest in Table 14.1 is the large proportion of administrators who marked the beginning of their present stage of life as the assumption of their present administrative position. Both the teachers and counsellors had a wider variation in the types of changes and the two latter groups were more likely to see a change of emphasis in their work as marking the major life change. There seemed to be little difference in the other categories of major life changes

Age of Major Change
The large number of female administrators reporting relatively recent major life changes is quite interesting. In all job categories, the men's life changes are spread more evenly. A sharp distinction can be noted between the patterns for the female administrators and female counsellors. Perhaps the recent lowering of barriers to women in administrative positions could account for some of these differences.

Emotions Reported at the Time of Changes
The data clearly show that most individuals experience feelings of anxiety or fear during the major life changes, though a surprising number of individuals reported feelings of elation as well. Females reported somewhat fewer feelings of anxiety

Table 14.1: Changes Reported as Marking the Beginning of the Present Stage of Life by Job Category

Type of Change	Administrators		Teachers		Counsellors		Totals	
	N	%	N	%	N	%	N	%
To take present position	22	85	6	26	8	40	36	52
Change emphasis in work	0	0	6	26	2	10	8	12
Reassessment of values	0	0	2	9	2	10	4	6
Separated from spouse	2	8	2	9	1	5	5	7
Marriage–coupling	0	0	1	4	2	10	3	4
To have children	1	4	2	9	1	5	4	6
Return to school	1	4	2	9	3	15	6	9
Change in emphasis in school	0	0	0	0	1	5	1	1
Immigration	0	0	1	4	0	0	1	1
Travel	0	0	1	4	0	0	1	1
Totals	26	101	23	100	20	100	69	99*

* Errors due to rounding

Table 14.2: Difference Between Reported Present Age and the Age Reported as the Onset of Major Life Change by Job Category and Sex

Age Difference	Administrators		Teachers		Counsellors		Total	
	Male	Female	Male	Female	Male	Female	N	%
0 Years	1	1	0	1	0	0	3	4
1–3 Years	6	4	2	5	7	0	24	35
4–6 Years	2	3	3	5	3	2	18	26
7–9 Years	6	0	1	4	2	1	14	20
10 Years or More	1	2	1	1	4	1	10	14
Totals	16	10	7	16	16	4	69	99*

* Error due to rounding

Table 14.3: Emotions Reported at the Beginning of the Present Stage of Life By Sex and Age

| Emotional | Male | | | | Female | | | | Total | |
| | <35 | | 40> | | <35 | | 40> | | | |
	N	%	N	%	N	%	N	%	N	%
Negative emotion against other-- rage, anger	3	9	1	4	7	17	2	9	13	11
Anxiety, fear uncertainty, stress	17	53	12	50	15	36	9	36	53	44
Failure, frustration depression	1	3	4	17	13	30	6	26	24	20
Elation, enthusiasm, excitement	11	34	6	25	6	14	5	22	28	23
Searching, stimulation	0	0	1	4	1	2	1	4	3	2
Totals	32	99*	24	100	42	99*	23	100	121**	100

* Errors due to rounding
** Multiple responses were permitted

Table 14.4: Numbers of Individuals Experiencing High Emotion at the Beginning of the Present Stage of Life By Sex

| | Experienced High Emotions | | |
	Yes	No	Total
Male	22	17	39
Female	24	6	30
Total	46	23	69

Chi square = 4.246 p<.05 (Phi Coefficient 0 .25)

than males and somewhat greater numbers of negative emotions toward other individuals. Perhaps, the most outstanding difference between the two sexes is the large proportion of females reporting emotions of failure, frustration, and depression.

Females expressed significantly more feelings of high emotions than did males. Table 14.4 reports the perceptions of high emotion at the time of the most recent major life change.

Antecedent Changes to the Beginning of the Present Stage of Life

The second part of the interview asked the participant to identify changes which might have been antecedent to the beginning of the present stage of life. Table 14.5 presents these data organised by job category.

There appear to be few important differences in the kinds of antecedent changes reported by individuals in different categories. Changes in job or career, places where the respondent lived, values, and relationships with other people were reported most often as antecedent to the beginning of the present stage of life.

Resultant Changes from the Onset of the Present Stage of Life

The third part of the interview asked the participant to identify changes which might have resulted from the beginning of the present stage of life. Table 14.6 presents these data organised by job category.

Tables 14.5 and 14.6 indicate that there are few important differences in either antecedent or resulting changes when examined by job category. There are approximately double the number of resultant changes reported compared to antecedent changes.

What is interesting, however, is the relationship between career decisions and other changes. Comparing Tables 14.2, 14.5, 14.6, it can be seen that some individuals viewed career changes as important turning points in and of themselves, while others viewed the career changes as being antecedent to or resulting from some other major life event. Administrators, as noted, seem to be more prone to make their life changes with job shifts, while the teachers and counsellors have selected a more varied set of life changes.

No one interviewed reported that a major life change occurred in isolation. Most reported significant changes in values and relationships around life changes. Marital separations were almost always accompanied with changes in jobs or places of residence. Changes clearly occurred in clusters rather than as isolated events.

Table 14.5: Changes Reported as Being Antecedent to the Beginning of the Present Stage of Life

Category of Change	Administrators N	%	Teachers N	%	Councellors N	%	Total N	%
Change in job or career	17	19	11	18	14	21	42	19
Change in where you lived	13	15	10	16	7	11	30	14
Change in values	14	16	8	13	9	13	31	14
Major changes in income	4	4	6	10	5	7	15	7
Changes in size or composition of family	4	4	5	8	7	11	16	7
Changes in relationships with other people	13	15	10	16	7	11	30	14
Change of health	7	8	4	7	5	7	16	7
Change in marital relationship	11	12	6	10	9	13	26	12
Other important changes	6	7	1	2	4	6	11	5
Totals	89	100	61	100	67	100	217**	99*
N (Respondents)	26		23		20		69	
Average number of changes per respondent	3.43		2.90		3.35		3.14	

* Error due to rounding; ** Multiple responses permitted

Table 14.6: Changes Reported As Resulting or Following From the Beginning of the Present Stage of Life

Category of Change	Administrators N	Administrators %	Teachers N	Teachers %	Counsellors N	Counsellors %	Total N	Total %
Change in job or career	26	16	17	15	15	17	58	16
Change in where you lived	18	11	12	10	9	10	39	11
Change in values	29	18	21	18	17	19	67	18
Major changes in income	19	12	19	16	9	10	47	13
Changes in relationships with other people	33	20	19	16	13	15	65	18
Changes in the size or composition of family	7	4	3	3	2	2	12	3
Changes in health	11	7	9	8	7	8	27	7
Changes in marital relationship	9	5	11	9	11	12	31	8
Other important changes	12	7	6	5	6	7	24	6
Totals	164	100	117	100	89	100	370**	100
N	26		23		20		69	
Average number of changes per respondent	6.31		5.37		4.45		5.36	

DISCUSSION

What Kinds of Life Crises or Major Changes Have Adult Educators Experienced?

The major marker events or changes reported were changes in jobs or job orientations. If those returning to school or changing emphases in school are included, more than half of the sample reported a change in career as the significant change which began their present stage of life. The second most important kind of change related to forming or dissolving marriages or changes within marriage. These data seem to corroborate the kinds of changes described by developmental literature, with perhaps a greater emphasis on career changes than would be indicated by theoretical writings.

What Kinds of Emotions Predominated During These Changes?

Fully three-quarters of all emotions reported were unpleasant, though interviews indicated that pleasant emotions were more likely to occur following the major life change. There were important sex differences noted with a much higher proportion of females reporting anger, feelings of failure and frustration than males.

How are Career Changes Related to Life Cycle Concerns?

For this sample of adult educators, most life cycle concerns seemed to be marked either by job changes or changes in the nature of jobs. There were differences among individuals in different job categories, but as a total group, the job or career is interwined deeply with the perceived life stage.

Are There Differences in Life Cycle Patterns Among Educators Who Identify themselves as Administrators, Teachers or Counsellors of Adults?

Administrators were much more likely to make life cycle changes with a change in job than were either teachers or counsellors. Teachers were less likely to report positive emotions during the major life change than were either administrators or counsellors.

Are There Sex Differences in the Relationship Between Career Changes and Life Cycle Concerns?

Females in this sample showed a tendency to have more recent life cycle changes than men, though this difference was more marked in the administrators than either teachers or counsellors. The females were more likely to have experienced high emotions at the time of change, and these emotions were clearly more negative than the emotions reported by the males. The sharp differences between the females and the males clearly indicate a qualitative difference between the way in which careers are experienced by the two sexes.

REFERENCES

Abbey, D., Davie, L., Fales, A., Griffin, V., and Ironside, D. 1978, Career Life Understanding of Mature Practitioners: Year One Interviews, Department of Adult Education, Toronto. The Ontario Institute for Studies in Education, Mimeographed.

Erickson, G.H., 1959, Identity and the Life Cycle, Internation Universities Press, New York.

Gould, R., 1972, "The Phases of Adult Life: A Study in Developmental Psychology," American Journal of Psychiatry, 129:5, November, pp. 521-531.

Lowenthal, M. F., and Chiriboga, D. 1973, Social Stress and Adaptation; Toward a life-Course Perspective, in: "The Psychology of Adult Development and Aging," C. Eisdorfer and L. Powell (eds.), American Psychological Association, pp. 281-311, Washington.

Sheehy, G., 1974, Passages; Predictable Crises of Adult Life, Dalton, New York.

Wilson, S. E., 1973, The Status of Women in the Adult Education Association of the United States of America, Unpublished paper, Department of Adult Education, Federal City College, Washington, D.C., June.

Chapter Fifteen

THE ADULT EDUCATION PROFESSORIAT OF THE UNITED STATES AND CANADA

Reynold Willie, Harlan Copeland and Howard Williams (1985)

Although its roots can be traced to the Middle Ages, the university as a social institution has not been subjected to close scrutiny until very recently. Only in the last 25 years has serious attention been turned to it. The soaring enrolments and proliferation of new subjects and services of the 1950s created serious problems in higher education. It was those problems that led Caplow and McGee (1958) to undertake one of the first studies of a very important part of the university - the academic staff. In their study of working conditions and performance, they found that the literature of the day held several speculative writings about the university and its staff but very few empirically based studies.

Caplow and McGee's study was quickly followed by others. During the next 25 years several national and many local studies of college and university professors were completed and reported in the literature. Some studies included professors from all teaching fields and types of institutions across the continent while others confined themselves to college teachers from specific subject fields or from institutions conforming to a specific criterion such as kind of institution or geographical location. The most widely cited studies of professors are those of Gustad (1960), Ladd and Lipset (1975-76), and Baldridge, Curtis, Echer and Riley (1978).

Gustad, surveying professors of psychology, chemistry and English, sought answers to two major questions: Why do some individuals choose to become college teachers? Why do some of them later decide to leave teaching for other positions? Ladd and Lipset, in a survey of slightly more than 4000 regular, full-time college and university faculty members at 111 institutions, searched for an expression of opinion on issues facing higher education and for information about participants' backgrounds, career expectations, attainments and aspirations. Baldridge et al., in a study of 9000 college teachers, addressed the state of faculty morale as a part of a larger study of academic management and governance.

Despite the studies of the 1960s and 1970s, the National Education Association (1979:5), in a recent study of higher education, found the information on faculty work loads and opinions to be 'meagre, sporadic, and somewhat dated'. It confirmed not only the continued existence of the problems identified by Caplow and McGee but also their intensification. Noting that most of the money spent in higher education is invested in faculty, the NEA predicted that even more critical public attention will be given to the quantitative and qualitative dimensions of the job of college teacher in the 1980s than was given in the 1970s.

There are many reasons why we should study the professoriat. Perhaps Blackburn (1974:92) expressed one of the most compelling reasons when he wrote, 'After all, the college's faculty · is the institution's principal capital. To permit human depreciation and to fail to realise human potential is an administrative sin'. This paper presents information about a portion of the capital of higher education in Canada and the United States - the professors of adult education. It is the report of a study designed to answer such questions as the following: Who are the people who comprise the adult education professoriat? What led them to their present positions in higher education? In what professional activities do they spend their time? Are they satisfied with their jobs and their careers? Do they reaffirm their career choice at this time in their lives? Answers to these questions are presented in the following pages. The possession and utilisation of this information may help us avoid the human depreciation and achieve the human potential noted by Blackburn.

METHODOLOGY

The study, focusing on the five questions above, took the form of survey research. The Spring 1982 membership roster of the Commission of Professors of Adult Education was used as the subject source. This source was chosen because the Commission confines its primary membership category to:

(a) people
(i) appointed on at least a half-time basis to the faculties of accredited institutions of higher education in Canada and the United States, and

(ii) involved not less than half-time in instruction and/or research activities directed towards the preparation of adult education professionals and scholars and

(b) people who have retired from such service.

After eliminating from the roster those not meeting the subject definition of the study - a currently active professor of adult education in a Canadian or American college or university - 215 professors remained as potential participants in the study.

A questionnaire was selected as the information gathering tool. It was adapted from one developed and used by Stecklein and Eckert (1958), Eckert and Williams (1972) and Willie and Stecklein (1982) in the Minnesota College Teacher Study, a series of surveys of professors teaching in Minnesota colleges and universities in 1956, 1968 and 1980. Most questions were phrased in closed form with respondents being asked to select from a list of phrases one or more that described them or their positions. An other category was included with some questions to accommodate unexpected responses. Several questions were phrased in open form with respondents being asked to generate statements about their feelings toward their jobs.

Questionnaires with three follow-up reminders (the first a postal card, the second another copy of the questionnaire, and the third a personal letter inviting participation) were mailed to the 215 eligible members of the Commission of Professors of Adult Education during April and May 1982. One hundred and seventy-seven professors (82.3%) returned completed, usable questionnaires. Three (1.4%) returned questionnaires with notations that they did not wish to participate; seven (3.3%) provided information indicating that they no longer met the subject definition; and 28 (13.0%) did not respond. (The number of non-respondents was reduced to 23, 10.7%, at the end of summer break when five professors returned completed forms. Their responses are not included in this report but will be included in subsequent analyses). Table 15.1 reports subject response rate.

The Statistical Package for the Social Sciences (SPSS) was used in the analysis of the data. Measures of central tendency were applied to selected frequency distributions and Chi-square tests of statistical significance of relationships among variables were applied to selected crosstabulations.

Table 15.1: Subject Response Rate

	Total		Canada		United States	
	N	%	N	%	N	%
Professors						
Meeting subject definition	215		34		181	
Returning usable forms	177	82.3	24	70.6	153	86.4
Not responding	28	13.0	8	23.5	20	11.0
Excluded	10	4.7	2	5.9	8	4.4

FINDINGS

The Respondents

Of the 177 professors electing to participate in the study, 153 (86.4%) were employed in American* institutions and 25 (13.5%) in Canadian institutions. They ranged in age from 29 years to 70 years with a mean age of 48.3 years, a median age of 47.6, and a modal age of 50. There were 31 women (17.5%) and 146 men (82.5%) in the total group. Eighty-five per cent (85.3%) of the respondents were born in the United States and 8.5 per cent in Canada. The regions of the United States given as birthplace by the greatest numbers of American and Canadian professors were the Midwest (21.5%), the South (20.3%), the Middle Atlantic States (13.0%), and the Upper Midwest (11.3%), the New England States (4.5%), and the West Coast States (6.8%). Fifty-seven per cent (57.1%) of Canadian professors were born in Canada and 28.6% in the United States. Ninety-six per cent (96.0%) of American professors were born in the United States and 2.0% were born in Canada.

Career Choice and Education

People do not ordinarily choose college teaching as a career early in their lives. It is unusual for people in professional fields to move directly from the role of student to that of teacher. The two are ordinarily separated by time in practice. Professors of adult education appear to follow the common route: 55.9% reported that first thoughts of teaching adult education came during graduate study and 27.1% reported that first thoughts came only after receiving the highest degree. Half of the group (50.8%) recalled a non-education career goal at college entry, one-fifth (20.3%) a secondary education career goal, and only one in twenty (5.1%) an adult education career goal. Slightly over one tenth of the group (11.9%) were undecided at that time. The percentage recalling a non-education career goal at receipt of the baccalaureate degree dropped to 33.3, the percentage reporting secondary education rose to 33.9, and the percentage giving adult education rose to 13.6 At the Master's level non-education career goals were still recalled by 13.6% of the respondents while secondary education as a career goal was recalled by 20.9%, adult education by 32.8% and higher education by 18.5%. At the doctoral level career goals in adult education

---

* Since there is no other commonly accepted term for people of the United States, we shall accept common usage and apply the term Americans to professors of the United States, recognizing at the same time that those in Canada are also Americans.

were recalled by 18.1% and career goals in higher education by 68.9%. Figure 15.1 illustrates changes in career plans over time.

Sixty per cent (59.3%) of the respondents reported a non-education major in their undergraduate programmes, 22.0% reported an elementary or secondary education major, and 13.0% reported a vocational-technical education major. Only one respondent (0.6%) reported adult education as an undergraduate major. At the Master's defree level the percentage of respondents reporting a non-education major dropped to 28.8%, an elementary or secondary education major to 13.0%, and a vocational-technical education major to 7.9%. Twenty-seven per cent (26.6%) reported an adult education major. At the doctoral level the most frequently given major was adult education (64.4%). The second most frequently cited major at this level was educational administration (7.9%). Five per cent (5.6%) continued to report a non-education major.

Most of the respondents completed their degrees at midwestern and southern institutions. Forty-three per cent (42.9%) completed their baccalaureate degrees at institutions located in the Midwest, Upper Midwest, and Plains States and 21.4% completed degrees at institutions located in the South. Forty-two per cent (41.8%) completed Master's degrees at institutions in the former group of states and 24.9% in the latter group. Half of the respondents (49.6%) earned doctorates at institutions in the Midwest, Upper Midwest, and Plains States and 23.1 per cent at institutions in the South.

The year 1957 was both the median and modal year for receipt of the baccalaureate degree, 1964 the median year and 1962 the modal year for receipt of the first Master's degree (11 reported a second Master's defree), and 1970 the median year and 1969 the modal year for the doctorate. Six of the respondents (3.4%) reported currently being active in a degree programme. Two reported enrolment in Master's degree programmes such as the MBA, one in a doctoral programme in higher education, and two in other degree programmes.

The Job: Professor of Adult Education
Ninety per cent (89.8%) of the respondents reported previous employment of a kind other than teaching adult education with 23.35 reporting a first job teaching in Kindergarten-Grade 12 and 14.1% a first job working in adult education areas. Thirty-six per cent of the respondents (36.2%) reported experience in an adult education teaching position elsewhere prior to acceptance of their present position. The mean number of years in another adult education teaching position was 5.7, the median 3.4, and the mode 3.0. The mean number of years in present position was 9.9 years, the median 8.7, and the mode 5.0.

Figure 15.1: Career goals at educational milestones: College entry and reciept of batchelor's, master's and doctor's degrees

What led these professors to their present institutions? The challenge of the job was the reason most often selected from and ranked first, second or third on a list of 13 reasons compiled from the responses given by professors in other studies. Challenge of the job was selected by 58.2% of the respondents and ranked first by 27.7%, second by 17.5%, and third by 13.0%. Other reasons selected and ranked by at least one-fifth of the respondents were the programme, the geographical location of the institution, the type of institution, the faculty, and the offer of a job. Table 15.2 summarises the reasons as they were selected and ranked by respondents.

Rarely did Canadians and Americans differ in a statistically significant manner in their responses to the questions in the inventory. They did on reasons for selecting their present institution, however. They responded differently to three reasons for becoming a professor of adult education at their present institution: 'I liked the challenge of the job opportunity' was ranked first, second, and third by 30.9, 18.4 and 13.8% respectively of American professors and by 8.3, 12.5 and 8.3% respectively of Canadian professors (p=.03). 'I liked the students' was ranked first, second, and third by 5.9, 3.3 and 5.3% respectively of American professors and by 0, 12.5 and 4.2% respectively of Canadian professors (p=.001). 'There were opportunities for me to do research' was ranked first, second and third by 5.3, 3.9 and 3.9% respectively of American professors and by 8.3, 16.7 and 4.2% respectively of Canadian professors (p=.005).

Of the 177 respondents 42.9% were professors, 35.0% associate professors and 21.5% assistant professors. Nearly half (49.2%) reported an administrative position with department or programme head the most frequently reported title (25.1%). The next most frequently reported title (5.1%) was one indicating co-ordination of an all-college or all-university activity. Half (51.6%) of the American professors reported an administrative position while only one-third (33.3%) of the Canadian professors did so. Adult education was given as the primary teaching assignment by 59.3% of the respondents, extension education by 6.2%, human resource development by 5.6%, adult literacy by 2.8%, educational gerontology by 1.7%, vocational and technical education by 1.1%, and other unidentified assignments by 6.8%. More than one primary teaching area was mentioned by 16.4% of the professors.

More than two-thirds of the respondents (68.4%) indicated that their positions are full-time positions in adult education. Table 15.3 shows the percentages in various time categories.

Nearly equal percentages reported holding nine and twelve-month appointments (40.1% and 41.2%, respectively). However, only 34.6% of the American professors hold twelve-month appointments while 83.3% of the Canadians do so. A ten-month appointment was reported by 10.2% and an eleven-month appointment by 7.3%.

201

Table 15.2: Reasons for Selecting Present Institution

Reason	Ranking 1	2	3
Challenge of the job opportunity	27.7	17.5	13.0
Job offered	11.3	7.9	4.5
The faculty	10.2	9.0	7.3
Type of institution	7.3	13.6	9.6
The programme	7.3	12.4	11.3
Transferred from another position	6.8	.6	2.8
Research opportunities	5.6	5.6	4.0
The students	5.1	4.6	5.1
Geographical location	4.5	10.7	15.8
Reputation of the institution	4.0	4.5	6.8
Salary package	1.1	0.0	3.4
Working conditions	.6	2.8	4.0
Declining opportunities elsewhere	.6	1.1	2.3

Table 15.3: Percentage of Time Assigned to Adult Education

Percentage of time assigned	Number of professors	Percentage of professors
100%	121	68.4%
67-99%	9	5.2
34-66% (50%)	25 (18)	14.2 (10.2%)
10-33%	19	10.8
Not reporting	3	1.7

Participants in the study were asked to indicate a range in which their salaries fell and to give terms of appointment. To allow comparisons, the midpoint of the salary range of each American professor was divided by the reported term of appointment and multiplied by nine to yield an academic year salary. The midpoint of the salary range of each Canadian professor was multiplied by .834, the average annual currency exchange rate in effect at the time 1982 salaries were determined, before being subjected to the same treatment as American salaries. Professors reporting an eleven-month term of employment were not included in the salary conversions because it was uncertain if they constituted a group distinct from those reporting a twelve-month term of employment. See Table 15.4 for a comparison of American and Canadian salaries.

Table 15.4: Selected Canadian and American Converted Academic Year Salaries Reported in American Dollars

| | | American | | | | Canadian | | |
	All	Cf%	Full time	Cf%	All	Cf%	Full time	Cf%
15,000-19,999	8.6	8.6	6.4	6.4	4.5	4.5	5.3	5.3
20,000-24,999	27.2	35.8	26.6	33.0	31.9	36.4	36.8	42.1
25,000-29,999	20.7	56.5	25.5	58.5	54.5	90.9	47.4	89.5
30,000-34,999	25.0	81.5	22.3	80.8	0	90.0	0	89.5
35,000-39,999	11.4	92.9	11.8	92.6	*9.1	100.0	10.5	100.0
40,000-44,999	5.7	98.6	5.3	97.9				
45,000 or over	1.4	100.0	2.1	100.0	*$35,000 or over			

What percentage of their time in an academic year do professors of adult education ordinarily devote to the functions associated with the job, i.e. teaching, scholarly writing, counselling, committee and administrative duties, and off-campus service? An analysis of the responses of those indicating a full-time assignment to adult education revealed the following median percentages of time devoted to each function: teaching, 39.8%; advising, 14.8%; research and scholarly writing, 10.4%; counselling, 9.9%; committee and administrative duties, 10.2%; off-campus service, 5.4%; and other activities, 10.3%. Respondents were asked the one or two activities to which they would like to give both more and less time. Nearly 70% (68.9%) would like to give more time to research and writing while over 50% would like to give less time to committee and administrative assignments. Table 15.5 gives respondents' time preferences.

A measure of productivity commonly applied to college and university professors is that of publication frequency. The inventory requested that participants report publications in certain categories for the five-year period preceding the study (1 July 1977 to April 1982). The most popular form of publication was the journal article with 57.1% of the respondents reporting one to five publications in professional journals and 22.1% reporting six or more. Over half of the respondents reported the publication of books and monographs (56.5%) and book chapters (54.8%). The least used publication outlet was ERIC with 39.0% reporting such publications. Unpublished but presented papers were reported by 88.1% of the respondents. Table 15.6 summarises the publication record of adult education professoriat.

Nearly 90% (88.7%) of the professors reported that they advise Master's degree students. The mean number of advisees for those reporting advisees at this level was 18.6,

Table 15.5: Activities to which Professors Would Like to Give More and Less Time

Activity	More Time (%)	Less Time (%)
Research/writing	68.9	2.3
Teaching	22.6	11.9
Thesis advising	15.3	8.5
Off campus service	13.6	3.4
Counselling	4.5	7.3
Committee and administration	4.5	55.9
Selected one only	71.1	81.9
Selected none	7.3	30.0

Table 15.6: Percentage of Respondents Reporting Publications for the Five-Year Period Preceding the Study

Type of publication	None	1-2	3-4	5-6	7 or more
Journal articles	20.9	24.3	21.5	13.0	20.4
Book chapters	45.2	36.1	11.9	3.4	3.4
Books and monographs	43.5	35.0	13.0	3.9	4.5
ERIC	61.0	20.4	8.0	4.5	6.2
Book reviews	51.4	24.9	13.0	5.1	5.7
Unpublished presented papers	11.9	13.5	26.0	16.4	31.2
Study guides	44.1	20.9	18.1	6.2	10.7

the median was 12.4 and the mode 10. Sixty-nine per cent (68.9%) reported that they supervise Master's theses. The mean number of students for those reporting was 7.9, the median 4.6 and the mode 1. A further (24.3%) reported specialist advisees. The mean number of advisees for those reporting was 4.3, the median 3.5 and the mode 3. Seventy-two per cent (72.9%) reported Doctor's degree advisees. The mean number of advisees for those reporting was 13.3, the median 10.1 and the mode 15. Nearly three-quarters (74.0%) supervise doctor's dissertations. The mean number for those reporting was 7.8, the median 5.3 and the mode 3.0.

Job and Career Satisfaction
Participants were asked to select from a list of potential job satisfactions and dissatisfactions and then rank those that best applied to their current situations. Working with

students, interesting and challenging work, opportunities for research and writing, and opportunities for teaching were the most often selected sources of satisfaction. Pressure to research and publish, ineffective administration, poor administrative support, and inadequate resources were the most frequently cited sources of dissatisfaction. Table 15.7 presents the sources of satisfaction and dissatisfaction that were selected and ranked by at least 10% of the respondents.

Canadian and American professors differed significantly in their responses to two of the questions addressing sources of job satisfaction and dissatisfaction. The opportunity to engage in research and professional writing was ranked first as a source of satisfaction by 37.5% of the Canadian respondents and by 7.2% of the Americans. The item was selected and ranked first, second or third by 54.2% of the Canadians and by 21.5% of the Americans. Working with other faculty was selected and ranked first, second or third as a source of job dissatisfaction by 20.9% of the Canadian respondents and by 6.6% of the Americans. Statistically significant differences were found between the responses of the two groups to these questions addressing research opportunities (p=.0001) and working with other faculty (p=.0002).

Participants were asked to check one of five terms that best described their present attitude toward their careers as professor of adult education. Nearly nine out of ten (87.5%) selected a term that indicated satisfaction - 44.6% checked the very satisfied category and 42.9% the satisfied. Three per cent (3.4%) of the respondents indicated that they were indifferent to their career as professor, 7.3% indicated that they were dissatisfied, and 1.1% indicated very dissatisfied. Asked if they would again choose the career of professor of adult education if they could remake the decision, 78.0% indicated that they would, 5.1% replied that they would not and 15.3% were uncertain. Two per cent (1.7%) did not respond to the question. Table 15.8 shows the percentages choosing each satisfaction category.

Retirement

When do they plan to retire? 'Never!' according to 7.3% of the respondents. Thirty-five per cent (35.0%) of their colleagues indicated that they would like to retire prior to or at age 62, 26.5% between ages 63 and 67, 20.9% between ages 68 and 70, and 3.4% between ages 71 and 80. Seven per cent (6.8%) did not respond to the item. Asked if there should be a mandatory retirement age, 28.2% indicated that there should be such a requirement and 48.6% that there should not be. More than one in five (22.5%) indicated uncertainty.

Table 15.7: Satisfactions and Dissatisfactions Reported by Professors of Adult Education

| | Per cent ranking | | |
	1	2	3
Satisfactions			
Students	34.5	20.9	14.7
Interesting work	16.4	11.9	11.3
Opportunities for research and writing	11.3	5.6	9.0
Opportunities of teaching	9.0	10.7	9.0
Dissatisfactions			
Research pressures	16.4	5.1	4.5
Inadequate resources	14.7	8.5	10.7
Administration	14.1	7.9	6.8
Poor administrative support	9.6	15.8	11.9

Table 15.8: Career Satisfaction of Adult Education Professors

	%
Very satisfied	44.6
Satisfied	42.9
Indifferent	3.4
Dissatisfied	7.3
Very dissatisfied	1.1

DISCUSSION

The data gathered in this study of the adult education professoriat of the United States and Canada suggest that:

1. The adult education professoriat is heavily populated with men who are middle-aged and older and, if the group is similar to the professoriat in general, the median age is increasing.

Eighty-two per cent of the respondents were male. other studies have similarly reported high percentages of males (Ladd and Lipset, 79%; National Education Association, 71%; Willie and Stecklein, 74%).

The median age of the professors was 47.6 years. Six or more of every ten professors were middle-aged and older. If one accepts 35 as the lower limit of middle age, 97% of the respondents could be described as middle-aged and older. If either one of the more commonly accepted lower limits - 40 or 45 years - is accepted, then either 79% or 62% of the respondents would merit such a description.

The National Education Association (1979) reported a 1978 median age of 43 years for faculty in four-year institutions and noted that the percentage of faculty under age 35 in all institutions had dropped from 32.0 in 1948 to 18.3 in 1978 while the percentage of those aged 35 to 49 rose from 45.6 to 52.6 and of those aged 50 years and over from 22.5 to 29.0. Ladd and Lipset (1976: 12-13) predicted changing median ages of faculty members in general from 39 years in 1970 to 48 years in 1990. They cited expert predictions of the virtual disappearance from the teaching ranks of the under-35 age group and the statement by Allan Cartter that academe is becoming a "gerontocracy" in which the attitudes and behaviours of the older generation will dominate.

Studies of college and university faculties indicate that age is a major variable affecting attitudes, opinions and actions and that increasing age is accompanied by increasing conservatism. Ladd and Lipset found older faculty more conservative than younger faculty and noted that 'on the responses to question after question, there is a steady progression from left to right in tandem with increased age'. (College and university faculty identified with professional fields have also been found to be more conservative than their counterparts in non-professional areas. Ladd and Lipset found 48% of the faculty members 55 years and older in professional fields to be in the most conservative fifth of professors in general and only 7% in the most liberal fifth.)

The studies reveal older faculty members to be clearly less liberal on social and political issues, on the rights of students, and on such issues as collective bargaining. The studies also suggest that older members are less inclined to be involved in research and they they are less productive in their research than are younger members.

If one accepts the hypothesis that an increasingly conservative professoriat is developing, one can cast a sombre scenario in which the adult education programme in our colleges and universities will change very little over the next decade, that there will be little movement within the group, that instructional methods will not soon or easily accommodate innovations such as those of educational technology. The base on which the professional field rests will soften as smaller percentages of faculty membership involve themselves in research. The professors will grow old together in a cohort whose membership is closed. Fortunately, one can also cast a scenario as exciting as the other is sombre. Studies of faculty vitality are now underway and they present a very powerful argument for emerging staff development programmes. They also present a convincing argument for the continued institutional support of sabbatical leaves, research grants, reimbursement for expenses connected with attending national and regional professional meetings, and the like.

2. Professors attach major importance to six factors in their decision to accept positions in adult education. The challenge of the job, the type of institution, the programme, the faculty, geographical location, and the actual offer of the job were reported in this study as the major attractions to positions. Respondents reported attaching lesser importance to type of student, the reputation of the institution and the opportunity to do research, and least importance to working conditions and salary package. Since national searches to fill position openings have become very costly and time consuming, job descriptions and position announcements that highlight factors professors identify as important may at least in a small way, ease the cost and time demands of such searches.

3. Teaching and activities related to teaching occupy the major portion of faculty members' time. Professors of adult education report spending slightly over half of their job time in teaching and advising and only one-tenth of their time in research and scholarly activities.

Since in most studies professors report spending the largest block of time in teaching and advising, one would tend to assume that teaching and advising are the most highly esteemed activities in which professors engage. Such apparently is not the case. Ladd and Lipset found that, while higher education as an institution esteems research more highly than it does teaching, 91% of the professors indicated spending 25% or less of their time in research activities, and 62% spending 10% or less of their time in such activities. They also found that three-quarters of the respondents agreed with a statement that teaching effectiveness, not publications, should be the primary criterion for promotion of faculty. Yet publish-or-perish continues to be perceived as a very strong force in many institutions. One can only wonder why faculties place so great an emphasis on a criterion for tenure and promotion when they devote such relatively small percentages of their time to these activities.

4. Most professors of adult education find their careers satisfying. Nearly nine out of ten respondents described themselves as satisfied with their careers, with half of those describing themselves as very satisfied and the other half as satisfied. These responses are generally consistent with those of other studies. Baldridge et al., found 66% of respondents to be high in satisfaction and 34% to be low but they limited satisfaction to four specific aspects of the work situation. An important finding in the Minnesota College Teacher Study was that, while the percentage of professors describing themselves as satisfied has remained stable over the last three decades, the percentage describing themselves as very satisfied has

steadily declined while the percentage describing themselves as satisfied has increased.

5. Most professors of adult education reaffirm their career choice. Seventy-eight per cent indicated that they would still choose to work as a professor of adult education were they to begin anew, 15% expressed uncertainty. These percentages are generally consistent with those reported in other studies. Ladd and Lipset, for example, reported that 88% would want to be college professors if they were to begin a new and Willie and Stecklein reported 72%. In the latter study, however, the percentage of those ready to reaffirm their academic career choice dropped 13 percentage points since 1968.

The purpose of this report has been to present information on the adult education professoriat of Canada and the United States. Findings have been drawn from the responses of 177 professors to questions designed to gather information about the people who comprise the adult education professoriat, the factors that led them to their present positions in higher education, their professional activities, their job satisfactions and dissatisfactions, and their attitudes toward their career. The information presented in this report should be especially useful to us at this time as we are called upon to examine our programmes and our faculties. It may help us preserve what a generation of adult education professors has built.

REFERENCES

Baldridge, V., Curtis, D., Ecker, G., and Riley, G., 1978, "Policy Making and Effective Leadership, A National Study of Academic Management," Jossey-Bass, San Francisco.

Blackburn, R., 1974, The meaning of work in Academia, in: "Assessing Faculty Effort," J. Doi, (issue ed.), Jossey-Bass, p.92, San Francisco.

Caplow, T., and McGee, R., 1958, "The Academic Marketplace," Basic Books, New York.

Eckert, R., and Williams, H., 1972, "College Faculty View Themselves and Their Jobs," University of Minnesota Press, Minneapolis.

Gustad, J., 1960, "The Career Decisions of Teachers," Research Monograph 2, Southern Regional Education Board, Atlanta.

Ladd, E., and Lipset, M., 'The Ladd-Lipset Survey,' "The Chronicle of Higher Education," 11 and 12 ('What professors think', 11:1; 'Faculty women; little gain in status', 11:3 'Faculty income favourably compared' 11:4; 'How faculty spend their time', 11:5, 'What do professors like best about their jobs?' 12:1; 'Nearly all professors

are satisfied with their choice of an academic career'
12:10; 'The Aging Professoriate', 12:13.

National Education Association, 1979, "Higher Education
Faculty: Characteristics and Opinions," National Education Association, p. 5, Washington.

Stecklein, J. and Eckert, R., 1958, "An Exploratory Study of
Factors Influencing the Choice of College Teaching as a
Career," University of Minnesota Press, Minneapolis.

Willie, R., and Stecklein, J., 1982, A three decade comparison of college faculty characteristics, satisfactions,
activities, and attitudes, Research in Higher Education,
AIR Forum Issue, 16:1 pp. 81-93.

Chapter Sixteen

PHILOSOPHICAL ORIENTATIONS OF ADULT
EDUCATORS

Leon McKenzie (1985)

Classification is a fundamental intellectual process by which
ideas and phenomena are sorted, compared, analysed, and
integrated into a coherent whole. Classification, therefore,
aids understanding in its quest for intelligibility. The fruit-
fulness of classification becomes evident when we evaluate the
schema provided by Elias and Merriam (1980) vis-a-vis philosophies of adult education. Their review of the philosophical
literature in the field of adult education enabled them to
delineate six categories of theoretical principles that govern
the practice of adult education. Adult educators, using the
Elias and Merriam schema, are able to compare and contrast
philosophical principles in a systematic manner, and are also
able to determine more clearly the relationship between these
principles and the practice of adult education.

To paraphrase Elias and Merriam, liberal adult education
emphasises the transmission of a body of organised knowledge
and the development of intellectual powers. Progressive adult
education stresses learning as problem solving, the acquisition
of practical skills, and the promotion of social change. Behaviorist adult education focuses on behavioral modification,
learning through reinforcement, and instructional management
by objectives. Humanistic adult education embraces principles
that view education in terms of enhanced personal growth and
development. Radical adult education has as its major theme
the initiation of social, political, and economic change.
Analytic adult education is concerned primarily with the need
to clarify concepts and arguments used in theoretical discourse. (pp. 9-11)

No doubt there is overlap among these philosophies of
adult education. We can hardly expect that any thoughtful
person would espouse a particular philosophy to the exclusion
of the values contained in other orientations. The Elias-
Merriam schema, however, remains a helpful device for
organising philosophical thinking about adult education.

A valuable tool for measuring the extent to which a
person values philosophies of adult education is the

Philosophy of Adult Education Inventory (PAEI) developed by Zinn (1983). The inventory assists individuals in determining the degree of their adherence to liberal, progressive, behaviorist, humanist, and radical philosophies. The PAEI does not include the analytic philosophy of adult education since this orientation is more of a methodological approach to philosophy than a definite philosophical system.

The instrument is comprised of 75 Likert-type items. The items yield responses which result in summated scores ranging from 16 to 112 for each of the philosophical orientations. Examination of the five scores provides an indication of the respondent's prevailing philosophy of adult education. The PAEI was used in the research reported here.

Research Problem and Null Hypothesis

The author sought to determine empirically whether a relationship existed between the philosophical orientations of adult educators and their experiences as educators in different adult education contexts. The research problem was: To what extent are the PAEI scores of adult educators from three different contexts congruent?

The null hypothesis was: There are no significant differences in the philosophical orientations of adult educators who represent three different contexts. It was assumed that the PAEI would be sensitive enough to detect differences if these differences actually existed.

Data Collection and Analysis

The PAEI, with the permission of the author, was administered to three convenience samples of adult educators, all of whom were involved at some level in the practice of adult education. The inventory was completed by 22 trainers in business and industrial settings, who were students in an undergraduate course, 48 religious educators of adults attending an adult education workshop, and 32 beginning graduate students in adult education who had not as yet studied the philosophical foundations of adult education. This latter group was comprised of persons who represented a diversity of adult education settings.

The data yielded by the PAEI were submitted to oneway analyses of variance. That is, the data for each of the five philosophical orientations were compared across the three samples.

Findings

The means and standard deviations for each philosophical orientation across the three groups are displayed in Table 16.1.

Table 16.1: Five Philosophical Orientations Across Three Samples: Means and Standard Deviations

	Liberal		Behaviorist		Progressive		Humanistic		Radical	
Business Trainers (N = 22)	81.3	(9.3)	85.9	(9.3)	86.0	(7.8)	75.0	(10.3)	68.2	(13.6)
Religious Educators (N = 48)	64.8	(12.5)	67.0	(11.8)	79.2	(9.7)	82.9	(12.7)	72.3	(9.4)
Graduate Students in Adult Education (n = 31)	70.5	(9.7)	75.9	(7.3)	82.3	(7.5)	78.4	(11.1)	66.5	(9.3)

The 22 trainers in business and industry scored highest in the liberal, behaviorist, and progressive orientations, and lowest in the humanistic orientation. The religious educators scored highest in the humanistic and radical orientations, and lowest in the liberal orientation. The adult education graduate students had moderate scores in the liberal, behaviorist, progressive and scored lowest in the radical orientation.

Table 16.2 displays the results of the one-way ANOVA's. There were significant differences at the .05 level of confidence among the three groups for each philosophical orientation. The null hypothesis was rejected.

CONCLUSIONS

The findings lend themselves to a number of inferences. Given the differences among the three groups of adult educators representing specific contexts it is suggested that the philosophical orientations of the adult educators in the study are rooted in professional practice and derive more from concrete experiences in organisational settings than from logical analysis or the evaluation of abstract philosophical arguments.

This suggestion does not deny, however, that a person's adult education philosophy is unrelated to his or her overall philosophy of life at least in part. Also it may be that some adult educators chose to work in particular specialised areas in adult education because their overall philosophies of life lead them into those career areas.

Table 16.2: Oneway Anova's

	Liberal	Behaviorist	Progressive	Humanistic	Radical
Between Groups Mean SSQ	2057.6	2781.4	358.9	519.3	349.4
Within Groups Mean SSQ	126.2	104.2	77.1	141.0	111.5
F Ratio	16.3	26.7	4.7	3.7	3.1
Significance	.0000	.0000	.0117	.0287	.0479

Table 16.3: Correlations Among Philosophical Orientations
(N = 102)

	Behaviorist	Progressive	Humanistic	Radical
Liberal	.84	.67	.35	.52
Behaviorist		.78	.42	.53
Progressive			.73	.73
Humanistic				.74

The 22 trainers representing business and industry scored highest in the liberal orientation.. This may not be due, it is suggested, to their keen interest in the curriculum we have come to associate with the liberal adult education agenda, e.g., the Great Books programme.

Table 16.3 presents the correlations among the five orientation scores for the total sample. While all of the correlations are significant at the .05 level for a two-tailed test, the highest correlation obtains between the liberal and behaviorist orientations. This suggests that what is shared in principle by these orientations is a pronounced concern for instructional content. Intuitively this makes sense. Liberals have been traditionally apprised as being concerned with the transmission of a predetermined body of knowledge. Behaviorists, by definition, are concerned with the acquisition on the part of learners of a predetermined set of behaviours.

The correlation between progressive orientation scores are high when the progressive orientation is compared to all other orientations. The progressive orientation seems to enjoy a commonality with the other orientations because it includes select values that are not incompatible with the main thrusts of the liberal, behaviorist, humanistic, and radical orientations.

Implications for Practice
It has been pointed out by Phillips (1981) and Suttle (1982), among others, that theory and practice are inextricably linked. What seems to be indicated by the limited study reported here is that the practice of adult education in particular settings controls theoretical orientation more than theoretical orientation conditions practice. Theory and practice may vary according to specific content areas of instruction. This should not be surprising to anyone who believes that one's personal experience imparts a particular character to one's philosophical ground.

The findings of this study could be the basis for the conclusion that many adult educators merely accept patterns of practice (and corresponding theoretical assumptions) to which they have been exposed without testing these patterns critically. It is not altogether uncommon for some adult educators to be enthusiastic about techniques, procedures, instructional aids, and fads while at the same time avoiding a critical examination of the philosophical grounds of practice.

Adult education practice should include theoretical reflection. One of the differences between a proficient adult educator and a marginally effective adult educator is that the practice of the proficient adult educator refers continually to theoretical principles which allow the individual to move in a creative manner beyond repetitive actions. The marginally effective adult educator, confronted with totally novel situations, is unable to adapt to these situations on the basis of theoretical considerations.

Thinking and doing ideally exist in a balanced reciprocal relationship. What we do unavoidably affects our internal interpretive structures. Action must be anchored in reflection. The theoretician who distances self from the real world becomes an ivory tower isolate. The practitioner who is unencumbered by theoretical reflection eventually becomes a shallow activitist.

REFERENCES

Elias, J. and Merriam, S. (1980), "Philosophical Foundations of Adult Education," Krieger Publishing Company, Huntington, New York.

Phillips, J. (1981), Theory, practice and basic beliefs in adult education, Adult Education, 31:93-106.

Suttle, B. (1982), Adult Education: no need for theories? Adult Education, 32: 104-107.

Zinn, L., (1983), "Development of a Valid and Reliable Instrument to Identify a Personal Philosophy of Adult Education," Unpublished doctoral dissertation, Florida State University, Tallahassee.

PART SIX

CRITERIA OF GOOD PRACTICE IN
GRADUATE ADULT EDUCATION

Chapter Seventeen

CRITERIA FOR THE EDUCATION OF ADULT
EDUCATORS

C.O. Robinson (1964)

During January 1961, the author interviewed twenty-four
adult educators in the Mountain-Plains Region in order to
obtain information for a study titled The Educational and
Experiential Backgrounds of Adult Educators in the Mountain-
Plains Region. These twenty-four educators interviewed
included the director or dean of the General Extension
Division of each state university, the director of each
Agricultural Extension Division in each land-grant university
or college, and the person in each state department of edu-
cation responsible for adult education in the states of
Arizona, Colorado, Idaho, Montana, New Mexico, Nevada,
Utah, and Wyoming.

In order to construct a set of criteria which would
reflect the best thinking of these adult educators concerning
both desirable experience and educational backgrounds for
persons entering the field of adult education, the following
questions were asked of each of the persons interviewed: How
important do you feel courses in adult education are for
persons in the field? Is there a particular experience you
believe important to success in adult education?

Each interviewee was asked several other questions in
order to gain information pertinent to the study. In every
case the investigator recorded the answers given and used
additional questions to probe for additional information. Each
of the persons interviewed cooperated not only during the
interview but also in many other ways, such as identifying
other adult educators, making sure that each adult educator
received a copy of the questionnaire used, and completing a
questionnaire themselves.

The answers to the questions above were listed and
grouped as to content in order that criteria for choosing
persons to enter adult education and criteria for educating
these persons could be written. The author found that by the
careful grouping of all answers it was possible to have all of
the statements represented by only sixteen criteria.

Table 17.1: Rating of the Criteria by the Jury

Criteria in Rank Order as Marked by Total	Average Rating of Agricultural Extension n = 9	Average Rating of NUEA n = 10	Average Rating of NAPSAE n = 9	Average Rating of Professors n = 7	Average Rating of Jury n = 35
1. The adult educator should have the qualities of a leader and should be mature enough to be accepted by adults.	4.77	4.77	4.77	4.43	4.69
2. The adult educator should possess initiative in programmes development.	4.88	4.50	4.88	4.36	4.67
3. The adult educator should understand adult psychology.	4.11	4.45	4.72	4.85	4.51
4. The adult educator should understand group leadership and be able to work with groups.	4.66	4.50	4.66	3.78	4.44
5. The adult educator should be a competent teacher.	4.77	3.60	4.50	3.93	4.20
6. The adult educator should be proficient in the use of communication media.	4.00	3.90	4.33	4.36	4.13
7. The adult educator should understand community organisation, community power structures, and community development.	4.33	4.33	3.83	3.85	4.10

8. The adult educator should have experience in working with adults.	3.66	4.27	3.72	4.14	3.94
9. The adult educator should have the ability to do public relations, promotional work, and organisational work.	3.88	3.75	3.78		3.93
10. The adult educator should have competence in an academic area.	4.11	4.35	4.27		3.89
11. The adult educator should have a course background in adult education.	3.44	3.15	3.72	4.07	3.53
12. The adult educator should have a broad course background in the liberal arts.	3.22	3.70	3.16	3.78	3.46
13. The adult educator should possess a master's degree.	3.44	3.25	3.61	2.33	3.29
14. The adult educator should have training and experience in educational administration.	3.05	2.61	3.61	3.71	3.22
15. The adult educator should have an internship as a part of his professional training.	2.77	3.20	3.31	2.83	3.05
16. The adult educator should have occupational experience outside of school experience.	2.55	3.15	2.88	3.28	2.96

CRITERIA

JURY OF EXPERTS

A jury of experts was then asked to place each of these criteria on a simple five point scale from a low value of one to the highest value, which was five. This jury of experts was obtained by asking officers in the following organisations to submit a list of ten persons qualified to serve on such a jury: NAPSAE (National Association of Public School Adult Educators), NUEA (National University Extension Association), the Professors of Adult Education, and the Agricultural Extension Division of the Land-Grant Colleges Association. Of the forty persons nominated, thirty-five were willing to serve on such a jury. The criteria and the average rating given them by the jury of experts is given in the accompanying table.

The author did not expect the jury to agree as much as they did either in the relative importance of each of the criteria or in the numerical value assigned each of the criteria. The four groups who served on the jury of experts agreed, generally on the approximate value of each of the criteria. The professors of adult education would value a course background in adult education much more than the other three groups. Although this criterion was placed eleventh by the total jury, it would have been placed sixth in importance by the group of professors of adult education. Conversely, the NUEA members of the jury placed the criterion concerning teaching competency in eleventh place, whereas the total jury placed it as sixth in importance.

COMPETENCE

The professors of adult education also placed the criterion relative to competence in an academic area lower than the other three groups. This criterion was fourteenth in importance in the professors' judgment; however, it was rated as sixth, fifth, and ninth in importance by the other three groups of the jury. This disparity might be caused by the fact that the professors do believe in a course background in adult education. If we could agree that this is an academic area, perhaps the ratings are even closer than is indicated by this seeming difference.

The persons interviewed and the jury of experts believed that certain competencies are of greater importance to adult educators than either particular experience backgrounds or particular formal course backgrounds. The author believes, however, that these competencies, at least in part, will have to come from learning that occurs either in particular experiences or in particular courses taken by those who enter the field of adult education.

Chapter Eighteen

PRINCIPLES OF GOOD PRACTICE IN
CONTINUING EDUCATION

Jack Mezirow (1984)

"A major breakthrough in this field," heralds Malcolm
Knowles. "For the first time in history we have a single
statement of the best knowledge and understanding of how
adults can learn most effectively" (The Learning Connection V
[July 1984] p. 4).
   The Council on the Continuing Education unit, in collab-
oration with the National University Continuing Education
Association, sponsored a study of current standards used in
continuing education, convened a conference and promulgated
a set of principles"... for general use by business and
industry, professional associations and organisations, educational institutions and organisations, government agencies,
health-care organisations and institutions and others involved
in continuing education and training as either providers,
users, learners or regulators." (1).
   Continuing education is defined here as "formal education
programmes/activities for professional development and
training, or for credentialing... or of personal interest to the
learner, for which academic credit is not awarded." The
purpose of continuing education is "... to help maintain,
expand and improve individual knowledge, skills
(performance) and attitudes and, by so doing, equally meet
the improvement and advancement of individuals, professions
and organisations. Therefore, a primary emphasis ... is on
the individual learner." Learning needs are "the difference
between the current level and the desired level of the
learner's knowledge, skills or attitude" and "may include the
individual participant's expressed needs or personal interest,
deficiencies in an individual's performance or deficiencies in
the quality and effectiveness of an organisation."
   The "Principles," reproduced below, are predicated upon
the notion that continuing education must be understood in
terms of anticipated learning outcomes; outcome is "a specified
change that is measurable or observable."

Principles of Good Practice in Continuing Education
Part 1 - Learning Needs in Continuing Education

1.1 Sponsors or providers of continuing education programmes/activities utilise appropriate processes to define and analyse the issue(s) or problems(s) of individuals, groups, and organisations for the purpose of determining learning needs.

Part 2 - Learning Outcomes in Continuing Education

2.1 The continuing education provider has clear and concise written statements of intended learning outcomes for the continuing education programme/activity.

2.2 The statements of intended learning outcomes of a continuing education programme/activity focus on learning that can be applied by the learner to situations beyond the boundaries of the learning environment.

2.3 When a continuing education programme consists of several interrelated activities, courses, seminars, and workshops, the contribution of the intended learning outcomes of each to the total programme is clearly designated.

2.4 The agenda of the continuing education programme/activity clearly specifies when each learning outcome will be addressed.

2.5 Learning outcomes are sequenced so that learners are able to recognise their progress toward achieving the stated learning outcomes.

Part 3 - Learning Experiences in Continuing Education

3.1 Learning experiences are designed to facilitate the role of the learner and are organised in such a manner as to provide for appropriate continuity, sequencing, and integration of the programme/activity to achieve the specified learning outcomes.

3.2 The statements of intended learning outcomes of a continuing education programme/activity determine the selection of instructional strategies, instructional materials, media and other learning technology, and create an appropriate learning environment.

3.3 Programme content, instructional materials, and delivery processes are relevant and timely for achieving intended learning outcomes.

3.4 Instructional staff in continuing education programmes/activities are qualified by education or experience to provide quality instruction in the subject-matter area.

3.5 The physical environment for the continuing education programme/activity is conducive to learning.

Part 4 - Assessment of Learning Outcomes

4.1 Continuing education programmes/activities are evaluated through assessment of learners' performance in terms of intended learning outcomes.

Part 5 - Continuing Education Administration

5.1 Each continuing education provider has a clearly stated, written statement of its mission, which is available to the publics served.

5.2 The continuing education provider has appropriate, sufficient, and stable human, fiscal, and physical resources to provide quality programmes/activities over an extended period of time.

5.3 The continuing education providers' promotion and advertising provide full and accurate disclosures about its programmes, services, and fees.

5.4 The continuing education provider ensures the maintenance of a set of limited access, permanent records of participants and the provision of documentation for accurate, readily available transcripts.

5.5 The continuing education provider makes available to participants recognition and documentation of achievement of learning outcomes specified for the continuing education programme/activity.

5.6 The continuing education provider ensures that appropriate quality control systems are in place and in use within its organisation.

A principle, according to Webster, is either a source of origin from which anything proceeds, an ultimate basis of a fundamental truth, a comprehensive law or doctrine, a governing rule of conduct or the essence of something. Whether "Principles" fulfills the meaning of any of these definitions and, more importantly, whether they have validity as a representation and a prescription for continuing education should appropriately lead to critical analysis and a vigorous professional dialogue. Discriminating adult educators may find "Principles" more an April Fool's deception and a snare for the unsophisticated than a truth, law, rule or essence to be taken seriously.

The fallacy of "Principles" is reductionist: they reduce all significant personal learning needs to expressed personal needs; they reduce all significant adult learning interests to those fostering individual performance and organisational efficiency; they reduce the learning process to content mastery and problem solving; they reduce learning gains to measurable outcomes; they reduce continuing education to a training ground for production and consumption and they reduce adult education to a technology divorced from any responsibility for social change and serving to maintain the status quo. "Principles" are uninformed about the nature of adult learning and misdirected about the purpose of adult education.

Perceptions and interest are generally consistent with a world view or system of values and priorities - a meaning perspective - which guides thought and action. It is not always feasible to specify learning outcomes in advance because understanding will come only through new structures - cognitive, conative, and affective - to be learned. Perhaps the most important adult learning involves problem posing rather than content mastery or problem solving - becoming critically aware of the reasons for one's needs embedded in taken-for-granted structures of assumptions which we have internalised.

This learning process is crucial for becoming aware and critically assessing structures of cultural and psychological assumptions which distort the way we perceive and act upon our situation. Belief systems, or meaning perspectives, predicated upon racial, sexual or age stereotypes are familiar examples. An integral element in this learning process is to come to recognise the way these dependence-producing assumptions are supported and legitimated by social practices, ideologies, institutions and systems.

Adult learning and education does not occur in a social vacuum. What is important for us to learn, where, how and why we learn are all determined by a value system manifested and sustained by social practices, ideologies, institutions, and systems. Learners need to know about them. "Practices" is just such 'an educational ideology, a commonly encountered belief system in adult education. When we, as learners, become aware of how these professional assumptions distort the reality of adult learning and its facilitation, we will, naturally, take action to change our educational practices accordingly.

There is an ultimate interactive relationship between learning about how society has influenced the shaping of our perspectives and taking action to change social practices and institutions when they reinforce assumptions we have come to see as distorted and dependency-producing. This is why it is not viable to formulate a set of guiding principles of adult education bereft of any vision of what kind of society or quality of collective life it should strive to achieve.

Adult educators have a commitment to foster both educational and social conditions essential for free and full participation in dialogue by which autonomous and responsible adults may come to understand the meaning of their experience. Social and political conditions which enhance the possiblity for such participation in learning include democratic participation in decision making, social justice, freedom, respect for human and civil rights, and equality of opportunity, among others. To educate to realise these values is to educate for perspective change – to help learners understand the connection between their personal needs and interest and larger social and economic forces which impact upon them. This is no less true of job-related adult education. Adult educators have social and political action commitments inherent in the function they perform.

"Principles" limits learning appropriate for continuing education to felt needs or to individual performance and organisational efficiency. (Since when was organisational efficiency a goal of education? Adults are not "human resources" for organisational efficiency. Organisations are resources for human development.) Certainly, learning how to do something better is important. But to suggest that this instrumental learning is all that is important in adult learning is patently a distortion. What about dialogic learning – involving understanding what others mean and whether what they say is valid or authentic when they communicate to us about ideals, about moral questions, about abstract ideas like justice, authority, rights, responsibility, power, oppression, ideology or about their feelings? What about self-reflective learning by which we learn about ourselves? In dialogic and self-reflective learning, we learn to acquire understanding rather than to establish cause-effect relationships in order to gain greater control over performance.

Crucial to dialogic learning and central to self-reflective learning is the exercise of critical reflectivity, of transforming meanings and perspectives – a learning process not amenable to anticipating measurable learning outcomes. (The notion that learning which cannot be measured is to be ignored by continuing education is too inane to warrant further comment.) Clearly, most dialogic and self-reflective learning are significant factors in much of instrumental learning. It may be possible to anticipate some learning outcomes, but when understanding involves critical reflectivity, to anticipate learning outcomes becomes a function of indoctrination, not of education.

Adult education fosters critical reflectivity by helping learners go beyond their initial learning needs to examine the reasons for their needs and to see the relationship of their needs to larger social and economic forces. This involves participation in a dialogue in which a critical analysis of assumptions and an exploration of alternative meaning perspectives open new ways of seeing with new learning priorities and outcomes. What is involved is a creative collaborative exploration, not a trip with a predetermined itinerary leading to an anticipated destination. Adult learning is not a one-dimensional linear process as "Principles" implies.

Knowles' endorsement of "Principles" is curious inasmuch as he is so indentified with andragogy, defined recently by a British study group as an orientation "aimed at enabling

227

people to become aware that they should be originators of their thinking and feeling." Where is the andragogy in "Principles"?

1. Report of the CCEU Project to Develop Standards and Criteria for Good Practice in Continuing Education. Silver Spring, MD: Council on the Continuing Education Unit (1984).

Chapter Nineteen

SOME FURTHER THOUGHTS ON PRINCIPLES OF GOOD
PRACTICE IN CONTINUING EDUCATION

Michael Collins (1985)

In the November, 1984 issue of Life-long Learning, Professor
Jack Mezirow reviewed the recent report published by the
Council on the Continuing Education Unit on Principles of
Good Practice in Continuing Education. Although it would be
difficult to resurrect Principles in the wake of Mezirow's
impressive analysis, the document does merit our further
consideration. All too often, authoritative looking publications such as Principles are quickly embraced by practitioners in adult and continuing education eager for any
guidelines which purport to clear away some of the aggravat-
ing ambiguities which confront them on a day-to-day basis.
     Certainly, Principles of Good Practice in Continuing
Education is enthusiastically endorsed by distinguished
figures in the field of adult and continuing education.
Malcolm Knowles (1984) describes it as "a major breakthrough
in this field" and adds that "our challenge now is to get this
(Principles) into the bloodstream of every educator or trainer
of adults." Another distinguished adult educator, Professor
Alan Knox, rendered enthusiastic acknowledgment to
Principles in his keynote address to the Sixth Annual
Conference of the Council on the Continuing Education Unit at
Columbus, Ohio in June of 1984. Such unstinted support from
prominent adult educators automatically gives credence to
Principles in the eyes of many continuing educators.
     These are not trivial observations. The endorsements of
well-known figures in adult education and the commitment of
respected practitioners gives legitimacy to the Principles
document. Such weighty endorsements are persuasive and
could lead us to overlook the fact, noted by Mezirow, that
Principles represents a particular educational ideology. It is
one ideology among several important alternatives most of
which attend, to some extent or another, to the problem of
competent performance - albeit, less simplistically than
Principles.
     The particular ideological orientation embedded in
Principles - that of technical competence - lends itself readily

to the expression of simplistic, taken-for-granted, statements which can be contained within relatively short documents. Since such stipulations have the aura of being manifestly true, they draw little in the way of critical engagement with their implicit assumptions. The economy of statements derived from the ideology of technical competence may be appealing, but it is not apparent they have much to do with ensuring competent performance in everyday practical and ethical projects of adults.

Except for observing that guidelines emanating from an ideology of technical competence are in no way a guarantee of "good practice," it is not feasible within the context of this article to undertake an analysis of the problems associated with legitimation through systematic endorsement and the pursuit of technical competence. However, the preceding commentary suggests, with regard to Principles and similar kinds of guideline documents, practitioners of adult and continuing education should begin to grapple with the following questions:

1. To what extent does the legitimising of technical competence as the paramount guiding force for practice in continuing education run counter to the basic needs of andragogy or self-directed learning?
2. Do guiding statements couched in technical language have a practical pay-off in terms of improved performance when applied to a value laden activity like adult education?
3. How can we achieve a meaningful rational perspective on what constitutes good practice in continuing education without giving primacy to prescriptive technical formats which run counter to practical and ethical dimensions of self-directed learning?

Professor Mezirow's commentary on the fallacy entailed in the reduction of good practice in continuing education to 18 general directives (designated as "principles") and 70 elements should not be overlooked by those of us who are serious about adult and continuing education as a distinctive vocation. The fully fledged reductionistic design of Principles was adopted in the face of recent published critiques (Collins, 1983, 1984) in the field of adult education showing the shortcomings and dangers of naive reductionism when it attempts to account for adult learning experiences. These critiques have not been adequately countered and yet the designers and endorsers of Principles are surely aware their document lays them wide open to the charge that they have been excessively reductionistic. Such remarkable confidence in the reductionistic compilation of stipulations on the part of the designers of Principles would suggest they and the well-known professorial advocates of the document "believe the kind of critical analysis and reflection integral to the nature of adult education as a vocation, and to the adult learning process, is merely a sideline interest with no practical or ethical impact."

Despite the short "discussion sections" which are intented to justify the stipulations ("elements" of good practice), Principles of Good Practice in Continuing Education can hardly be rescued from the charge that it is absurdly reductionistic. Most of the statements are little more than superficial taken-for granted directives. Practitioners who already adhere to the "technical competence" ideology will find nothing new in them and are bound to concur. Perhaps this is the basis on which Principles can be resurrected: that is, as a compendium of the obvious for those who embrace the ideology of technical competence as a panacea for ensuring effective practice in all areas of educational endeavors. However, they are left to ponder on why the Principles document contains only "18 principles and 70 additional elements." Why not triple, or quadruple, the numbers? There are only five categories. Do we need five? Could we do with more? Perhaps Principles could have short-changed us in this regard. How many is enough? Such are the trivia confronting the determined reductionist and those who believe that practitioners are unable to engage, on their own account and in more serious terms, with the problem of what constitutes good practice in continuing education.

According to Principles of Good Practice in Continuing Education, there is really nothing new about the kind of statements it contains but "what is new, and different, are the consolidation and refinement of principles and elements from a variety of sources into a single set of principles." (p.2) So what we have for the first time is a comprehensive (though not exhaustive) list of stipulations for the practice of continuing education. Credit must be granted to Principles for this deliberate move towards a comprehensive accounting. But why the continuing quest for comprehensiveness throughout the field of continuing education? It is certainly not merely a concern for competent performance which is always displayed in and from a particular context. Why this endeavour to construct an umbrella of stipulations over the field of continuing education? Is it a move towards staking out the turf and parameters of a distinctive profession which we know requires some central authority - some font of knowledge - for collective action? If so, practitioners of adult and continuing education would be advised to consider the following questions with regard to collective action:

1. Is the drive for comprehensiveness in defining the field along the lines of Principles an effective and proper (ethical) strategy for achieving the larger political ends?
2. What are effective and proper strategies for achieving

substantial recognition for continuing and adult education, bearing in mind that some notable commentators view adult education as a bulwark against the increase of modern professionalisation as it stakes out and claims more and more areas of expertise?

Unless questions such as these are culled from the document for the purpose of disclosing the underlying motivations and concrete problems which inspired its creation, Principles represents for us nothing more than yet another ponderous list of reductionistic, attenuated stipulations of a kind that continuously crop up on the North American public education scene.

Even so, one might still argue that the Principles document is to be commended for reminding us of the need for technical competence. Unfortunately, the document does not distinguish, because of its technical format, between the technical and the ethical (or practical) domains of adults' everyday experience. It is the failure to account for ethical and practical concerns when human experience (or learning) is depicted according to technical dependency-producing tendencies mentioned in Mezirow's review.

Of course, we should be concerned with technical competence and instrumental modes of action. Both ethical or practical questions (requiring critical reflection) are crucial aspects of technical performance as well as being integral to the meaning of adult education. It is important for us to recognise that the epsitemology of the particular educational ideology which undergirds Principles - and documents like it - cannot generate for us what our ends (values) ought to be

This brings us back, inevitably, to the problem of excessive reductionism. It is really nonsensical to describe, or capture, through technical formultions, practical day-to-day endeavors like adult learning. They are not amenable to technical representation and the attempt leaves us with a series of adumbrated, insufficient, statements which trivialises the field. The Principles document is a case study of how stilted and artificial the language becomes when determined attempts are made to render ethical and practical concerns within a technical framework.

So if Principles has provided a service in reminding us that it is a good idea to be competent, to plan activities carefully, to take our commitments seriously, we have yet to ask ourselves whether yet another reductionistic set of stipulations is the best way to go about it. Even with all the hoopla and promotion, Principles will hardly impress colleagues in related fields who believe that adult continuing education is "up for grabs" and can be readily incorporated within their already legitimised areas of speciality. If this is the best kind of representation of our vocation that can be offered, it might even encourage their expansionist ambitions.

Assuming we do resurrect the Principles document for the purpose of critical appraisal, let's not hitch our wagon to it. Otherwise, we will have to give more credence to the cynics among our colleagues who fear that distinguished adult educators, while advocating self-directed learning for adults, are really selling us out to the experts of pedagogy who have been putting out puerile lists of stipulations like Principles for over half a century. We deserve better.

At a recent adult education conference, an experienced Francophone continuing education administrator from Quebec who had taken up full-time graduate work was sharing with colleagues the excitement she felt about her research and theoretical studies. However, she added that she is appalled by the way so much of adult education literature "infantilises" adults. It turns out there is no such word as "infantilise" in the English lexicon, but it is clear what our Francophone colleague means by the term. A great deal of effort has gone into producing the Principles document, but it serves to "infantilise" us.

Surely, adult educators have moved beyond the need for prodding by long lists of formal stipulations (whether we want to call them standards, or criteria, or principles). Such stipulations to guide the experts or - "providers" - of adult continuing education imply that adults are not capable of making relevant decisions about the direction and nature of their own learning experiences. As the kind of approach to professionalisation characterised by Principles gains ascendancy, the possibilities for self-directed learning, and adulthood itself, surely decline. This is not the way to lay out the parameters of a vocation.

REFERENCES

Collins, M., (1983), A critical analysis of competency-based systems in adult education, Adult Education Quarterly, 33(3), 174-183.

Collins, M. (1984), Competency-based adult education and variations on a theme: A reply to my critics, Adult Education Quarterly, 34(4), 240-246.

Council on the Continuing Education Unit (1984), "Principles of Good Practice in Continuing Education," Silver Spring MD: Author.

Knowles, M.K. (1984), Principles of good practice in continuing education, in: Pamphlet, Silver Spring, MD: Council on Continuing Education Unit.

Chapter Twenty

STANDARDS FOR GRADUATE PROGRAMMES IN ADULT EDUCATION

Commission of Professors of Adult Education (1986)

INTRODUCTION

Since the Commission of Professors of Adult Education was established in 1955, the number of graduate programmes in adult education has increased dramatically. A major reason has been the demand for qualified adult educators to meet the growing needs of adults for further learning as they cope with the effects of technological changes, with a desire for advancement in careers, with career shifts, with increased leisure time, etc. One result has been the shift of graduate study in adult education from an emerging field to a recognised field of graduate study with distinctive features. These include theory, research, and practice relating to adult learners, adult educators, adult education processes, providers, and programmes.

RATIONALE FOR STANDARDS

A concern for quality dominates the planning, conduct, and evaluation of graduate programmes in adult education. Quality is also a central concern in such outcomes as preparation of adult educators with needed competencies and with a commitment to lifelong learning; their placement and their contributions to the field, including leadership and scholarship; and the continued contributions of university faculty to theory, research, and practice in adult education.

It is axiomatic that quality outcomes result from a combination of quality input and processes. Input embraces curriculum, faculty, resources, students' programmes, and other services; while processes are those forces operating within an organisation to give it is dynamic nature.

While there is no assurance that the setting of standards will guarantee the high level of quality sought in formal graduate programmes in adult education, the standards presented here at least point the way. They provide established programmes with guidelines for review and new programmes with guidelines for establishing graduate study in adult education.

STANDARDS FOR GRADUATE PROGRAMMES

Standards for adult education programmes must take into account guidelines and standards for graduate programmes, requirements for teaching loads, advising, etc., set by the school or college in which the adult graduate programme is located; and other constraints. It is also recognised that, given the variety and scope of graduate study in adult education, the standards cannot apply uniformly to every programme. Nevertheless, these standards are deemed to be basic, and graduate programmes should strive to observe them. Finally, it should not be assumed that the following discussion implied an endorsement of one-person programmes, which have obvious limitations. However, the reality is that such programmes do exist, and the discussion might assist their further development.

The standards are grouped under the following categories: curriculum, faculty, organisation of graduate study, students' programmes, resources and facilities, and scholarship.

CURRICULUM

The adult education curriculum clearly distinguishes between Master's and doctoral levels in terms of beginning and advanced graduate study.

At the Master's level, the core areas include the following:

- introduction to the fundamental nature, function, and scope of adult education.
- adult learning and development.
- adult education programme and process-planning, delivery, and evaluation.
- historical, philosophical, and sociological foundations.
- an overview of educational research.

These core areas are supplemented by additional study appropriate to students' needs and goals, which may emphasise specific leadership roles (e.g., administrator-manager, teacher, counsellor, etc.). The area of speciality may relate to study of particular clientele (e.g., disadvantaged, career-changers, aged) or to programmes serving them (e.g., adult basic education, career education, gerontology). That special-

ity might involve study in other faculties. In general, because it is unlikely that any adult education programme will
contain all the courses that students require (e.g., business,
educational psychology, philosophy, political science, sociology), the should be encouraged to seek resources in appropriate faculties.

At the doctoral level, the core areas include study that
is at once more far-ranging and more intensive than study at
the Master's level. At the doctoral level, the core areas
includes the following:

- advanced study of adult learning (e.g., theory and
  research relating to specific issues).
- in-depth analysis of social, political, and economic
  forces that have shaped the historical and philosophical foundations of adult education.
- study of leadership, including theories of administration and management.
- study of issues that impinge on policy formation.
- advanced study of methods of inquiry, in order to
  conduct adult education research.

As at the Master's level, the core areas are supplemented by additional study appropriate to students' needs and
goals. This study might be pursued as a formal cognate area
or simply as specialised study therein. At the doctoral level,
the core curriculum may differ at institutions offering both
the Ph.D. and Ed.D. In general, the distinction between the
two degrees is one of orientation. The Ph.D., which emphasises theory and research, aims at producing a scholar-
researcher who has, as his or her major goal, the advancement of knowledge. The Ed.D., which focuses on translating
scientific findings into practice, aims at producing a practitioner who will give leadership to the field. Institutions
offering only the PhD. or Ed.D. can provide for both orientations through individual programming.

FACULTY

It is expected that institutions offering a graduate
degree, major, or specialisation in adult education (whether in
small programmes attached to or combined with another programme area, or specific adult education programmes of
varying sizes, or multidisciplinary programmes) will have
several faculty members. At least one full-time faculty member
will have an earned doctorate in adult education. (Other
designations include continuing education, community education, and cooperative extension education.) Other full-time
faculty members will have a doctorate in adult education or an
earned doctorate in a relevant field (e.g., philosophy,

psychology, sociology), with knowledge of adult education. Other criteria are as follows:

- at the outset, at least one person will possess a minimum of three years of graduate level full-time teaching experience in adult education. All faculty members will possess some graduate or under-graduate teaching experience.
- academic rank necessary for graduate status in a tenure track position.
- a record of leadership, as evidenced by significant positions in the field, profession, and university.
- a record of contributions to scholarship in adult education.
- a continuing commitment to adult education theory, research, and knowledge of current practice.

Part-time faculty consist of individuals whose adult education assignment is limited due to any of the following conditions:

- a full-time administrative role at the university (e.g., dean of extension, programme planner, counsellor).
- a major commitment in another faculty (e.g., educational psychology, instructional technology, philosophy).
- a research appointment relating to a grant or a graduate assistantship.
- a full-time assignment outside of the university (business, government, voluntary agency, or as a private consultant).

Although selection of part-time faculty members belonging to a multidisciplinary group is based on their particular expertise and contributions, they will still need to meet the following criteria:

- an earned doctorate in the area of their competency. However, suitable experience may be substituted when appointing a part-time faculty member from the field.
- evidence of interest in and concern for problems and issues in adult education.
- a record of contributions to scholarship relating to courses to be taught, or to particular areas of theory, research, and practice, (e.g., adult basic education, community development, continuing professional education, human resource develop-ment).

ORGANISATION OF GRADUATE STUDY

A graduate programme in adult education may be housed in a variety of colleges (e.g., education, agriculture) or form part of a multi-disciplinary group. At least one faculty member will be a full-time member of the graduate faculty and a member of the policy making unit that administers the graduate programme in adult education. The strength of that programme is determined by the calibre of the graduates it produces and their distinctive contributions to adult education. To enhance this process, while ensuring that faculty have freedom to continue making their contributions, the following organising principles apply:

- the student admissions committee consists of at least one full-time or part-time faculty member with a degree in adult education.
- the programme committee for Master's students is chaired by a member of the adult education faculty. Whether a student selects the thesis or non-thesis option, the chair and student select committee members who will increase a student's competencies through advisement or mentoring.
- the load for Master's advisement depends on certain variables (e.g., number of thesis and number of non-thesis students, and number of doctoral advisees). For advisement and counselling, a distinction is made between full-time and part-time students.
- these variables suggest the following student-faculty ratios for quality programmes:
  - for students not writing a thesis or major paper-25 to 1.
  - for students writing a thesis or major paper-10 to 1. (Where a faculty member has a large proportion of thesis students, the number of non-thesis students would be reduced.)
- The programme committee for doctoral students is chaired by a member of the adult education faculty. The chair and student select committee members who will increase a student's competencies through advisement or mentoring.
- the dissertation committee is chaired by a member of the adult education faculty with an interest in a student's research. For special topics, co-chairs are selected from other faculties. Other committee members are selected on the basis of their contributions to the research problem or design.
- the load for doctoral advisement depends upon certain variables (e.g., number of Master's advisees, number of doctoral students at programme

stage, number of doctoral students at dissertation stage). A distinction is made between full-time and part-time students as applied to advisement and counselling.

- these variables suggest the following student-faculty ratios, which are maximum ratios for quality programmes:
  - for students at the programme stage prior to intensive dissertation advisement-15 to 1.
  - for students assigned to a faculty member at the dissertation stage-8 to 1, with no more than 4 students actually writing. (Where a faculty member has a large proportion of dissertation students, the number of programme committees or memberships on other dissertation committees will be reduced.) The ratios suggested above are based on the fact that students at the programme stage require much less commitment from faculty members in terms of time and effort than do students at the dissertation stage. In particular, students actually writing dissertations typically require many hours of intensive help from faculty members.
  - the teaching load of faculty members varies according to the number, level (Master's or doctoral), and status (programme, thesis, or dissertation) of students. A graduate load for a faculty member with fewer than 3 Master's thesis students, or fewer than 2 doctoral dissertation students, will not exceed six courses (3 semester hours each) during the year. Programmes on quarter systems will have a higher number of hours, whereas programmes on a year-long system will have fewer hours.
- the suggested teaching load for faculty members having 3-6 Master's thesis students is 5 courses per academic year; and, for those having 7-10 Master's thesis students, 4 courses.
- the suggested teaching load for faculty members having 2-4 students at dissertation stage is 5 courses per academic year; and, for those having 5-7 at dissertation stage 4 courses.

  The above teaching loads will vary according to whether an institution is research orientated or practice oriented.

Other ways to enhance the process aimed at desirable outcomes are as follows:

- formal and informal contacts with other faculties, in the interest of developing fruitful relationships that

>   will benefit adult education faculty and students
>   alike.
> -   systematic review of courses, programmes, and pro-
>   cedures to provide evaluative data for improving
>   the programme; and peer review by external pro-
>   fessors of adult education.

STUDENT PROGRAMMES

Since undergraduate programmes in adult education are rare,
students enter graduate study with little or no formal preparation and, frequently, with some experience. Hence, the
orientation of many is narrowly directed to serving the field,
rather than directed to scholarly pursuits. In order to acquire competencies needed to function in particular roles
(e.g., administrator, teacher, researcher), students will
complete the following:

- the core curriculum discussed above.
- a special area of study. On the Master's level, it
  takes the form of certain courses of a limited research study; whereas, on the doctoral level, it
  consists of courses in particular areas of adult
  education and/or a cognate area of study in another
  faculty.
- research. At the Master's level, it entails an understanding of basic statistics and research; whereas,
  on the doctoral level, research methodology entails
  methods of inquiry as preparation for writing the
  dissertation.
- internship. To broaden the horizons of some
  Master's students, an internship is incorporated
  into his or her programme. This experience equips
  a student to function in a particular setting as
  administrator, teacher, evaluator, etc., and to
  apply theory and research to practice. At the
  doctoral level, internships are more intensive and
  demanding, i.e., a person would actually assume a
  certain role in an organisation, and even conduct
  evaluation or research.
- independent study. On both Master's and doctoral
  levels, students investigate specific topics in-depth
  through independent study. Such study draws upon
  the strengths of adult education faculty members
  and/or the strengths of faculty members in relevant
  disciplines.
- thesis and dissertation. The Master's thesis or
  project is much more limited in nature and scope
  than a doctoral dissertation. Typically, the dissertation requires investigation of a more complex

problem, a broader theoretical base, a more sophisticated methodology, and the expertise of outside faculty.

RESOURCES AND FACILITIES

Graduate programmes need funds to support full-time students in the interest of providing them with varied experiences through internships, which commonly offer administrative experience; assistantships, which commonly offer teaching experience; and research associateships, which offer experience in conducting research. Additional resources consist of assignments with extension divisions, where students can make contributions while acquiring experience; and stipends to aid students in completing their dissertations.

Other resources consist of a comprehensive professional library, including new periodicals, and access to ERIC and other databases.

SCHOLARSHIP

Outcomes of a quality graduate programme are as follows:

- publications in referred journals by faculty members, students and alumni.
- books and reports by faculty members, students, and alumni.
- contributions of faculty members, students, and alumni to conferences at local, regional, national, and international levels.
- exchanges, both formal and informal, of faculty members and students including international exchanges.
- service to the field and profession by faculty members, students, and alumni.
- placement and performance of the alumni of the programme.

PART SEVEN

CURRICULA AND PROGRAMS OF
GRADUATE ADULT EDUCATION

Chapter Twenty-One

OBJECTIVES FOR GRADUATE PROGRAMMES IN
ADULT EDUCATION

Watson Dickerman (1964)

Objectives of graduate programmes in adult education must be
rooted in the characteristics and needs of their students. As
Houle says, most graduate students in this field are

> "... people who were trained in some other discipline,
> who happened to enter the field, who were educated in
> its essentials by the school of hard knocks, who decided
> to build a career for themselves, and who returned
> (usually between the ages of 35 and 45) to embark on a
> graduate programme."

Their educational and occupational backgrounds are thus
extremely varied,* they are long on experience but short on
previous training in adult education, they vary greatly in
their attitudes toward adult education and their values about
it, and they tend to be somewhat older than most graduate
students.

Both Houle and Liveright believe the number of young
inexperienced students, now few, will gradually increase.
Another way of saying this is that graduate study in adult
education will eventually be preservice education for more
students than it is now.

Liveright invites attention to five objectives which are
common to programmes of professional education for a number
of professions, and which, slightly modified as follows, are
suitable for professional education for adult educators:

Competence to practice his profession with sufficient
knowledge and skill to satisfy its requirements.

Social understanding with sufficient breadth to place his
practice in the context of the society which supports it,
and to develop the capacity for leadership in public
affairs.

Philosophy and set of values which make possible effective practice.

Zest for continued study which will steadily increase knowledge and skill needed by practice.

According to Knowles,[1] planning a programme of graduate study in adult education is more complex than merely establishing objectives. He suggests a five-step process and illustrates the outcome with the chart reproduced here. First, he says, we must decide what general functions our students will have to perform as full-time careerists in adult education (Column 1 in the chart). Second, we must decide what competencies these functions require (Column 2 in the chart). Third, we must decide what learnings these competencies require - i.e., what understandings, skills, attitudes, values, and appreciations. (Column 2 of the chart combines competencies and learnings.) Fourth, omitted in the chart, we must formulate objectives in terms of behavioural change which are to result from the aforementioned learnings. Fifth, we must decide what learning activities will best produce the desired behavioural changes (Column 3 in the chart).

Knowles' list of "relevant competencies" (Column 2) is intended to be suggestive rather than complete. A recent study by Chamberlain carries this exploration farther. he secured the judgment of 90 leaders in adult education and

---

* For example, the 1962, graduate students in adult education at one of the participating universities between 1953 and 1961 showed the following diversity in occupational background: administrators of university extension, 48; administrators and supervisors of Cooperative Extension, 23; executives of national associations, 9; foreign adult educators, 8; university faculty members, 8; administrators and supervisors of public-school adult education, 7; labour union officers and staff, 7; Cooperative Extension county workers, 6; public-school education teachers, 6; staff members of group-work agencies, 6; Cooperative Extension specialists, 5; clergy, 4; staff members of national facilitative agencies of adult education, 4; armed services personnel, 3; instructional staff of community agencies, 3; lay citizens, 2; librarians, 2; nursing administrators, 2; others, 9. The phrase, "one of the participating universities," which will be used frequently in this chapter, means one of the universities listed in Table 1 of Chapter IV.

[1]References in this chapter may be found at the end of this chapter.

A Model for the Development of Competencies for Adult Educators

Required Functions	Relevant Competencies	Appropriate Learning Activities
A. Formulation of policies, objectives, and programmes in institutions of adult education.	1. An understanding of the function of adult education in society.	Study of the nature and scope of the adult educational field.* Practice in using basic programme planning processes.*
	2. Ability to diagnose adult educational needs and translate these into objectives and programmes.	
	3. An understanding of the unique characteristics and processes of adults as learners.	Systematic inquiry into research findings about adult psychology and developmental process.*
	4. Ability to plan and execute strategies of institutional and community change.	Laboratory experience in performing the role of change agent.**
B. Organisation and administration of programmes of adult education.	1. Same as A-2.	Same as A-2*
	2. An understanding of the theory and dynamics of organisation.	Study of organisational theory theory and dynamics.*
	3. Skill in the selection, training, and supervision of leaders and teachers.	Laboratory and field experience in practice of supervisory skills.*
	4. Skill in institutional management.	Study and practice of principles and methods of financing, staffing, interpreting, etc.*
C. Performance of special functions required in particular adult education roles.	Such specialised competencies as use of mass media, preparation of materials, organisational and community consultation, human relations training, etc.	Guided independstudy, supervised field experience, systematic study in related fields, group projects, skill exercises, research projects, etc.

* Most appropriate at the master's level
** Most appropriate at the doctor's level

produced a list of 45 desired competencies, of which the ten rated highest are reported by Liveright. Chamberlain further refined his list of competencies by screening them according to Tyler's curriculum theory and obtaining the reactions of professors of adult education to them. In this way he derived a list of objectives for programmes of graduate study in adult education, explored the extent to which such programmes at thirteen universities are based on these objectives, and proposed a list of fourteen courses which might well comprise a desirable curriculum of graduate study in adult education.[2]

Knowles' fourth step calls for stating objectives in terms of behavioural changes sought. He does not illustrate these changes in his chart, but a recent study by Aker[3] attempts to establish them. From a review of the literature of adult education, Aker derived a list of 410 objectives, competencies, and behaviours. He then subjected these findings to various screening and testing procedures, including the judgment of 18 professors of adult education and 287 persons who held graduate degrees in adult education or were working toward them and arrived at the following list of 23 "essential behaviours" of the adult educator considered to be observable and measurable:

1. He helps people control and adjust to change rather than to maintain the status quo.
2. Intelligently observes and listens to what is being said or done and uses this information in guiding his response.
3. Selects and uses teaching methods, materials, and resources that are appropriate in terms of what is to be learned and in terms of the needs and abilities of the individual learners.
4. Helps his clientele acquire ability for critical thinking.
5. Provides an atmosphere where adults are free to search, through trial and error, without fear of institutional or interpersonal threat.
6. Identifies potential leaders and helps them to develop their potentials and capacities.
7. Makes use of existing values, beliefs, customs, and attitudes as a starting point for educational activities.
8. Is actively involved in continuing study that will increase his professional competence.
9. Understands the role of adult education in society and is aware of the factors and forces that give rise to this function.
10. Actively shares, participates, and learns with the learners in the learning experiences.
11. Helps adults actively to set their own goals, and provides a variety of means and opportunities for intensive self-evaluation.

12. Identifies and interprets trends that have implications for adult education.
13. Has clearly defined his unique role as an adult educator and understands his responsibility in performing it.
14. Arranges learning experiences so that the learners can integrate theory and practice.
15. Is effective in building a teaching team among lay leaders and group members.
16. Uses the process of appraisal to evaluate programmes and help clarify and change objectives.
17. Is creative and imaginative in developing new programmes, believes that innovation and experiment are necessary for the expansion of adult education.
18. Makes use of the contributions of all group members through the utilisation of individual talents and abilities.
19. Works with schools, teachers, parents, and pre-adults to assist them in developing the motivation, attitudes, understanding, and skills necessary for lifelong learning.
20. Objectively presents contrasting points of view.
21. Assumes the initiative in developing a strong national perception of the importance and essentiality of continuing education.
22. Recognises when the communication process is not functioning adequately or when it breaks down.
23. Identifies, critically evaluates, and discusses scholarly work by investigators in adult education and related fields.

The graduate students and doctorates whom Aker queried rated the following behaviours from the above list as most essential in the work of adult educators: 2, 3, 16, 22. They expressed need for increasing their competence in all 23 behaviours but especially in Items 16 and 23. They considered that graduate study was "extremely important" in helping them develop the competencies indicated in these two items and "quite important" in Items 3,8,9,11,13,14 and 17. They did not feel that a high degree of competence was needed in any of the 23 behaviours before undertaking graduate study. However, they did feel that an entering student needed some competence in Items 2, 7 and 22 and that if he didn't have this before undertaking graduate study he probably would not be able to acquire it through formal graduate study.

Aker inferred that the very high need which these students expressed for greater competence in Items 16 and 23 meant that current graduate programmes are not placing sufficient emphasis on developing competence in these two behaviours. He suggested that their professors try to determine how they might do this more effectively.

The statements about objectives which have appeared in the foregoing pages all differ somewhat. And it is certain that when each professor of adult education establishes objectives for his programme, as he must, his statement will differ somewhat from those of his colleagues. This is not important. What is important is that each professor of adult education familiarise himself with the Chamberlain and Aker studies or go through some such process as Knowles has suggested, that more studies like those of Chamberlain and Aker be made, and that theorising about objectives for programmes of graduate study in adult education continue.

BUILDING THEORY FROM THE PRACTICE OF ADULT EDUCATION

Jensen says adult education is trying by two processes to develop a unique body of knowledge suited to its purpose. (1) From experience gained in dealing with past problems of practice it develops principles which provide guides for future practice. (2) It seeks needed knowledge from relevant disciplines and reformulates it for use in adult education. The present section deals with the first of these two processes and the following one with the second.

Clarification of Terminology

Adult educators have been lax about trying to define the terms they use in talking about their work. Apologists have sought refuge in the lame excuse that it was too early to do this, that attempts to define might hamper the lusty growth of adult education. Growth there has certainly been. But if adult education is to merit the status of "an emerging discipline," which the authors of several of the chapters in this book confer on it, its professionals must begin the task of precise definition.

Verner addresses himself forthrightly to this formidable task. Is and adult to be defined in terms of age or of maturity? Does adult education include efforts at self-education? What is the difference between adult education, further education and continuing education? Between a programme and a curriculum? Between process, method, technique and device?

Since attempts to define lead inevitably to argument, it is predictable that no chapter in the book will be more debated than Verner's. However, it should make it less easy for adult educators to talk past each other. It should also introduce more exactness into graduate courses in adult education. And, most important, it should foster precision in research on the problems of adult education. As Verner says: "Without such precision it is difficult to determine whether comparisons are made of like objects or whether the phenomena under the study are free from contamination by related but dissimilar phenomena. Furthermore, (precision) limits research to a manageable area that can be easily recognised and studied."

Thomas takes one of the terms which Verner explores at the first level of definition, programme, and examines it exhaustively. He justifies this by saying that this term is, of all words employed by adult educators, "the most pervasive in use, and the most elusive in definition."

He shows that adult educators use "programme" to mean a nation-wide programme of adult education such as that of the Cooperative Extension Service, all the adult education activities of a community, an institution's programme of adult education, an educational activity which involves a series of meetings, a one-shot activity, an individual student's schedule of studies, and many more. Not to mention "programme planning," "programme materials," "programme evaluation," and "programmed instruction."

We now need a Verner to assign preferred terminology to the many uses of "programme" in adult education, with definitions to fit. And we need someone to differentiate among the many terms which we saw associated with the word "objectives" in the preceding section: "knowledge," "understanding," "skills," "abilities," "attitudes," "values," "appreciations," "competencies," "behaviours," "learnings," etc. And others to tackle similar troublesome clusters.

Ways of Looking at Adult Education as an Institution
Hallenbeck reviews the efforts of Bryson, Floud and Halsey, Peers, and others to present systematic statements of the functions of adult education. He then offers a statement of function which he hopes is inclusive enough to be recognised by all who work in the field "as a common denominator of their efforts": to keep the machinery of our civilisation in operation and to help individuals realise their aspirations. As concomitant contemporary requirements he adds that of helping adults face up to the facts of change, to the need for foresight and planning, and to the need for cooperation in an increasingly specialised society.

Adult education has long been noted for the complexity of its field of operations. The epithets "chaotic" and "jungle" have not been too strong for some of its despairing chroniclers, and there have been few attempts at critical analysis. Knowles offers a new perspective of the field of operations of adult education in terms of its institutional sponsorship, content, levels, personnel and programme forms. His analysis represents the most comprehensive and sytematic view that has appeared in the literature to date, and is likely to be generally used in courses in adult education for some time to come.

Reexamination of Some Responsibilities of Leaders

Choosing Programme Objectives. Miller does not underestimate the difficulties which adult educators face in choosing programme objectives. They have to embrace too many objectives because of the multitude of problems which confront adults in our fast-changing society. And even when they do choose an objective, they may not be allowed to mount the necessary programme, either because it won't make money for the parent institution of because the latter think something else is more important. But though he sympathises with those adult educators who, for these reasons, abdicate professional responsibility for choosing objectives and settle for trying to meet whatever demands come their way, he does not condone this. He insists that they choose as wisely and responsibly as they can among the welter of possible objectives.

To help them do this he presents a mode which enables us to see that if we wish to foster certain kinds of behaviour (The Adaptor, The Well-Informed, The Expert, or The Intellectual) and to communicate certain kinds of content (from the worlds of work, form, nature, or the social world) we are thereby selecting <u>this</u> category of objectives rather than <u>that</u> one.

Miller reveals his own preference for objectives which aim at developing the individual rather than at the solution of social needs. But he warns that we will have little success with any objective which does not have relevance to needs which adults really feel. Finally, he says, if we are to stand a chance of realising the objectives we have chosen as wisely and as responsibly as we can, we must transform these objectives into desired behavioural outcomes which are specific enough for programme planning (as we saw Chamberlain and Aker doing in the first section of this chapter).

Teaching and Learning in Adult Education. McKinley analyses minutely the multitude of factors that can help or hinder adult learning. These influences may come from the teacher, from the learner, from the group, from the institution, or from outside. They may relate to the content which is being communicated or to the processes by which this is being done. He traces how these influences make themselves felt and some of the ways in which some of them can be managed, and his suggestions regarding their management are supported by many of the principles which Jensen develops in the closing pages of Chapter VII.*

For some, the chapter's chief value will be its comprehensiveness. One has encountered some of these ideas in research on adult learning, some in communications research,

---

* Refers to original publication

and some in the literature on the study of groups. But this is the first time so many of them have been pulled together and focussed on the adult learning situation.

Another reason why the chapter will be valuable in graduate programmes in adult education is that many of the concepts are deliberately stated as testable propositions. Further, McKinley has made some attempt to indicate which propositions already have considerable research support and which ones need verification.

Evaluating Programmes. Programme evaluation in adult education tends to be slighted for a number of reasons. For one thing, most adult educators believe that adults don't like to be tested. Could it be, rather, that adults don't mind being tested as long as the results, if unflattering, are not made public? This suggests self-evaluation for adult students. But in the opinion of some of the authorities whom Thiede cites in his chapter, self-evaluation doesn't come off very well. It looks as though more research is needed in this area.

Another reason why adult education programmes are infrequently evaluated is that adult educators tend to feel that as long as the number of their students increases the programme must be all right, especially since attendance is voluntary and tuition often high. Furthermore, most adult students have specific and immediate reasons for attending, and if these aren't realised they evaluate themselves out of the course. Fourth, programme evaluation is not an easy process. Fifth, most adult educators are so busy running their programmes that they feel they haven't time to evaluate them. Finally, they fear evaluation might point to the need to make troublesome changes, or reveal programme weakness to outsiders.

Thiede develops a convincing rationale for programme evaluation in adult education, of which it suffices to mention here the point that the marginality of adult education makes it particularly vulnerable. Programme evaluation can provide the best defence against attack.

Many professors of adult education have the responsibility of helping adult educators evaluate their programmes. They will find especially helpful the detail in which Thiede elaborates this process and the fidelity with which he applies it to situations in adult education. They will also be especially interested in his hypotheses about programme evaluation in adult education, as follows:

1. Adults will more readily accept external evaluation and
2. Evaluation will be more feasible when programmes are:
   a. formal rather than informal
   b. long-term rather than short-term
   c. based on simple rather than complex objectives

  d. based on objectives derived from social rather
   than individual needs.

Learning to Live with an Occupational Disease

Ever since John Powell told adult educators that they were in
for trouble so long as their programmes are sponsored by
institutions whose primary function is something else, and
Burton Clark gave them a name for this disease, they have
been trying to find a cure. They haven't and they aren't
likely to. But Hallenbeck suggests some ways of learning to
live with their affliction. For one thing, they can exploit the
advantages of marginality, which are not inconsiderable. For
another, they can seek greater acceptance and support by
explicating the roles of adult education in our society and
demonstrating its contributions.

  Hallenbeck then develops this second possibility at some
length. In the course of doing this he comes up with new
data which professors of adult education will not be slow to
incorporate in their courses. He shows that more adults
participate in education than do children and youth: 58 million
against 41.5 million. Also, we spend almost as much on adult
education as we do on education for children and youth:
$16.5 billion against $18 billion. Little of this money for adult
education comes from public funds. Adult educators would like
to see more public money available for adult education; they
find it hard to understand why citizens and legislators (and
even educators) seem inattentive. Maybe, now that it is
becoming impossible for a man to drink his morning coffee
without seeing headlines about automation, unemployment and
retraining, he will eventually get the message that this is
adult education he is reading about and that without it we
stand little chance of coping with some of the most crucial
problems of our times.

  Hallenbeck looks forward to the day when most citizens
will take it for granted that they will have to resort to education throughout their lives if they are to realise their
aspirations (even so simple a one as eating regularly) and
when most educational and many other institutions will come to
regard adult education as a normal function instead of the
peripheral one it usually is today. Will people learn that they
must go on learning only from such harsh teachers as bore-
dom, obsolescence, and unemployment? Or will schools and
colleges try to make them aware of this need as they pass
through their classrooms? If there are experiments in doing
the latter, they are not appearing in the literature. Research
on ways of doing this is needed.

  Essert too makes a point which may help adult educators
live with their old enemy, marginality. If they realise that
marginality is inevitable for all institutions (educational,
business, or government) which are part of larger insti-

tutions, they can accept its consequences with better heart. More, they can learn how other institutions deal with the problems of marginal status, and perhaps adapt these solutions to their own problems.

SEEKING HELP FROM RELEVANT DISCIPLINES

The preceding section was concerned with attempts to build theory from the practice of adult education. But the objectives presented earlier suggest that graduate students in adult education also need knowledge from outside their field. For example, they need understanding of community power structure and community development, social class, human development, human relations, problems of inducing change, and so on. Professors of adult education have long known that their students need such relevant theory from certain disciplines, and have in fact been conducting border raids into these disciplines and making off with valuable booty, including occasional struggling colleagues as captives.

Chapters VII–XI* make far more clear than before some of the wealth to be mined in related fields of study. And Chapter VI* suggests a process for fashioning this rich ore into tools for the hand of practicing adult educators.

Are we to conclude that no other disciplines contain knowledge of value to adult education? Of course not. Anthropology and economics certainly do and other disciplines may. The reader will understand why education is omitted: most programmes of graduate study in adult education are located in schools of education, so their students get as much of this discipline as they need. (Indeed, some of them feel they get far more of it than the need.)

Explorations of Five Disciplines

Sociology. In Chapter VII* London suggests several ways in which the study of sociology can be helpful to adult educators:

(1) Since adult education is an emerging discipline which hopes to become an established one, and since sociology has been through this process, professors of adult education can profit by studying how it became a discipline. (2) One of the concerns of professors of adult education is to study the institutions which carry on adult education and the study of institutions is one of the principal functions of sociology.

---

* Refers to original publication

Professors of adult education can therefore gain by learning how sociologists do this. (3) Sociologists can be used as consultants to facilitate the application of knowledge from their field to the problems of adult education.

As one example of helpful content from sociology London mentions understanding of large-scale organisations. Many adult educators employed in such organisations are puzzled and dismayed by the problems of bureaucracy which confront them. Another example is understanding the concepts of social role, social class, and social image. London himself has recently made a study of the effects of social class on attitudes toward adult education. [4] A related suggestion is that adult educators should seek more understanding of the role of informal associations as a means of attracting persons of lower social status - one of the most puzzling problems in adult education. Another suggestion is understanding of the concept of reference groups, which bears directly on the behaviour of mass-media audiences. His plea for studying the adult classroom as a social system illuminates McKinley's chapter on teaching and learning in adult education. These are but a few of the many areas of the content of sociology which London commends to the attention of adult educators and which he is able to relate shrewdly to their day-to-day problems.

Social Psychology. In Chapter VII* Jensen applies to the discipline of social psychology a systematic process for borrowing knowledge from another discipline - a process that will be described in more detail later. Jensen uses the adult instructional group as the situation on which light is wanted, and develops an impressive array of principles for application and testing. Inspection of these principles will reveal that many of them support the propositions which McKinley develops in Chapter XIV* for dealing with adult learning groups.

Psychology. In Chapter IX* McClusky selects from research in psychology a number of highlights of great interest to adult educators. He feels that we can no longer accept the view that people grow up through childhood and settle down in adulthood; adults continue to develop, and an understanding of this fact and of its stages is "an important prerequisite to the theory and practice of adult education." He reviews the research on adult learning and concludes that it supports the hopes of adult educators and lights their path. He shows how past experience can either help or hinder adult learning, and how one's perception of the amount of lifetime remaining to him affects his attitudes toward life and

---

* Refers to original publication

learning. Finally, he deals with perceptions concerning the ratio between one's load in life and one's power to carry that load, and how one can adjust this ratio - an extremely significant concept for adult educators and gerontologists.

Administration. In Chapter X* Essert places the administration of adult education in its proper focus in relation to the administration of all large-scale organisations. He then invites attention to lines of convergence in recent research in public administration, business administration, and educational administration. Finally, he develops a number of propositions which he suggests can profitably be examined and tested in order to arrive at dependable principles for the administration of adult education and for teaching adults.

History. The author of Chapter XI* suggests several ways in which the discipline of history can serve adult education. He also makes suggestions about the methodology of historical research which will be of great value to the graduate student who chooses a historical problem for his dissertation topic. More to the point, he applies these suggestions to specific problems in the history of adult education and makes reference to actual dissertations in the history of adult education. Furthermore, he indicates some dark corners in the history of adult education which may provide more than one graduate student with a dissertation topic.

In summary, the authors of Chapter VII-XI* give the professor of adult education some part of the priceless legacy of a relevant discipline. Armed with such legacies, the professor of adult education is no longer one man but many men. If he be scholar enough and bold enough, he can now translate and integrate these legacies in such fashion that his students will have the chance to grow into the kind of adult educator he himself would like to be.

A future responsibility of the professors of adult education as a group is to arrange for the winnowing of equally golden grain from other relevant disciplines.

Present Ways of Getting Help From Other Disciplines

The authors of Chapters VII-XI* have performed a signal service for professors of adult education by identifying needed knowledge in certain disciplines, and showing its revelance to problems in adult education. But it is one thing to know what this knowledge is and where it lies and quite another thing to know how best to make it available to one's students.

The most obvious way to do this is to encourage students in adult education to take courses in other departments. Professors of adult education at all the participating

---

* Refers to original publication

universities do this. In fact, at one institution where doctoral candidates in adult education are held responsible for three fields of knowledge on their comprehensive written examinations, Ed.D. candidates may, and Ph.D. candidates must, choose one of these three fields from outside the department of education. Another of the participating universities requires students specialising in adult education to take one-fourth of their course work outside the department of education.

Encouraging students in adult education to take courses in other departments involves some problems. For one thing, unless they choose wisely they are likely to pick up a smattering of unrelated knowledge. For this reason, the professor of adult education at one of the participating universities requires his students to take a block of related courses in a single discipline rather than single courses in several disciplines. And he requires this discipline to be sociology because of the values he feels it holds for careerists in adult education. Another problem is that adult educators often fail to see that knowledge from other disciplines can be useful to them. For example, many adult educators protested when the journal Adult Leadership began to report findings from research in human relations and community development in the 1950's. So one of the tasks of the professor of adult education is to convince his students of the relevance for them of knowledge in other disciplines.

Another means of making relevant content from other disciplines available to students in adult education is to ask professors in such fields to organise special courses for students in adult education. This is, of course, an inordinate request. Yet this is precisely how the late Professor Irving Lorge's course in adult learning at Teachers College originated some years ago. And professors of adult education, knowing that this has been brilliantly accomplished once, devote a good deal of time to plotting the seduction of innocent colleagues in psychology, sociology, and other disciplines with special relevance for adult education.

It is of course easier to persuade professors in other disciplines to give only a lecture or two, or to serve as a consultant, in a course in adult education. But the process of communicating research findings by experts from one field of knowledge to practitioners in another is less easy than it sounds. For example, at one participating university it was thought that some of the findings from research in human relations would be valuable to directors of public school adult education. About twenty such persons were invited to a meeting at which three or four human relations specialists were asked to describe some of the fruits of research in human relations. The only trouble with this conference was that it didn't work. The public school men were overwhelmed by the research reports, went away bewildered, and never made any known use of the information. This conference failed because the human relations experts were not properly briefed about the problems on which help was wanted. If the directors of public school adult education had been invited to identify their problems in advance, and if this information had been communicated to the human relations specialists in time to enable them to screen human relations research known to them for findings relevant to these problems, then the directors would have been better motivated and the specialists would have had a better chance of hitting the target.

A Proposal for Systematic Borrowing

Professors of adult education use all the foregoing ways to make relevant knowledge from other disciplines available to their students. But they are still unable to make available to their students in these ways all the needed knowledge from other disciplines. Inevitably, they have to assume actual personal responsibility for appropriating and communicating some of it, which they find easier to do in connection with disciplines in which they themselves have had considerable graduate training. But no professor of adult education can be a specialist in all the relevant disciplines. Inevitably he is going to have to do the best he can to appropriate and communicate the knowledge of some discipline in which he has not specialised. This is not easy. However, in Chapter VI* Jensen makes it easier than therefore by presenting a careful exposition of the steps which he feels are necessary if the borrowing is to be successful.

First, says Jensen, the adult educator must familiarise himself with five "operational indices" which indicate whether or not a given programme is functioning properly. (Is the programme facilitating the progress of the various instructional projects which are being used to develop the desired behaviours? Is the programme holding together to the degree required for effective implementation of instructional activities? Etc.) Second, if there is trouble he identifies the problem. Third, he screens the theory and research of other disciplines for concepts related to this problem. Fourth, he coordinates the appropriate concepts from the discipline with the operational indices, seeing the former as independent variables and the latter as dependent variables. Fifth, he formulates propositions which describe the relationships between these two sets of variables and which specify what changes need to be made in order to improve the instructional programme. Sixth, if there are still knowledge gaps after the foregoing process, he may need to try to create theory and research to take care of them.

---

* Refers to original publication

SOME PROBLEMS OF GRADUATE PROGRAMS IN ADULT EDUCATION

Location and Organisation of Programmes

One problem in the development of any programme of graduate study is where to locate it and how to organise it. The programmes of graduate study in adult education at most, if not all, of the participating universities are located in schools of education. Houle mentions some problems resulting from this fact which sometimes lead professors of adult education to wish that their programmes were located elsewhere. Most of the problems, however, would still exist in any other university school or department. They are inherent in the nature of adult education as an emerging field of graduate study and an emerging profession, and in the characteristics of graduate students in adult education. These conditions require, as we have seen, a complex system of linkages between the programme of adult education and other fields of study, organisations, and personnel in the university.

It would save a lot of trouble if this process of linkage were begun at the time a graduate programme in adult education is contemplated. For example, when one participating university was thinking about starting a graduate programme in adult education, a university-wide committee was appointed to explore the matter. For a full year the committee deliberated on the need for such a programme, consulting with other members of the faculty and hearing testimony from visiting adult educators. In the end it not only recommended that such a programme be established and that a professor of adult education be employed, but also "that any major development in the training of leadership for adult education should be an outgrowth of an overall integrated programme which considers the total resources of the University."[5] It was further proposed "that a Faculty Study Group on Adult Education be constituted for an indefinite period of time consisting of one representative from each of the schools and colleges having an interest in the education of adults, and one or more representatives of the university administration, including the Division of Continuing Education."[6] Thus at the outset of its programme this university took two important steps toward developing lines of communication, cooperation, and support.

Provision of Learning Activities

The two preceding sections have to do with the identification and borrowing of essential principles and concepts by professors of adult education and with the assimilation of these by their students. This is of the utmost importance, and we have much to learn about both. But it is equally important that our students learn how to generalise this knowledge and apply it to problems of practice.

We suspect that one way to help them do this is through imaginative use of such techniques as case studies, incidents, role-playing, and so forth. Articles on how to use these techniques have appeared in Adult Leadership, but one has heard little about their use in graduate courses in adult education. Research on this would be welcome.

We are slightly better off when it comes to information about field work, another valuable means of fostering the application of knowledge to practice, and to this we now turn.

In a study of field work provisions in programmes of graduate study in adult education, Booth[7] distinguished three kinds of field work: observation, practice, and internships. He found that graduate students in adult education participated in these three kinds of field work in decreasing order of frequency. Those who had participated in any of the three activities testified that it was as valuable as, or more valuable than, their academic courses. On the other hand, only about half the students took advantage of these opportunities. This could mean that those students who needed field work were getting it and profiting from it, and that the others didn't need it.

Aker found that students who did not participate in field work as part of their graduate training in adult education felt that they were missing something important and wished that they might have had actual job experience in adult education before entering their graduate training, while those who did participate in fieldwork as part of their graduate training in adult education saw little need for actual job experience before entering their graduate training. This suggests that fieldwork during graduate training in adult education can replace to some extent prior experience in adult education, which is after all the function of fieldwork.

A number of the participating universities require observation (often in connection with an introductory survey of adult education) and at least one requires that its students serve an internship. It is perhaps no accident that this last institution has the most highly developed programme of fieldwork for students in adult education. Within its extension division it has a bureau which provides services to community institutions that have educational programmes: business firms, churches, hospitals, public schools, etc. Its professors of adult education are employed part-time by the department of education and part-time by this bureau. Their work for the department of education consists of two kinds of teaching: courses in adult education in the department of education and supervision of fieldwork in the bureau. Their work for the bureau consists of whichever of its activities they are best qualified for: planning programmes, teaching off-campus in-service training courses, leading conferences, consulting, making community studies, evaluating programmes, and the like.

This institution requires its graduate students in adult education to devote 200 hours to fieldwork. This consists of (1) field practice (165 hours minimum), (2) field observation (20 hours minimum), (3) literacy training (15 hours), and (4) lectures. Of the 165 hours of field practice, at least 75 hours (more typically 100-120) must be devoted to a long-term project in a cooperating community institution. The student actually plans, conducts, and evaluates an educational programme for the cooperating institution. The other 45 to 90 hours of the student's field practice are devoted to experience as a trainer in adult education institutes, in churches, hospitals, public libraries, service clubs, or other community institutions. The cooperating community institutions submit reports to the university on the quality of the intern's field practice. The 20 hours of field observation are devoted to field trips to community institutions and to observation of the educational programmes being conducted by these community institutions, with follow-up critiques. The 15 hours of literacy training are acquired at an annual university institute on literacy training. The lectures are designed to contribute to the student's growth as an adult educator.

Variations of this plan are in use at several of the participating universities. At one the tie-up between the department of education and an operating department is with the extension division, minus the special bureau described above. At a second it is with agricultural extension; at a third, with an institute of adult education; at a fourth, with an institute of community development; at a fifth, with a continuation study centre; and at a sixth, with a variety of community agencies of adult education.

In all these cases the nature of the tie-up differs. But in general it can be said that they provide graduate students one or more of the following advantages: observation, practice, internships (sometimes paid), real experience in contrast to merely listening or reading, opportunity to discuss problems in adult education with a professor of adult education on the spot as the problems arise, individualisation of learning activities, and research opportunities. And they offer the professors a chance to maintain and enlarge their expertness in the practice of adult education, to extend their contacts with adult education in the community, and to do research.

As the proportion of inexperienced students in programmes of graduate study in adult education increases, demand for fieldwork opportunities may also be expected to increase.

It is not too soon to begin thinking about the overall design of learning activities for graduate courses in adult education - what Knowles was working up to in the analysis which is set forth early in this chapter. As mentioned in footnote 2, Chamberlain has done some thinking about this. So have Houle and Liveright. If their efforts were published, it would give us something to make a start on. We should also make use of efforts to design learning activities for related fields of graduate study, notably Clark's thoughtful and provocative monograph concerning the use of behavioural science in business education.[8]

Individualisation and Flexibility

Much that has been said in this chapter suggests the need for individualisation and flexibility in graduate programmes in adult education. The fact that students differ so from one another, the sort of objectives thought suitable for them (especially certain attitudes and values, zest for continued learning, research skills), the kinds of help which Aker's and Chamberlain's respondents expressed need for, the necessity to borrow from other disciplines, the fact that fieldwork is needed and is almost inevitably done individually - all these conditions cry aloud for individualisation.

Accordingly, Liveright urges effective means of evaluating the student's previous education and experience, of discovering his needs, of counselling, of programme planning. Professors of adult education at several of the participating universities have developed statements of objectives for their programmes. They give these to their students and use them as the basis for personal conferences, encouraging self-analysis and probing for evidence of progress in achieving the desired competencies and values. The studies of Chamberlain and Aker might be used in the same way.

We could do all these things and still rely overmuch on courses. The chief justification for organising learning into courses is to save the instructor's time and the institution's money. As long as we have comparatively few students in programmes of graduate study in adult education, we should take advantage of it. Wherever possible we should encourage them to pursue their own learning, under guidance. This can be a bridge to the art of self-directed learning. Our students will have had few enough opportunities to cultivate this art up to this point in their educational careers. It is time to get them started.

All the participating universities offer individual study and research "courses" in which the instructor-student relationship is one-to-one. These are ideal means of cultivating self-directed learning. They are also ideal means of realising the individualisation of learning opportunities. Through these individual courses, through fieldwork, through papers and projects, through examinations and self-evaluation, through establishment of credit by examination, through minimising course and unit requirements, and most of all through encouraging the student's own study and reflection, we should do all we can to individualise our programmes and give them flexibility.

Houle asserts that zest for continued learning (in which self-directed learning is likely to play a large part) is the most essential of all values for an adult educator.[9] Hallenbeck, Liveright, Chamberlain and Aker all assign great importance to it. But let us not limit this to professional study. Professionals tend toward narrowness. They need breadth not only in their field but beyond their field. Of all professionals, adult educators must be the least tolerant of narrowness. Their business is to help people enlarge their lives. They must do no less themselves.

One participating university uses a novel means of fostering zest for continued learning in its students. It requires doctoral candidates in adult education to cultivate some special interest: intellectual, artistic, literary, community service, and the like. The student is asked to make a plan for developing this interest, or to give evidence that he has made progress on a plan which he may have made previously.

CONCLUSION

Graduate study in adult education is in an emerging stage and is advancing through four processes: building theory by developing guidelines from practice in adult education, borrowing appropriate knowledge from relevant disciplines and reformulating it into new theory for adult education, creating new theory by research, and devising ways to help its students appropriate and apply this knowledge. This is at once our challenge and our compass.

REFERENCES

1. Malcolm S. Knowles, (1962), "A General Theory of the Doctorate in Education," Adult Education XII, 3, Spring, pp. 136-41.

2. Martin N. Chamberlain, (1960), The Professional Adult Educator, Unpublished doctoral dissertation, University of Chicago. An article on Chamberlain's dissertation appeared in 1961 (Chamberlain, Martin N., "The Competencies of Adult Educators," Adult Education, XI, 2, Winter, 1961, 78-83) but it covers his study very incompletely. Chamberlain's dissertation deserves wider circulation and careful study, especially by professors of adult education. It is the only attempt known to the writer to construct systematically a curriculum of graduate study in adult education.

3. George F. Aker, "Criteria for Evaluating Graduate

Study in Adult Education," (no date). Findings of a study conducted for the Commission of the Professors of Adult Education. Chicago: The University of Chicago, Centre for Continuing Education, mimeographed.

4. Jack London, Robert Wenkert and Warren O. Hagstrom, "Adult Education and Social Class," (December 1963), Survey Research Centre, University of California, Berkeley.

5. Malcolm S. Knowles, "Boston University's Adult Education Programme," (Autumn, 1959), Adult Education, X,I, p. 49.

6. Proposal For a Continuing Study of Boston University's Role and Program in Adult Education, mimeographed, 3 pages, not dated.

7. Alan Booth, "A Study of Field Work Programs," (Autumn, 1960), Adult Education, XI, 1, pp. 14.18.

8. James V. Clark, "Education for the Use of Behavioural Science," (1962), Institute of Industrial Relations, University of California, Los Angeles.

9. Cyril O. Houle, "The Development of Leadership," (not dated or paged), The Fund for Adult Education, White Plains, New York, Mimeographed.

Chapter Twenty-Two

A CURRICULAR AND PROGRAMMATIC ANALYSIS OF
GRADUATE ADULT EDUCATION IN NORTH AMERICA

Stephen Brookfield (1988)

As is evident from the selections in the historical perspectives
section of this volume, the question of what comprises a
suitable curriculum for those who are training to become
educators of adults has been debated at least since the con-
ferring of the first doctoral degree in adult education in the
United States (in 1935 at Columbia University, Teachers
College). There is a substantial body of literature examining
the forms of knowledge to which aspiring or practising adult
educators should be exposed, and the skills they should
develop or improve. Guidelines regarding curricula and proficiencies appropriate to the training of educators of adults
have been issued by Lindeman (1938), Overstreet and Overstreet (1941), Hallenbeck (1948), Liveright (1964), Verner
and Booth (1964), Grabowski (1976, 1981), Miller and Verduin
(1979) and Carter (1983). Analyses of the specific competencies required by practising adult educators have been
undertaken by Chamberlain (1961), Knowles (1962), Robinson
(1962), Mocker and Noble (1981) and Daniel and Rose (1982).
In 1964 the Commission of Professors of Adult Education
issued its first concerted attempt to define and delineate what
appropriately comprised the field of adult education as it
related to graduate study (Jensen, Liveright and Hallenbeck,
1964). In 1987, the same Commission approved a policy document outlining appropriate standards for graduate programmes
in adult education (also included in this volume). Yet a
recent paper argues that the diversity of views regarding
how graduate adult education should be organised "raises
serious questions about adult education as a field of specialised study - questions regarding who will prepare adult
educators in the future, and what knowledge base should be
required of those to whom will be entrusted the responsibility
of mapping future directions" (Weaver and Kowalski, 1987,
p.14). Evidently, then, debate on methods and curricula
suitable for inclusion in a programme of graduate study has
been concerted and continuous.

In this chapter the debate is placed in the context of accurate information regarding the organisation of programmes of graduate adult education within universities and the curricula they adopt or develop. The works comprising the frame of reference upon which this analysis is based are the second revised edition of the UNESCO Director of Adult Education Training and Research Institutions (UNESCO, 1982), Peterson's annual guide to Graduate Programmes in the Humanities and Social Sciences 1986 (Goldstein and Frary, 1986), and the recent surveys of graduate programs conducted by Goyen (1983), Daniel and Kasworm (1985), Cross (1985), Kowlaski and Weaver (1986), and Knott and Ross (1986).

CHARACTERISTICS OF GRADUATE PROGRAMMES

In reviewing the characteristics of graduate programmes in adult education, and the literature surrounding the development of this field as an area of academic study, it is apparent that there is a strong divergence of opinion as to how the doctorate in adult education should be conceived in terms of its purpose and functions. At the master's level, there seems to be a consensus of agreement that this is essentially a practitioner's degree, though the split between the M.A. and M.Ed. degree in some departments does represent an attempt to distinguish between a theoretically and research inclined master's degree (the M.A.) and an advanced practitioner's degree (the M.Ed.). Where the doctorate is concerned, however, there is a divergence. On the one hand there are those who, like Boyd (1969), p.191) maintain that in graduate work the "emphasis is on research and not service in the sense of preparing professionals to meet the demands of current needs". According to Boyd, the purpose of graduate education is to "observe, analyse, and develop evidence and theory to explain that which we are examining and studying". Contrary to this, Daniel and Rose (1982) argue that the emphasis of practitioners on real life problems in planning and facilitating adult learning means that graduate study should make a much greater integration of theory and practice than is presently the case. A middle position is represented by the many who see the Ed.D. as a practitioner oriented degree and the Ph.D. as suitable for those who wish to become scholars, researchers and professors. My own belief that graduate study should be concerned chiefly with developing critically reflective practitioners is argued elsewhere in this volume.

Definitively accurate information on the number and organisation of graduate programmes is notoriously difficult to obtain. At the master's degree level, Peterson's Guide (1986) lists 153 Master's degree programmes in adult education in the United States and Canada. Although information on the providing institutions is not provided, we can speculate that of these 153 programmes many offer adult education only as a minor or specialisation within a wider programme of studies. The greatest numbers of degrees in adult education offered at master's level are those of M.Ed. (58 in number), M.A. (38), and M.S. (34). Others offered are the M.S. Ed. degree (12), M.A. Ed. (4), A.M. Ed. (3), M.A.T. (2) and M.A.E. (2). The following degrees are each offered at only one of the schools listed; 6th Year Diploma, M.S. Cont. Ed., M.C. Ed., M.G.S., M.P.S., M. Higher Ed., M.A.P.M. and M.A.J. Ed. The UNESCO Directory (1982) lists 24 Master's degrees in the United States (14 at the M.A. level, 6 at M.Sci. and 4 at M.Ed.) and 9 in Canada (3 at the M.Ed. level, 2 at M.A., and 1 each at M.A. Ed., M.A. Ad. Ed., M. Cont. Ed., and M.S. Ext. Ed.). A number of non-master's degrees in adult education are offered in Canada according to the UNESCO survey, including those of Diploma in Adult Education (at 2 institutions), Diploma in Post-Secondary Education, Postgraduate Diploma, 4th Year Course for Education Majors, B.A. (with a major in adult education), Certificate in A.E., Certificate in Andragogie, Certificat de Perfectionnement en Ensiegnement Collegail, Diplome de Formation en Ed. des Adultes, Niveau Baccalauriat and Maitrise en Ed. (each at one institution). The survey of graduate adult education programmes conducted by Knott and Ross (1986) lists 27 reponding institutions offering the M.Ed. or equivalent degree, 14 offering the M.S. and 9 the M.A. Kowalski and Weaver's (1986) survey obtained responses from 34 institutions offering the master's programme, and 2 offering the bachelor's degree in adult education.

With regard to doctoral degrees, Peterson's (1986) guide, lists a total of 91 doctoral programmes in adult education in the United States and Canada. 42 of these are at the Ed.D. level, 27 at the Ph.D. level and 22 at the Ed.S. level. The UNESCO directory (1982) lists 27 doctoral programmes in adult education in the United States, (14 at the Ed. D level and 13 at the Ph.D. level) and 6 in Canada (2 at the PH.D. level., 2 at the Ed.D. level, and one each at the level Docteur and Docteur en philosophie). Goyen (1983) studied 38 doctoral programmes, 16 of which offered both the Ph.D. and Ed.D. degree, 15 offering only the Ed.D., and 7 offering the Ph.D. Daniel and Kasworm (1985) collected data from 41 institutions offering doctoral programs in adult education in the United States, 18 of which offered only the Ed.D. degree, 11 of which offered only the Ph.D. degree, with the remaining 12 offering both doctoral options. Questionnaires were sent to directors of 50 graduate programmes offering doctoral work in adult education by Kowalski and Weaver (1986), of which 37 returned a response. Of this number 12 programmes offered only the Ed.D. degree, 10 the Ph.D. and 15 granted both degrees. Knott and Ross (1986) identified 21 programmes which offered the Ed.D. or D.Ed. degree, 17 which offered the Ph.D., and 11 which offered both.

In the two most recent surveys available (Kowalski and Weaver, 1986; Knott and Ross, 1986), certain features emerge prominently as common to programmes across the range of the responding universities. In the majority of programmes, for example, the mechanism of some form of student practicum or internship is a central feature, though there are variations in whether or not such work is required or optionally available. At the doctoral level, written comprehensive examinations (or certification examinations as they are sometimes called) are required for all candidates in all the doctoral programmes surveyed by Knott and Ross (1986), though Kowlaski and Weaver (1986) report contradictory findings to the effect that 13 of the 37 doctoral programmes in their sample do not require these. The great majority of programmes (34 of 37) in Kowalski and Weaver's (1986) study require a period of residency for doctoral candidates, though this period varies from institution to institution with the most common require-ment being two consecutive semesters of residential, full time study. The study reported that a majority of programme directors polled (58 per cent) 'agreed' or 'strongly agreed' that such residency was important to the doctoral experience, with 28 per cent 'disagreeing' or 'strongly disagreeing' with this requirement.

FACULTY AND STUDENT CHARACTERISTICS

The size of graduate programs varies considerably from institution to institution. According to Daniel and Kasworm (1985) 3 of the doctoral programmes have 200 or more students annually, 6 have 100, 7 have between 50 and 100, and 25 have less than 50. 2 programmes have over 10 faculty members, 8 have between 5 and 9, and the remaining 33 have less than 5 full time faculty in adult education. The insti-tutional context within which these programmes are located also varies. Kowalski and Weaver (1986) report that of the 37 doctoral programmes they reviewed, only 4 were housed in a separate department of adult education. 10 were within a department including adult education and another specialis-ation. 2 were a programme area in a department of curriculum and instruction, 4 in a department of educational adminis-tration, 2 in a general education department, 2 in a depart-ment of educational leadership, 3 in a department of second-ary or higher education, and the remainder in "other types of departments" (p. 2). This means that a majority of doctoral programmes in adult education are sub-programmes of a department which does not include adult education as a des-criptor in the department's title. We can surmise that the marginality commonly supposed to afflict adult education programmes in the wider sphere of higher and continuing education institutions is paralleled by the position of graduate programmes within their host universities. 5 of the 37 doctoral programmes reported that none of the faculty involved in teaching and research held a doctorate in adult education. 8 reported having only one faculty member with a doctorate in adult education, 11 had 2 faculty members with this doctorate, 4 had 4, 4 had 5, and one had 6 faculty holding the doctoral degree in adult education. The mean age of graduate students in adult education programmes was between 34 and 40 years of age, and in the majority of programmes female students outnumbered males, accurately reflecting the predominantly female nature of the wider profession. Students from ethnic minorities were, on the whole, poorly represented according to Kowalski and Weaver, with 14 of the 37 programmes reporting a minority enrolment of less than 5 per cent, and 8 with a minority enrolment of 5-10 per cent. The majority of students in these programmes are reported to have a professional background in some form of education. However, 31 of the 37 programmes stipulate no requirement regarding students' having some form of educational experience as a condition for admission. None of the 38 doctoral programmes studied by Knott and Ross (1986) required a master's degree in adult education as a condition of admission; however, 11 of the Ed.D. programmes would not accept students without practical experience in the field of adult education, while 6 of the 17 Ph.D. programmes required such experience.

CURRICULUM OF GRADUATE ADULT EDUCATION

Information on the courses comprising the master's and doctoral programmes of graduate study in adult education are available in the UNESCO Directory (1982) and the surveys by Cross (1985), Daniel and Kasworm (1985) and Knott and Ross (1986). In the United States the UNESCO Directory lists a total of 147 identifiable courses given in the graduate programmes surveyed. Five clusters of courses stand out as comprising a 'core' curriculum according to this survey:

Courses	Number	Percentage
Programme Development in Adult/ Continuing Education	30	20.41
Survey/Introduction/Foundations of Adult/Continuing Education	18	12.24
Instruction/Teaching Methods	14	9.52

Management and Administration of Adult/ Continuing Education	14	9.52
Adult Learning and Development	12	8.16

The Programme Development category includes courses in programme development, programme development and evaluation, evaluation, curriculum development, designing adult education programmes, designing training programmes, analysing community needs and others which included programming or programme design in their titles. The Survey/ Introduction/Foundations category includes course titles such as introduction to adult education, continuing education, survey of adult education, foundations of adult education, nature of adult education and philosophy of adult education. The Instruction/Teaching Methods category includes courses such as instruction of adults, teaching methodology, adult teaching strategies, methods in adult education, methods and materials, principles of adult education, and instruction of adult learners. The Management and Administration category includes courses with titles such as programme management, organisation and administration, administration of adult education agencies and programmes, continuing education agency supervision, continuing education leadership, educational management, leadership theory and practice, and administration and supervision. The Adult Learning and Development category includes courses on adult learning, adults as learners, learning and development, independent adult learning, motivation and participation of adult learners, psychology of adult education, and issues in adult learning.

In descending order, the smaller clusters of courses are those of research methods (8 or 5.44%), the societal context of adult and continuing education (5 or 3.40%), educational gerontology (5 or 3.40%), adult basic education (4 or 2.72%), the community college (3 or 2.04%), community education (3 or 2.04%), issues in adult education (3 or 2.04%), vocational education (3 or 2.04%), cooperative and extension education (3 or 2.04%), vocational education (3 or 2.04%), history of adult education (3 or 2.04%), client-consultant relationships (3 or 2.04%), teaching English as a Second Language (3 or 2.04%), small group dynamics (2 or 1.36%), international adult education (2 or 1.36%), practicum in adult education (2 or 1.36%), leisure education (2 or 1.36%), and paraprofessionals in adult education (2 or 1.36%). Single courses taught were non-traditional education, non-formal education, career education, business and industry education, technical education and grant proposal writing. A remarkable congruence regarding 'core' curricula of graduate programmes in adult education is evident from comparing the analyses of Daniel and Kasworm (1985), Cross (1985) and Knott and Ross (1986) with the UNESCO Directory content analysis of courses. Daniel and Kasworm's study of 41 doctoral programmes reported the following clusters of required courses in adult education:

Adult Learning and Development (36.84%)

History and Philosophy of Adult Education (23.68%)

Administration and Development of Adult Education Programmes (10.52%)

Introduction to Adult Education and Adult Learning (5.26%)

Introductory Seminar (2.63%)

Teaching Methods and Group Processes in Adult Education (2.63%)

Community Development (2.63%)

Working with a much smaller sample of syllabuses drawn from 43 courses taught at 9 universities, Cross (1985) reported the most common courses to be (in rank order) (1) introductory and survey courses, (2) programme planning and marketing, (3) adult learning, (4) organisation and administration of adult education, (5) aging/educational gerontology, (6) adult development, (7) international adult education and (8) research methods. Knott and Ross (1986) reported their findings regarding required courses by breaking these down into required courses at the master's level and required courses at the doctoral level. At the master's level, they report that of the 159 required courses recorded, the following clusters of courses emerge:

Course	Number	Percentage
Adult Learning and Development	31	19.50
Introduction/Foundations/ Survey of Adult Education	26	16.35
Programme Planning	26	16.35
Teaching and Instruction	19	11.95
Administration of Adult Education	12	7.55
History/Philosophy/Issues	11	6.92

Adult Education Seminar	11	6.92
Research in Adult Education	10	6.29
Internship	9	5.66
Other	4	2.52
Total	159	100.01

(Percentages have been rounded off to two decimal points)

At the doctoral level, Knott and Ross reported data on 128 required adult education courses for graduate students as follows:

Course	Number	Percentage
Adult Learning and Development	20	15.63
Research and Statistics	18	14.06
Introduction/Foundations	15	11.72
Programme Development	14	10.94
Teaching/Instruction	12	9.38
Adult Education Seminar	10	7.81
History/Philosophy	7	5.47
Administration of Adult Education	7	5.47
Training	6	4.69
Dissertation Seminar	5	3.91
Internship	4	3.13
Miscellaneous	4	3.13
Community Education	3	2.34
Problems/Controversies	3	2.34
Total	128	100.2

(Percentages have been rounded off to two decimal points)

CONCLUSION

There are problems raised by attempts to generalise on the basis of the seven curricular analyses provided. Ambiguities remain regarding how different authors clustered different course titles; for example, is a course title on 'principles of adult education' to be interpreted as a methods course, one on philosophical analysis or a foundations type review? Should educational leadership be placed under programme development or management and administration? Are foundations and introductory and survey courses similar enough to warrant inclusion in the same generic category? Should history and philosophy be placed in discretely separate categories? Are not courses on history and philosophy of adult education in effect contained within many foundations courses? There are marked variations in the degrees of importance accorded to very similar clusters of courses in surveys which, presumably, used essentially the same sampling frame for their investigations. For example, adult learning and development is ranked fifth in the UNESCO Directory, but first by Daniel and Kasworm and Knott and Ross, and instruction and teaching methods as a category is not mentioned by Cross at all.

Notwithstanding these ambiguities in definition and classification, and the variations in ranked importance, the core elements of the graduate adult education curricula are remarkably consistent. Master's and doctoral students concentrate their adult education studies in five key areas; programme development, adult learning and development, foundations of adult education, teaching methods and instructional processes, and the management and administration of adult and continuing education institutions. The findings of this curricular analysis confirm Hiemstra's (1976, p.60) conclusion that "there is a fairly recognisable pattern to the nature of training received in adult education" based upon recognisable clusters of courses to do with adult learning and development, programme development and administration, the philosophical and historical underpinnings of adult education practice, a survey of the forms and institutions of adult education, and examination of societal issues relevant to practice within the field. A decade later Merriam (1985) observed that "a typical graduate programme consists of three types of core courses: adult learning, organisation of the field, and programme development and administration" (p.91). Not surprisingly, perhaps, this same concentration of interest is represented in the conduct and dissemination of adult education research as evinced in the professional journals, registers of dissertations and theses, and research conference proceedings in the field. In the twenty year span from Brunner's (1959) specification of 'core' categories of research to Verner's two (1970; 1980) reaffirmations of these, the focus of research attention has concentrated on studies relating to processes of adult learning, lifespan, stage and phase psychology in adulthood and its connection to learning, instructional design and method, participation studies, programme development for adults, and the societal function of adult education. Further attention is given to the research concerns and development of professional knowledge within the field in the 'Comparative Perspectives' section of this book.

With regard to the connection between graduate students' participation in programmes of graduate adult education, and any perceptible improvement in graduate practitioners' enhanced skill, sensitivity, proficiency or social commitment, very few causal claims can be made with any degree of certainty. In their study of the literature of graduate adult education Verner et. al., (1970, p. 48) concluded that "very little research has been done to assess the achievements of graduate study as a way of providing the field with skilled adult educators. Consequently there are unresolved questions about the content provided in graduate programs and whether or not graduate education in adult education provided the kinds of learning experiences that lead ultimately to an improvement in the field." In a debate a decade later Griffith (1980, p. 223) remarked that "The cold, hard facts are that we don't have any empirical evidence that people who have been trained academically in the field of adult education do any better in carrying out the roles of adult educators than those who have not been professionally trained." The continued lack of connection between graduate adult education and the practice of adult education was noted in a recent survey of employment opportunities in the field (Bruce, Maxwell and Galvin, 1986). Commenting on "the apparent discontinuity between the practice of adult and continuing education and academic preparation in the field" (p. 7), the authors reported that with regard to employment "experience with adult education programs and teaching are clearly valued; but apparently a degree in teaching or adult education is not, even in institutions that offer degree programs in the field" (p. 7). They raise the question whether or not a graduate programme in adult education can be justified if it is perceived by the wider field as irrelevant to practice. The same concern is voiced by Weaver and Kowalski (1987) who believe that the split between those who see adult education as a function of human resource development in business and industry, and those who see it as part of education proper, "is likely to devalue the doctoral degree as potential employers become even more uncertain about the quality of graduates" (p.27). In the next chapter a rationale is provided for organising graduate adult education which emphasises the need to focus such programmes on analysing students' past and current adult educational experiences as a way of developing their capacity to be critically reflective practitioners.

REFERENCES

Boyd, R. D., (1969), New designs for Adult Education doctoral programmes, Adult Education, 19 (3), 186-196.
Bruce, R., Maxwell, D., and Galvin, P., (1986), Graduate study and the practice of Adult Education: A problem of congruence, Lifelong Learning, 10 (3), 4-7, 20.
Brunner, E., (1959), An Overview of Adult Education Re search, Adult Education Association of the United States; Chicago.
Carter, G. L., (1983), A Perspective on Training Adult Educators, in: "Strengthening Connections Between Education and Performance," S. M. Grabowski ed., Jossey-Bass; San Francisco.
Chamberlain, M. N., (1961), The competencies of Adult Educators, Adult Education, 11 (2), 78-82.
Cross, K. P., (1985) "Adult/Continuing Education," Un- published paper, Graduate School of Education, Harvard University.
Daniel, R. and Kasworm, C., (1985), Evaluation of adult continuing education doctoral programmes within the Federation of North Texas Area Universities, Report presented to the Commission of Professors of Adult Education Annual Conference; Philadelphia, November 1983.
Daniel, R., and Rose, H., (1982), Comparative study of Adult Education Practitioners and professors on future knowledge and skills needed by Adult Educators, Adult Education, 32 (2), 75-88.
Goldstein, A. J., and Frary, A. C. eds., (1986), "Graduate Programmes in the Humanities and Social Sciences 1986," Peterson's Guides, Princeton; New Jersey.
Goyen, L. F., (1983), Survey of Doctoral programmes in North America, presentation to Commission of Professors of Adult Education Annual Conference; Philadelphia, November 1983.
Grabowski, S. M., (1976), "Training Teachers of Adults: Models and Innovative Programmes," Syracuse; Syracuse, University Publications in Continuing Education.
Griffith, W. S., (1980), Personnel preparation: Is there a continuing education profession? in: "Power and Conflict in Continuing Education," P. E. Frandson, ed., Wadsworth; Belmont, California.
Hallenbeck, W. C., (1948), The training of Adult Educators, in: "Handbook of Adult Education in the United States," M. L. Ely ed., Centre for Adult Education, Teachers College; New York.

Jensen, G., Liveright, A. A., and Hallenbeck, W. C., (1964), Adult Education: Outlines of an emerging field of university study, Adult Education Association of the United States; Washington D.C.

Knott, E. S., and Ross, J. M., (1986), Distinctions among degrees offered in Adult Education Graduate Programmes, Paper presented to the Commission of professors of Adult Education Annual Conference; Hollywood, Florida, October 1986.

Knowles, M. S., (1962), Philosophical issues that confront Adult Educators, Adult Education, 7 (4), 234-240.

Kowalski, T. J., and Weaver, R. A., (1986), Graduate studies in Adult Education; An analysis of Doctoral Programmes and professional opinions, Proceedings of the 1986 Midwest Research to Practice Conference in Adult, Community and Continuing Education, Muncie, Indiana; Ball State University School of Continuing Education.

Lindeman, E. C., (1938), Preparing Leaders of Adult Education, address to the Pennsylvania Association for Adult Education, November 18th.

Liveright, A. A., (1964), The Nature and aims of Adult education as a field of graduate education, in: "Adult Education: Outlines of an Emerging Field of University Study," G. Jensen, A. A. Liveright and W. C. Hallenbeck, eds., Adult Education Association of the United States; Washington D.C.

Merriam, S. B., (1985), Training Adult Educators in North America, Convergence, 18 (3-4), 84-93.

Miller, H. G., and Verduin, J. R., (1979), "The Adult Educator: A Handbook for Staff Development," Gulf Publishing Company; Houston.

Mocker, D. W., and Noble, E., (1981), Training part-time instructional staff, in: "Strengthening Connections Between Education and Performance," S.M. Grabowski, ed., Jossey-Bass; San Francisco.

Overstreet, H. A., and B. W., (1941), "Leaders for Adult Education," American Association for Adult Education; New York.

Robinson, C. O., (1962), Criteria for the education of adult educators, Adult Education, 12 (4), 243-245.

United Nations Educational, Scientific and Cultural Organisation (UNESCO), (1982), "Directory of Adult Education Training and Research Institutions," UNESCO; Paris.

Verner, C., Dickinson, G., Leirman, W., and Niskala, H., (1970), The preparation of Adult Educators: A selected review of the literature produced in North America, ERIC Clearinghouse on Adult Education/ Adult Education Association of the United States, Syracuse.

Verner, C., (1980), Academic education about Adult Education, in: "Towards a Learning Society," R. Boshier, ed., Learning Press; Vancouver.

Verner, C., and Booth, A., (1964), Adult Education. Centre for Applied Research in Education; New York.

Weaver, R. A., and Kowalski, T. J. (1987), The case for programme accreditation of doctoral degrees in Adult Education, Lifelong Learning, 10 (7), 14-15, 26-27.

Chapter Twenty-Three

GRADUATE ADULT EDUCATION AS A SOCIO-CULTURAL
PRODUCT: A CROSS-CULTURAL ANALYSIS OF THEORY AND
PRACTICE IN THE UNITED STATES AND GREAT BRITAIN

Stephen Brookfield (1988)

This chapter undertakes a micro-level comparative analysis of
one aspect of adult education practice and organisation; that
is, graduate adult education as organised and conducted in
university departments of adult education in the United States
and Britain. It argues that the methods, curricula, evaluative
criteria and modes, and intellectual terrain of graduate adult
education can be analysed as socio-cultural products; that is,
as practices, structures and attitudes rooted in and reflective
of the society and culture of which they are a part. Graduate
adult education is not viewed wholly as an isolated, idiosyncratic activity. In its organisation and intellectual emphases it
is seen as reflecting dominant political ideologies and prevailing cultural forms of the society in which it is located.
Analysing adult education structures and curricula as socio-
cultural products is, it seems, an unfamiliar activity to most
theorists and researchers in adult education. There are few
adult education equivalents to the analyses undertaken by
Bowles and Gintis (1976, 1986), Bourdieu and Passerson,
(1977) and Bernstein (1977)of how school curricula reflect and
perpetuate dominant cultural values. These writers are
commonly referred to as 'reproduction' theorists. They regard
school curricula, organisational structures and informal school
activities as hegemonic; that is, as serving to transmit,
maintain and reinforce the values of the dominant groups in
society. The radical pessimism of this reproductionist analysis
has been countered by a group of 'resistance' theorists
(Apple, 1981, 1982; Giroux, 1983; Aronowitz and Giroux,
1985) who see education as much more problematic. To resistance theorists schools are sites of contestation in which the
values of the dominant culture are countered and resisted by
pupils and teachers. Ethnographic studies of school life such
as those undertaken by Willis (1977), Corrigan (1979) and
Fine (1982) provide the empirical foundation for resistance
theorists' arguments concerning the possibility for teachers
and pupils to reject dominant cultural values and to develop
values more reflective of their own experiences. An account

of how adult education classes can serve as liberatory zones for consciousness change is provided in Shor's (1980) description of his work with working class adults at the City University of New York.

Common to reproduction and resistance viewpoints is an acknowledgment of school curricula as socio-cultural products. Curricula became social facts - sui generis realities which can be studied objectively in much the same way we examine political arrangements or economic systems. Curricula are analysed to the extent to which they reproduce and sustain prevailing political ideologies and economic arrangements. What comprises school curricula is seen as a political question, rather than one having to do with the idiosyncratic personalities of the teachers involved. Curricula are viewed as bodies of knowledge and clusters of values approved and sanctioned by dominant cultural groups. Since schools are viewed as perpetuating prevailing ideologies and socialising pupils to accept a majority culture, advocating curricular alterations which challenge the assumptions of that culture becomes politically contentious and professionally dangerous. In America school boards and state departments have become used to legislating what are to be regarded as legitimate curricula in schools. In Britain the recent move towards a national curriculum has drawn the reproductionist nature of schooling even more sharply into focus.

In 1985 in commenting on this body of reproductionist theory I observed that "analyses of adult education curricula employing a similar interpretative framework are noticeable only by their absence" (Brookfield, 1985b, p. 296). Since that time three books have been published (Jones, 1985; Youngman, 1986; Cowburn, 1986) which apply elements of this analysis to the organisation and functioning of adult education. Additionally, several works are in press which promise to develop this analysis even further (Armstrong, 1988; Evans, 1987; Lovett, 1988). Notwithstanding these recent works, however, very little attention has been granted to the culturally constructed nature of adult educational curricula. What work has been done (and what is promised to come) comes chiefly from British adult education analysts. In the work of Keddie (1980), Thompson (1983) and Griffin (1983, 1987) elements of the reproductionist analysis are applied to adult education curricula. Thompson analyses adult education for its reproduction of the patriarchal values of the dominant culture. Griffin argues that adult educators currently subscribe to an ideology of needs, access and provision, and that the criteria governing this ideology are administrative and organisational rather than deriving from any central philosophical rationale concerning the purposes of education. To Griffin, Gelpi's (1979, 1985) study of adult education curricula as a function of the social relations of production provides the most fruitful future direction.

In passing, it is interesting to note how this 'felt needs' rationale - that adult education is concerned with meeting the needs, wants and desires of learners as expressed by those same learners - has determined the 'core' curricula as uncovered in the analyses of adult education programmes undertaken by Thatcher (1956), Minich (1969), McCall and Schenz (1969) and Peters (1974) in the United States and by Lumsden (1977), Jarvis (1978), and Mee and Wiltshire (1978) in Britain. These analyses supply an important clue as to the surprising paucity of curricular analysis in adult education which applies variants of the reproductionist framework to the education of adults. In adult education, it appears, there is no 'core' curriculum (in the sense of fixed bodies of knowledge or sets of skills which programmers feel it important to provide) in the same way as there is in schools. Rather, programme developers provide curricula as diverse as the range of learner needs expressed. A consumer-service rationale seems to operate whereby adult educators feel duty bound to respond in some way to the entire range of psychomotor, affective and cognitive needs evident in the adult population. A 'typical' curriculum (though such an elusive animal cannot really be said to exist in adult education) comprises a variety of intellectual, social, aesthetic, economic and physical goals. Courses in literature, vegetarian cookery, art appreciation, microcomputers for small businesses and aerobics co-exist with no apparent sense of incongruence in many adult education programmes. Given this operating principle of there being no fixed curricular core in adult education, only an ever shifting array of diverse offerings organised in response to idiosyncratically expressed needs, it becomes more problematic to analyse how such curricula either sustain and reproduce dominant cultural values.

ORGANISING CONDITIONS OF GRADUATE ADULT EDUCATION: SOME TRANSATLANTIC DIFFERENCES

Before undertaking a detailed comparative analysis of how graduate adult education programmes reflect broader cultural forms and values in the United States and Britain, it might be useful to make some brief introductory comments regarding how adult education in each country has historically been conceived and practised. In exploring the literature of the field in the two countries concerned, it is impossible not to be surprised and intrigued by the apparent lack of common intellectual frames of reference. Scholars, researchers and theorists in each country appear to be remarkably ethnocentric, at least where the other's organising concepts are concerned. The history of American adult education as documented in standard texts such as those of Adams (1944), Grattan (1965) and Knowles (1977), is cast firmly within the liberal-democratic framework which informs the culture and political system of the country. Adult education is seen as existing to enhance the individual's creative powers, aesthetic capacities and economic opportunities. This tradition is discernible in Lindeman's (1926) early writings, through the Great Books programme of the 1950's, to the current popularity of the related concepts of andragogy (Knowles, 1984) and self-directed learning (Knowles, 1975). It is striking just how much this latter concern of self-directed learning has dominated the adult education research agenda and occupied the minds of American practitioners (Brookfield, 1985a). The finding that adults design, conduct and evaluate their own learning in an independent manner free of institutional control is a perfect enhancement to the American ethos of rugged individualism. Not surprisingly, writers, researchers and practitioners exploring this form of learning have found a ready and receptive audience in the United States.

In Britain, on the other hand, it is much harder to find any kind of consensual agreement as to what activities, concepts and philosophies comprise any kind of central tradition in adult education. To many, the adult education movement is inextricably bound up with the emergence of working class movements, collective organisations and structural forms such as trade unions, worker education and the Labour Party. This tradition is vigorously alive and well in recent works such as those by Thompson (1980), Lovett (1975, 1983), Youngman (1986), Ward and Taylor (1986) and Armstrong (1988). Some of their intellectual forerunners are Tawney, and the authors of the 1919 Report, and they fuse elements of Freire's and Gramsci's ideas with their own community development and community action experiences. According to this tradition adult education should be analysed according to the extent to which it buttresses and reinforces the prevailing wider social structures. Proper adult education practice as advocated by those who locate themselves in this tradition is concerned with assisting oppressed groups in the process of their collective advancement.

A tradition which runs markedly counter to this worker education rationale is that which views adult education as concerned with the development of aesthetic judgments and intellectual capacities. It emphasises the cognitive outcomes of learning over and above any alterations in wider social structures that might result from adult education participation. As conceived by Livingstone (1945) and more recently by Lawson (1979, 1982, 1985) and Paterson (1979, 1987) this orientation argues that adult educators should remain politically neutral and should refrain from exercising their positions of power to promote collective action on the part of their learners. An attempt has been made to redefine this liberal tradition in such a way that it encompasses those elements in adult education practice in Britain and America which are concerned with challenging dominant cultural values and political ideologies (Taylor, Rockhill and Fieldhouse, 1985). In my opinion (Brookfield, 1986) this is only partially successful and major differences between the liberal and socialist positions remain regarding the proper function of adult education. Irrespective of the merits of the claims laid by different writers to the correct interpretation of the liberal tradition, it remains clear that the American and British adult education traditions are very different. America has a largely consensual, liberal democratic tradition with no real polarities of opinion or divisions across the field regarding what should be the proper outcomes of adult education. In Britain, by way of contrast, there is a real and fierce debate over the connection between adult education and collective political action. Those who view adult education in terms of individual cultural enhancement, and those who see it as contributing to the collective advancement of oppressed groups, possess fundamentally unresolvable beliefs about the proper function of adult educators. No such public debate amongst those adhering to such clearly differentiated political positions is currently present in American adult education, though there is evidence that this was much more the case some forty years ago (Taylor, Rockhill and Fieldhouse, 1985).

A second important and major difference which needs to be acknowledged is the difference in the scale of the graduate adult education activity in the United States and Britain. In purely quantitative terms, at least, graduate adult education is treated more seriously in the United States. If we examine the number of university departments offering graduate adult education, the number of students enrolled for master's and doctoral degrees in these departments, the number of faculty teaching in these departments and the amount of advanced research undertaken, then it is clear that the graduate adult education enterprise in the United States is on an entirely different scale from that in Britain. Peterson's guide (Goldstein and Frary, 1986) lists 91 doctoral programmes in adult education in the United States and Canada, with many more offering only the master's degree, compared to the 14 institutions offering master's and doctoral degrees in the United Kingdom (SCUTREA, 1986). There are over 300 full, associate or affiliate members of the Commission of Professors of Adult Education, all of whom identify as their primary professional responsibility the teaching of courses on adult learning and adult education within university departments. It is not uncommon for single departments to have over 100 graduate students in adult education. In my own institution, the graduate programme in adult education has three full time faculty members and anywhere between 100 and 150 graduate students in adult education at any one time. This quantitative difference does not, of course, have any necessary correlation with any qualitative difference; indeed, British

283

lecturers could claim that there is a law of diminishing returns operating in the United States whereby once a certain faculty-student ratio is exceeded the intimacy between faculty and students necessary for quality research to be encouraged is lost.

Given the difference in numbers of departments, students and faculty engaged in graduate adult education in the two countries, it is not surprising that a great deal more research in adult education is generated and published in American than in Britain. For the last 29 years there has been an annual adult education research conference (AERC) meeting at which 45 to 50 papers and symposia are presented by graduate students and professors on aspects of research in adult education. Publication outlets and opportunities are far more numerous in the United States, a fact amply demonstrated by Long's (1977) finding that the professors of adult education he surveyed had published in over 300 academic journals. In Britain, by way of contrast, the principal adult education research meeting - the Standing Conference on University Teaching and Research in the Education of Adults (SCUTREA) - is comprised wholly of lecturers in adult education who present 10 to 15 papers at each annual meeting. Whereas AERC is open to all who can attend and maintains no roster of members (indeed, there is no standing organisation for anybody to join), SCUTREA is attended almost exclusively by lecturers and membership is granted only to those who teach within university departments of adult education and a few selected individuals who are voted the privilege of membership. There is currently no forum in Britain at which graduate students can present their research to a wider audience of interested academics and researchers. Neither does the range of publishing outlets for adult education research exist in anything like the quantity that can be found in the United States.

As with the number and size of graduate adult education programmes, there is no necessary correlation between the amount of research produced and published and its quality, merit or utility. Indeed, one could argue that the 'publish or perish' mentality which drives American professors of adult education to publish such a quantity of research in order to safeguard their employment, actually encourages research of a poorer quality. Researchable questions may come to be defined as those most accessible to quick investigation and easy conversion into published articles. This may explain the pre-eminence of quantitative approaches in adult education research in which instruments previously tested for reliability and validity are simply applied to new populations and the results tallied and compared to those drawn from previously studied groups. There are numerous studies of participation and self-directed learning using such approaches, in which doctoral students and junior professors apply developed instruments to collecting data on these themes with populations not previously studied. By way of contrast, qualitative research studies generally take longer to conduct and report since data collection and theory development are conducted concurrently. In qualitative studies, researchers begin with a generally defined theme of research and then pause periodically to review the data collected up to that point, to identify emergent themes, and to decide on new areas for exploration. This process is time consuming and, in terms of the 'publish or perish' syndrome, dangerously inefficient. The period needed to conduct and report on one well crafted qualitative study (say perhaps, three years) may be a period during which several quantitative studies could be conducted. This may be one explanation why British lecturers in adult education are more ready to conduct qualitative studies. Since, traditionally, granting of tenure after a probationary period has been much less problematic than in the United States, lecturers have not felt the urgent need to produce one or two books and twenty to thirty articles in the period leading up to the tenure decision. The re-election of Mrs. Thatcher's Conservative government in 1987 with their announced determination to end the tenure system in British universities may change this situation dramatically in the foreseeable future.

COMPARATIVE ANALYTICAL CATEGORIES IN RESEARCHING GRADUATE ADULT EDUCATION AS A SOCIO-CULTURAL PRODUCT

The preceding discussion makes it clear that differences in intellectual orientation and scale do exist between graduate adult education in the United States and Britain. Notwithstanding these differences, however, the unity of purpose shared by graduate adult education programmes in each country does provide a valid comparative base line for analysis. Programmes in each country are concerned to prepare educators for future employment as educators of adults, to assist in career shifting by those who are moving into adult education from another field, or to provide in-service professional development for those already working in the field. In each country curricula, methods, literature, research and evaluative criteria have been developed to inform these efforts. Taken together, these clusters of activities comprise a distinctive set of activities, structures and ideas which can be analysed for the extent to which each reproduces and reflects elements of the dominant culture of which it is a part.

This chapter applies five analytical categories to understanding graduate adult education as a socio-cultural product;

(1) historicity,
(2) political context,
(3) philosophical orientation,
(4) specified competencies of adult educators and
(5) paradigms of appropriate research.

The argument is made that programmes of adult education in the United States and Britain display marked differences in each of these analytical categories, and that these
differences can only be understood in terms of the values,
beliefs and structures of the host culture. They are socio-
cultural products; that is, the assumptions and criteria
governing what are considered to be appropriate curricula,
methods, evaluative procedures and research activities are
reflective of the dominant cultural values and prevailing
political ideologies of each of the two societies concerned.
Briefly stated, I argue that the pragmatic tenor, individual-
istic ethos and entrepreneurial values of American culture are
reflected directly in the organisation of programmes of graduate adult education. Conversely, I argue that the political
self-consciousness and historicity evident in British graduate
adult education programmes is a function of that society's
political culture.

The United States is a culture which values pragmatism
and in which a much greater degree of consensuality concerning political values and arrangements is evident than in
Britain. There is an overwhelming acceptance of the capitalist
ethic as the normal and natural mode of economic
arrangement, with the values of free enterprise and
entrepreneurial activity accepted almost as unchallenged
givens. Although there are policy differences between the
Democratic party's advocacy of higher levels of public
spending on public welfare programmes compared to the
Republican's much espoused aim of 'getting government off
the people's backs', these differences occur at points along a
relatively narrow continuum of ideological orientation compared
to that existing between the British Labour and Conservative
parties. Both American parties operate within a consensus
framework in which the capitalist free enterprise ethic is,
essentially, unchallenged. For both parties the capitalist mode
is viewed as the embodiment of the American approach to
economic management, reflecting the values of individuality
and entrepreneurial freedom which lie at the culture's core.
One American adult educator who deplored this consensuality
was Eduard Lindeman (1926), who condemned the manner in
which capitalist ethics had infused the practice of education.
To Lindeman, capitalism was a doubtful competitive ethic
designed to favour the crafty, strong and truculent. He
warned that the entire American educational system was
becoming determined by the need to respond to the needs of
business and industry regarding the kinds of skilled workers

required for more efficient production. As a major element in the post-World War Two reconstruction effort he urged that adult educators focus their energies on prompting adults to explore the suitability of different economic arrangements (such as socialism, capitalism and the mixed economy) for different societies (Lindeman, 1944).

As well as the virtually unchallenged acceptance of the capitalist, free enterprise ethic, there also exists in the United States a consensus on the range of ideological debate which is acceptable in the political sphere. America, alone amongst the members of the western alliance, does not contain within its political culture clearly articulated polarities of left and right wing persuasions. In European societies individuals are used to considering ideas, interpretations, policies, propaganda and party statements drawn from a broad philosophical spectrum. There are right wing, left wing and centrist groups in every political system and, at different times, ruling groups which subscribe to socialist, social democratic, capitalist and fascist ideologies. In European cultures, therefore, citizens are used to witnessing intellectual conflict between clearly articulated and opposed ideologies. Governments of different political hues rise and fall, but one enters adulthood with a perspective that there are highly differentiated alternatives available regarding how political and economic structures might be managed and altered. Adults are used at least to viewing, and sometimes to participating in, vigorous debates concerning the merits of contrasting ideologies. They are not unused to, or offended by, the possibility of debate about which of a number of ideologies are better, more humane or more efficient.

No such tradition of debate concerning a wide range of alternative political ideologies exists for the great majority of adults in the United States. There are, certainly, debates between Democratic and Republican politicians, activists and followers regarding the degree to which adjustments might be made to the free enterprise, liberal democratic system to ensure that it encourages production, economic growth and individual enterprise. The basic system, however, and its underlying assumptions are rarely criticised concerning their fundamental ethical validity and economic effectiveness. In contrast to European cultures, it is entirely possible to reach adulthood in the United States with little awareness of any alternatives to the free enterprise system, and with no understanding of, or acquaintance with, alternative political philosophies. In particular, discussion of the merits or validity of Socialist and Communist philosophies is rejected out of hand as entirely inconceivable and inappropriate to the American democratic tradition. Given the frequency with which Socialist parties have comprised ruling groups, or have been members of ruling coalitions in the governments of the chief European allies of the United States since 1945 (Britain and France), this apparently out of hand rejection of alternative political ideologies is often difficult for Europeans to understand.

In contrast to the United States, Britain is a society in which people are used to living under governments which represent clearly opposed political ideologies, even if the policy decisions of these governments have not always reflected their ideologies. Within each of the main parties themselves there is an additional level of debate between right, left and centrist groupings. Adults living within such a political culture are not as intimidated by considering widely diverging ideological interpretations as those who grow up in a culture which effectively excludes a whole ideological orientation as fundamentally evil or irrelevant, and which regards discussion of the contrasting merits of this orientation as unpatriotic and somehow undemocratic. In Britain, the workings of the economy, the distribution of power on a macro-societal level, and the way individuals perceive their life chances will frequently be understood in terms of warring class interests. When people view their society's economic and political arrangements, and perhaps their own biographies, as functions of wider competing class interests, they develop a world view very different from the consensual perspective so dominant in the United States. They become used to viewing society not as a plurality of mutually complementary subcultures in which individual initiative is rewarded with status and money, but as a perpetual arena of class and subcultural warfare. In such an arena education is frequently claimed to be a contested site in which alternative ideologies compete through institutional structures and representatives of those structures for the hearts and minds of students. Different activists claim education to be a central element in the struggle for equality, efficiency, revolution or productivity. In European cultures it is quite usual to view education as a tool of social engineering or reform. Education is assigned a pro-active function; it is seen as contributing to the creation and maintenance of a certain social order, rather than simply being required to adapt to the requirements and demands of free market forces.

Two cautions need to be issued at this point in the discussion. The first concerns the danger of invalid generalisability, always a central concern in any attempt at comparative educational analysis. In making cross-cultural comparisons it is all to easy to propose as empirically verifiable generalisations what are really intuitive insights. This is not to denigrate the value of intuitive insights, merely to caution against too ready an acceptance of generalisations concerning whole cultures, systems or ideologies. Secondly, in comparative analyses of educational systems it is possible to erect false, mutually exclusive dichotomies in which each contrasting system is represented as being comprised of elements found only in that particular system. In terms of the present analysis, the differing orientations evident in each of the six developed categories should not be interpreted as verdicts that all programmes in each country exhibit only the characteristics ascribed to them in each category. For example, there are programmes in the United States which exhibit some elements of what will be presented as essentially British preoccupations and practices, in particular the concern for placing adult education within the context of wider movements for social change. Many American adult educators have taken Paulo Freire's ideas as the starting point for an analysis of the liberatory function of adult education (Finlay and Faith, 1979; Monette, 1979; Minkler and Cox, 1980; Ewert, 1982; Knott, 1983; Heaney, 1984; Noble, 1983). The Highlander Folk School (Adams, 1975) represents a tradition of adult education in the context of social movements such as the civil rights and labour union movements in the United States. In the wider educational context, American writers such as Kozol (1985), Bowles and Gintis (1976, 1986), Gioroux (1983), Aronowitz and Girouz (1985), Apple (1981, 1982) and Livingstone (1987) have studied how American schools are sites for contesting ideologies. The converse of this caution also holds true. There are many British adult educators who hold the consensual viewpoint which I am arguing is quintessentially American, and who see no merit in discussing the merits of left wing political philosophies since, to them, it is self-evident that these philosophies are devoid of any merit. However, it is my contention that the differences do outweigh the similarities both in number and depth, and that valid comparisons and contrasts can be made between the two countries concerned, provided that they are always informed by a certain scepticism and concern to guard against over-statement and overgeneralisation.

CATEGORY (1) HISTORICITY

The term 'historicity' describes people's awareness of how their individual actions are affected by, and located within, past actions, ideas and developed structures. Those who possess this awareness place their lives, the social structures within which those lives are embedded and the belief systems informing them in a historical context. People with this out-look understand the present in terms of the past. They view contemporary events as being partially determined by pre-vious events, rather than as a-historical happenings. In British university departments of adult education, lecturers and graduate students exhibit a much greater degree of historicity than is the case in the United States. To American researchers, British academics seem to be preoccupied with investigating the historical origins of the development of adult education. Typical of this view is Boshier's (1977) comment that British adult educators display a "somewhat compulsive penchant for historical research" (p. 232).

To what extent is this stereotype of British adult education accurate? In analyses and bibliographies of research undertaken in Britain by Charnley (1974, 1984), Kelly (1974), Legge (1977), Mee (1978), Thomas (1984) and Thomas and Davies (1984) historical research is certainly a major category. Comparative analyses by Guy (1976) and Brookfield (1982) record that students and faculty in British university departments of adult education conduct research into the history of adult education much more frequently than to their American counterparts. In terms of historiography, Kelly's A History of Adult Education in Great Britain (1970) is probably the single best known piece of research in the field. A content analysis of the journal Studies in the Education of Adults (formerly Studies in Adult Education) reveals the pre-eminence of historical research. In the last few years papers by Field (1980), Marriott (1981), Marks (1982), Fieldhouse (1983, 1985), and McIllroy (1985) have been published in the journal dealing with topics such as 19th century views on workers' education, ideology in English adult education teaching from 1925 to 1950, unemployment and adult education in the 1930's, the Responsible Body tradition, and the Trade Union Congress education scheme from 1929 to 1980.

This academic concern with researching the historical dimensions of the field is reflected in the relative centrality (compared to the United States) afforded to historical matters in graduate adult education programmes in Britain. It is hard to imagine students leaving diploma, master's or doctoral degree programmes without some basic awareness of the history and traditions of the field of adult education. Bibliographies such as those of Charnley (1974), Legge (1977) and Thomas and Davies (1984) record the frequency with which historical themes and subjects form the focus of dissertations and theses within graduate programmes. Exposure to the history of the field means that students in these programmes are aware of the connections between workers' education, the development of the labour movement, and the growth of adult education provision. In particular, the political context within which the adult education movement was framed in Britain is emphasised. Students exploring this context can hardly fail to speculate on the political dimensions of adult education. In the most recent bibliography of adult education research, (Thomas and Davies, 1984) the category of 'History and Organisation of Adult Education' has by far the largest number of research projects listed.

It is intersting to note, however, that according to the 1986 Guide to University Courses for Adult Education in the United Kingdom and Eire (SCUTREA, 1986) courses of study in the history of adult education are mentioned less frequently, and with less emphasis as mandatory components of the curriculm than was the case in the previously published SCUTREA guide of 1983. Analysis of this 1986 guide also reveals a movement toward adopting some of the curricular concerns (and even course titles) of American graduate programmes. There is some ground to believe that the greater exchange of research perspectives occasioned by recent academic exchanges between American and British adult educators is having some real influence on the field. In the last three years there have been exchanges between groups of American and British professors and lecturers who have visited the chief research conferences (AERC and SCUTREA) of each other's countries. A register of the research interests of researchers and academics in each country has been published and distributed in both countries. A British and North American Network for Adult Education (BANANAE) is in place, and 1988 saw the first ever jointly sponsored AERC - SCUTREA conference held at the University of Leeds in England. In the United States, signs of a recent revival of interest in the historical foundations of the field can be seen in the recently created newsletter and journal titled Historical Foundations of Adult Education: A Bulletin of Research and Information which grew out of a series of AERC pre-conferences on historical aspects of adult education research. At the main AERC conference itself, there has been a marked increase in historical research papers such as those of Craver (1984), Hellyer and Schied (1984), Omolewa (1984), Rockhill (1984), Sisco (1985), Boshier (1985), Gainey (1986), Hellyer (1986), Wallace (1986), Hugo (1987), and Nel (1987). There has also been a revived interest in the works of Eduard Lindeman (Brookfield, 1987; Stewart, 1987).

Notwithstanding the greater exchange of personnel and increase in transatlantic discussion between academics and researchers in adult education, it is still true to say that the majority of professors and graduate students of adult education in the United States do not regard understanding the historical foundations of the field to be a major priority. Historical analyses of the development of adult education are rarely undertaken, either as major scholarship efforts by established professors, or for master's or doctoral dissertations. In the years between Brunner's (1959) review of research and Grabowski's (1980) analysis of Trends in Graduate Research, the emphasis has remained firmly on applied empirical studies. In the 1980 series of handbooks of adult education in the United States issued by the American Association for Adult and Continuing Education, none of the ten volumes published was concerned with tracing the history of the field. The most widely used foundations text of adult education (Darkenwald and Merriam, 1982) omits any discussion of historical foundations of adult education in the

United States. The analyses of adult education research in the United States undertaken by De Crow (1969), Copeland and Grabowski (1971), Hiemstra (1976) and Long (1983) note that "compared with the British condition, the historical dimensions of adult education in the United States are impoverished" (Long, 1983, p.264). The a-historical nature of American graduate adult education was well demonstrated by a study conducted by Day and McDermott (1980) at a large midwestern university. When graduate students in adult education were asked about significant adult education texts which had appeared over the last seventy years such as the 1919 Report, The Meaning of Adult Education (Lindeman, 1926), Ten Years of Adult Education (Cartwright, 1935), Adult Education (Bryson, 1936), Adult Education in Action (Ely, 1936) and Adult Education in a Free Society (Blakely, 1958) these students appeared to be generally ignorant of the existence or content of these works. They were also unfamiliar with general histories of the field such as those of Grattan (1965) and Knowles (1977). In a follow up survey the authors sent their original questionnaire to 37 additional graduate adult education programmes in the United States, and found this lack of historicity among graduate students to be confirmed.

CATEGORY (2) POLITICAL CONTEXT

This category refers to the extent to which lecturers, professors and graduate students self-consciously place the practice of adult education within a political framework. Do they study the organisation and curricula of programmes for the ways in which these reflect the values of dominant groups within society? Are they aware of the connections between learning, consciousness change and political action? Do they analyse participation patterns in adult education for the extent to which classes are disproportionately composed chiefly of learners drawn from certain limited socio-economic groups? Do they view the proper practice of adult education as being that of challenging the status quo, of revealing to learners the structural inequities in their societies, and of prompting the consideration of alternatives to the dominant ideology? Do they see the practice of adult education as centrally located wtihin movements for social, political and economic change?

These questions are viewed very differently, if indeed they are raised at all, in graduate adult education programmes in Britain and America. In Britain, adult education is much more likely to be seen as the educational arm of some movement for social reform. Practice in the field is seen as having some important origins in the growth of the labour movement. Standard histories of British adult education such as those by Harrison (1961) and Kelly (1970) devote a considerable amount of space to discussing the impetus given to the development of adult education through its connection to political movements such as the Labour Party, trade unions, working men's colleges, the Chartists, and the Workers' Educational Association. This political tradition is reflected well in recent works by Thompson (1980, 1983), Lovett (1975, 1983, 1988), Taylor, Rockhill and Fieldhouse (1985), Thomas (1982), Youngman (1985), Evans (1987), Cowburn (1986), Armstrong (1988), and Ward and Taylor (1986). In these analyses adult education exhibits a clearly defined political dimension. Adult educators are charged with assisting adults to take control over their personal and political worlds, and to view their own changes in consciousness as occasioned by, and inextricably linked to, collective action. The concepts of liberation, conscientisation and empowerment are placed at the heart of good practice in adult education and these analyses draw strongly on the work of Gramsci and Freire.

In the United States the connection between adult education and political change is, on the whole, ignored, at least if we take the professional and scholarly literature of the field to be at all representative of practice. The ten volume 1980 handbook of adult education series did not address directly how adult educators could work within the context of existing political movements to advance the interests and conditions of oppressed groups. In the volume in the series in which one might have expected this perspective to be explicitly dealt with - that on Serving Personal and Community Needs through Adult Education (Boone, Shearon, White and Associates, 1980) - no reference can be found to this approach. This absence of attempts to analyse and practice adult education within a political context is difficult to understand given that until the Second World War it was placed directly in the mainstream of the American adult education movement. Rockhill (1985) maintains that "the systematic denial of class in the USA" (p. 187) by dominant groups within the culture represents an exclusion of socialist and radical perspectives from American adult education since the 1930's and that this denial has prevented the development of a separate working class adult education movement. According to her analysis socialism "has been rendered invisible" and "the liberal tradition in adult education has contributed above all else to the silencing of socialism" (p. 207) within American adult education. To Rockhill "working class education was delegitimated by the newly emergent profession of adult education. Liberal educational values as they came to be institutionalised in university adult education, provided the basis for the annihilation of working class education as an approach to the education of workers" (p. 208).

In terms of the history of ideas in the field, it is interesting to note that Eduard Lindeman, arguably the single most influential figure in the intellectual development of adult education in the United States, was villified after World War Two for his supposedly socialist and communist leanings. And yet today Lindeman is placed firmly in the progressive educational tradition (Elias and Merriam, 1980) rather than in any radical tradition and is known by most graduate students and professors only through his first book on The Meaning of Adult Education (1926), which is chiefly concerned with methodological and conceptual aspects of adult education rather than with its social and political impact. Through Knowles's (1980, 1984) popularisation of certain of Lindeman's ideas, his chief contribution is seen as being in the areas of experiential learning and teaching methods. As recent works (Brookfield, 1987; Steward, 1987) have made clear, however, Lindeman's chief concern throughout his life was with the ways in which adult education could contribute to the creation and maintenance of democracy. To Lindeman, adult education was irrevocably and undeniably a political activity. At one point he wrote that "every social action group should at the same time be an adult education group, and I go even so far as to believe that all successful adult education groups sooner or later become social action groups" (Lindeman, 1944, p. 11). The contemporary view which holds Lindeman to be basically a useful source on participatory learning methods is one of the most serious intellectual misunderstandings current within American adult education.

Two other much neglected politically oriented traditions in American adult education deserve mention. The first of these is the Highlander Folk School and Research Centre (Adams, 1975; Kennedy, 1981) which since the 1930's has trained community activists to learn from their own, and others', experiences of political involvement. The involvement of Highlander staff in political movements such as the development of labour unions, civil rights campaigns, and land ownership reform represents an important counterpoint to the a-political element in the American adult education tradition which currently prevails in research and practice within the field. The second tradition is that of the American labour education movement. Apart from isolated papers such as those by Hellyer and Schied (1984) and Hellyer (1986) it is as if, to American scholars of adult education, the labour education movement in the earlier part of this century never existed. Union education programmes and union-management collaborations (such as those between the UAW and Chrysler or Ford corporations) certainly exist, but their activities rarely form the focus of adult education research.

CATEGORY (3) PHILOSOPHICAL ORIENTATION

The absence of a philosophical dimension from discussions

which are of central concern to American graduate students, professors, researchers and theorists in adult education is a surprising connundrum. It is a connundrum because discussion of this sort has in the past been central to the field. Currently, however, the research and professional literature is framed within the context of applications of technique. The habit of debating vigorously alternative philosophical perspectives on the nature and proper purposes of American adult education seems to have been lost. The 1980 handbook on adult education series contained no volume devoted to charting a philosophical mission for the field. In one of the volumes (Kreitlow, 1981) some controverisal issues were aired and contrasting positions stated in a dialectical fashion. Nowhere, however, was there a sustained analysis of the philosophical rationale which should underly adult education, an explicit attempt to state any fundamental purposes for adult education, or an elaboration of the criteria by which we might judge whether or not these purposes were being realised. Yet as recently as the 1950's a ferment of philosophical discourse bubbled within the pages of the two chief American adult education journals of the time; Adult Education and Adult Leadership. Concurrent with the founding in 1953 of the Adult Education Association of the United States (a successor to the American Association for Adult Education and a precursor to the American Association for Adult and Continuing Education), the Adult Education journal published accounts of a national debate conducted at the level of living room discussion groups on the central purposes of the proposed new association. One outcome of this discussion was the publication of seven principles which were agreed on as guiding the American adult education movement (Pell, 1952). Throughout the 1950's and 1960's the Adult Leadership journal featured a column in each issue titled 'Accent on Social Philosophy' in which different individuals explored the social relevance of adult education and addressed the kinds of responses adult educators should make to the political issues of the times. The AEA/USA 'Committee on Social Philosophy and Direction Finding' was the most influential committee among the range of different committees existing within the organisation in these decades, and it was not uncommon for discussion on the fundamental philosophical purposes of the field to be public and significant.

With the appearance in 1964 of the Commission of Professors of Adult Education first important professional publication - Adult Education: Outlines of An Emerging Field of University Study (Jensen, Liveright and Hallenbeck, 1964) - the movement toward greater professionalism and academic respectability for the field of adult education gained momentum. Concurrent with the attempt to define the distinguishing characteristics of adult education as a field of practice (briefly, to establish andragogy as the quintessential adult educational mode) and to discover the unique features of adult learning (briefly, to claim that adult learners are innately self-directed) that have formed the basis of most discussion in American adult education in the last quarter of a century, has been a decrease in philosophical debate regarding central purposes and rationales for the field, particularly politically contentious ones. It is as if the search for academic respectability and the quest for professional identity has effectively de-politicised the field. We have concluded that being seen to engage in public debate about fundamental philosophical questions and issues regarding the proper practice of adult education is unseemly and unprofessional. The search for respectability and professionalism has, in my view, removed much of the politically and socially motivated fire and passion from debate in the field. There is a very real danger of an academic orthodoxy prevailing in adult education which states, briefly, that:

(1) adults are self-directed learners,
(2) andragogical methods are the uniquely adult forms of teaching and facilitation, and
(3) adult educators should attempt to meet the felt needs of their learners as their first and overwhelming priority.

This service-oriented rationale is, in effect, an 'espoused theory' of adult education, and while its exclusionary nature has done much to grant a common identity to practitioners from a very diverse range of adult educational settings, it has also effectively removed from the arena of adult educational discourse philosophical debate concerning essential political and social purposes for the field. Monette, (1977, 1979) has offered some trenchant criticisms of this service oriented orthodoxy. The felt needs rationale appears admirably democratic, humanistic and learner-centred, yet it is one which removes from educators the need to make contentious judgments concerning the merits of alternative curricular offerings. The consummate professional, according to this rationale, is one who accurately assesses what adults want in educational programmes and who then successfully mounts course, workshops, seminars and other offerings which satisfy these expressed needs. The criteria by which successful adult education is determined which are implicit in this rationale are easily observable, external and unequivocal. They are the numbers of adults attending courses, the satisfaction they express with their participation, and the revenue they generate.

According to this rationale the responsibility for determining content and curricular direction rests largely with the learner. The educator's role becomes that of facilitating learners' acquiring those skills or that knowledge which learners themselves have specified. A good adult educator is seen as one who gives adults what they say they want, who markets programmes which leave learners satisfied, and who generates revenue for the sponsoring agency. One implication arising out of the adoption of this rationale is that educational activities in which learners are challenged, in which their existing assumptions and prejudices are called into question, and in which they are forced to confront aspects of their values and actions they would prefer not to examine, are likely to be avoided. Such activities are likely to be resisted because of the pain and anxiety accompanying many efforts at self-scrutiny. In seeking to offer programmes which leave participants feeling satisfied and pleased with the outcomes, the danger is that learners will never be provoked or challenged for fear of their feeling displeased and not returning with their enrolment monies. A second implication arising from the adoption of this rationale is that any discussion of the merit or worthwhileness of different curricula becomes meaningless and irrelevant. If the over-riding purpose is to attract large numbers of learners to programmes then 'good' curricula for adult education become, to all intents and purposes, those which meet learners declared wants. We can see, then, that behind the apparent democratic learner-centredness of the felt needs rationale lurks a wholly consumerist justification for how good practice in adult education should be conceived. With only occasional exceptions (Beder, 1987; Cameron, 1987) debates on the philosophical purposes of adult education will probably be seen by most professional adult educators as immature reflections of the last vestiges of amateurism in the field and as peripheral to the central task of creating a professional identity.

In British programmes of graduate adult education, however, such a debate still exists in a very active way. Because the striving for professional identity and academic credibility has not been anything like as strong in Britain, as in the United States (British professors frequently combine their academic role with a role as programme developer in extra-mural programmes or continuing education divisions), there has been no sense of embarrassment about admitting in public to very distinctively different philosophical orientations within the field. There are debates concerning the social role of adult education (Joyce, 1973; Paterson, 1973), calls to put politics on the agenda of the field (Simey, 1978), and calls for adult educators to attack current priorities in government policy (1974). Against the radical adult education orientation evident in works such as Thompson (1980, 1983), Armstrong (1988), Lovett (1975, 1988), Cowburn (1986), Thomas (1982), Youngman (1986), Evans (1987), and Ward and Taylor (1986) there is a vigourously argued liberal tradition which holds that the proper purpose of adult education is the development of personhood. In this tradition the emphasis is placed on developing individual qualities of intellectual discrimination, aesthetic appreciation and moral reasoning, none of which activities are seen as necessarily linked to adult education for social action (Wiltshire, 1976; Paterson, 1979, 1987; Lawson, 1979, 1982, 1985). It is not unusual, then, for graduate students in British university departments of adult education to be asked to consider contrasting philosophical orientations within their academic studies. There is much less of a consensus, or a clearly discernible espoused theory, about what comprises adult education. Instead, there are two broadly articulated competing paradigms, representing the radical and liberal traditions in British adult education. Graduate students are exposed to both these traditions and may well try to locate their own beliefs and practice within them. Whilst adherents and advocates for each of these traditions may believe the other's ideas to be fundamentally flawed, they value the debate generated by this polarity of philosophical orientation. A central concern of courses within graduate adult education programmes becomes that of identifying what ought to be the proper purposes of adult education, whether these are seen as the development of discriminatory capacities appropriate to a liberally educated adult, or as working in an adult educational capacity with political action movements.

CATEGORY (4) SPECIFIED PROFICIENCIES OF ADULT EDUCATORS

In the United Kingdom, a body of research is gradually accumulating on the content, methods and organisation of training for adult educators (Elsdon, 1975, 1984; Legge, 1981; Charnley, Osborn and Withnall, 1982; Graham, Daines, Sullivan, Harris and Baum, 1982; Magee and Alexander, 1986; Usher, 1987). Comparing those analyses conducted in the United States, we find identified a body of skills, knowledge and personal attributes which represents what the authors and respondents deem to be the desirable characteristics of effective adult educators. Aspiring adult educators are said to benefit from a familiarity with a wide range of skills and knowledge including techniques of needs assessment, objectives writing and setting, instructional design, instructional management, budgeting, marketing, counselling and evaluation. The paradigm from which this armoury of necessary proficiencies is drawn is that of a continuing education programmer in non-credit (that is, non-vocational) adult education. Despite significant discrepancies between the categories of employment open to graduates of university adult education programmes and the employment paradigm informing the organisation, methods and curricula of these programmes (Bruce, Maxwell and Galvin, 1986), the image of the non-credit continuing education programmer is the one which is uppermost in the minds of those responsible for developing graduate programmes. Graduate students in adult education in the United States typically take courses in programme planning and development (including evaluation of adult education programmes), design and management of instruction, organisation and administration of adult education, adult learning, and a survey or foundations course. Courses concerned with the development of these programmatic, instructional and administrative skills are the staple diet of the graduate adult education curriculum. In certification or comprehensive examinations, in dissertations and theses, and in their course work, American graduate students are expected to acquire a familiarity with techniques of needs assessments, models of programme planning, instructional design and evaluative procedures far beyond that typically required of students in British graduate programmes. The literature base for this acquisition of techniques is comprised of works such as those by Houle (1972), Davis (1974), Lauffer (1977), Farlow (1979), Langerman and Smith (1979), Knowles (1980), Knox and Associates (1980), Pennington (1980), Boyle (1981), Klevins (1982), Strother and Klus (1982), Deshler (1984) and Beder (1986). Apart from the works by Knowles and Houle, very few graduate students in British university departments would know of these books and they would not typically appear on reading lists distributed for diploma, masters or doctoral degree courses. The consummate adult educator, according to the paradigm underlying current provision in American graduate adult education, is one who exhibits a mastery of skills of needs assessment, objectives setting, programme development and evaluation, instructional design and management, and the organisation and administration of adult education programmes. Although courses designed to inculcate or refine these programme developmental, administrative and instructional skills would be offered along with survey or foundations courses, these latter courses would frequently be seen as preliminaries. A foundations course examining the historical, philosophical and sociological foundations of the field would be conceived as an introductory, ground clearing exercise to be undertaken before beginning the 'real' business of helping students become better administrators and programme developers.

Courses, assignments, theses, literature and research concerning techniques of needs assessments, programme development, budgeting, marketing and evaluation are most emphatically not the staple diet of graduate adult education in British universities. Within British departments, it is not uncommon for students to take separate courses on the history, philosophy and sociology of adult education. Whereas in the United States, these areas of scholarly concern would be compressed into one overview course to do with surveying the foundational elements of the field, in Britain they would more likely be felt to be deserving of separate courses. The paradigm within which the capable or competent adult educator is conceived within Britain is, therefore, in marked contrast to that evident within the United States. Instead of conceiving of a professional as one acquainted with, and skilled in, the application of a battery of programme developmental, instructional and organisational skills, the British paradigm of graduate adult education holds that capable and trained professionals are those who can place the organisation and functioning of adult education within some broader historical and sociological context, and who can develop a philosophical rationale which informs their practice. Graduates of British diploma, master's and doctoral programmes are much more likely to exhibit certain intellectual dispositions than would be the case with their American counterparts. They will be more aware of the historical antecedents to current organisation, practice and values in the field. They will have considered the extent to which adult education programmes function to enhance social mobility, to further social transformation, or to support existing economic and ideological structures. They will be able to articulate an explicit philosophical rationale which underlies their practice as educators of adults. They will be familiar with a range of contrasting ideological positions regarding the proper philosophical purposes of adult education. The paradigm of the professionally prepared practitioner in British university departments of adult education is one which is likely to emphasise the educator's awareness of the historical, sociological and philosophical contexts within which practice occurs, rather than the command of a range of specific practical techniques.

CATEGORY (5) PARADIGMS OF APPROPRIATE RESEARCH

British adult education researchers, as we have already seen, are usually characterised by their American counterparts as being interested primarily in philosophical and historical concerns which are explored through qualitative modes of enquiry. Their work is viewed as being characterised by a certain literary grace and an endearing, if misguided, amateurism. Conversely, British adult educators tend to view American researchers as preoccupied with quantitative measurement to the unfortunate exclusion of any appreciation of the subtleties and nuances of human behaviour. An earlier paper has found these stereotypes to be rooted in reality so that "the virtues which practising researchers in the two countries hold dear are regarded as unfortunate and misguided aberrations by their transatlantic counterparts" (Brookfield, 1982, p. 165). The data base for reviewing the research activities of professors, students and lecturers in graduate programmes of adult education is notoriously difficult to locate. For the purposes of this comparative analysis five sources of data have been used;

(1) the UNESCO directory of graduate programmes which lists the major areas of research conducted within each graduate programme involving faculty and students,

(2) reviews of research such as those conducted by Brunner (1959), De Crow (1969), Copeland and Grabowski (1969), Hiemstra (1976), Dickinson and Rusnell (1971), Long and Agyekum (1984), Long (1977, 1982), Sork (1979), Grabowski (1980), Charnley (1984) and Allcorn (1985),

(3) registers of completed research such as those compiled by Charnley (1974), Kelly (1974), Legge (1977), Mee (1978) and Thomas and Davies (1982),

(4) comparative analyses such as those conducted by Guy (1976) and Brookfield (1982),

(5) general statements on research by graduate faculty such as those issued by Knowles (1972), Houle (1961), Griffith (1979), Kidd (1981), Rubenson (1982) and Thomas (1984) and

(6) content analyses of the proceedings of the chief annual research conferences in Britain (SCUTREA) and American (AERC) and of the two chief journals reporting research in adult education in the two countries (Studies in the Education of Adults and Adult Education Quarterly, respectively). The series of twelve monographs on reviews of research published by the British National Institute of Adult Continuing Education (NIACE) has been excluded from this analysis since they are focused reviews of pre-selected research topics, rather than being overall reviews of the major research activities of scholars in the field as identified by inductive analysis.

Four trends are discernible from an analyses of the six data bases identified above. Firstly, there is a remarkable congruence of agreements between American professors and British lecturers in university departments of adult education regarding the acceptance of a wide range of research methodologies. Indeed, a reading of general statements on appropriate research approaches by researchers in both countries reveals no real difference in the principle of methodological triangulation. In terms of espoused theories of adult education research, there are no significant differences between the pronouncements of major researchers in Britain and the United States. Contrary to what many Britons might believe,

American adult education researchers are ready to admit the validity of qualitative, ethnographic and naturalistic approaches to research. Indeed, barely a year passes when the annual Adult Education Research Conference (AERC) does not hold a symposium on qualitative research.

Secondly, a clear division is evident in the two countries in terms of research methods most frequently adopted in the actual conduct of research. Despite the acknowledgment of the validity of qualitative approaches on the part of American researchers, American journals and research conferences still favour articles and papers which can be located within either the experimental design paradigm or the survey research paradigm. Research is frequently reported in terms which require a good knowledge of statistical techniques of analysis; something which is much less frequently found in British graduate students than in American students, probably because American graduate students are generally required to take courses in statistical analysis as part of their graduate programmes. It is also the case that American professors who conduct research primarily of a qualitative nature run real risks of being denied tenure and promotion and face many more entrenched prejudices in terms of their being taken seriously as intellectually credible researchers. They may also face real difficulties in convincing other faculty members from across their institutions that qualitative dissertations and theses undertaken by graduate students are as valid as ones using experimental or statistical approaches. In the face of such strong biases, professors and graduate students may well make a political decision not to fight the prevailing institutional culture, and to conduct research which fits much more clearly into identifiable and acceptable research paradigms. It is interesting to note that in Britain precisely the converse view probably holds sway. The institutional culture of British university departments of adult education holds that statistical analyses and survey questionnaire studies are probably camouflage for the researcher's lack of analytical capacities. Statistical research is seen as pure 'number crunching' and as having little to do with understanding and interpreting the real nature of educational interactions. Statistical significance is frequently scorned as a concept when compared to judgments of significance made from the viewpoint of the meanings that actions have for their agents. Survey questionnaire studies are seen as the last refuge of the intellectually incapable (Pilsworth and Ruddock, 1975). In terms which are precisely the opposite of those in American adult educational research, it may be very hard for British researchers to gain academic credibility unless they exhibit some proficiency in qualitative modes of analysis. In American universities the assumption is that statistical analyses, survey questionnaires and experimental designs are the 'natural' mode of research, and that research which departs from these three approaches needs an unusually strong justification for it to be taken seriously. In British universities the converse is much more likely to be the case. It is qualitative research which is the taken for granted norm and quantitative, survey and experimental research which requires additional justification.

Thirdly, certain emphases are evident in the substantive themes of research most frequently conducted in the two countries. The chief categories of research conducted in American graduate programmes are the following:

(1) the psychology of adult learning
(2) adult basic education
(3) instructional processes
(4) adult education personnel
(5) continuing professional, supervisory and management education
(6) self-directed learning
(7) participation in adult education, and
(8) programme development and evaluation.

In Britain the data base is much more restricted than that in the United States. However, from the information available it appears that the most common form of research is the qualitative case study of adult education programmes in which the development of various forms of adult education provision is documented. This is followed by six other important categories:

(1) community education and community development
(2) clientele analyses
(3) instructional and training methods
(4) adult education policy
(5) adult learning, and
(6) the history of adult education.

Fourthly, there are indications that the central themes in British adult education research are moving closer to those more traditionally known as 'American'. This may be connected to the ravaging of British higher education in the last ten years and the attempt to make the research activities of British universities more connected to the operations of business and industry. This is a connection which is seen as natural and inevitable by most American academics, so that questions concerning its advisability are rarely raised. But there does seem to be a real increase in the interest of British adult education researchers in the activities of their American counterparts. There have been many more exchanges of faculty and researchers in recent years than has ever before been the case. There is a British and North American Network for Adult Education in place. A major

British academic publisher, Croom Helm, has just started a series of books under the title of 'Theory and Practice of Adult Education in North America' (of which this volume is a part), which will make current research, analysis and practice in the United States much more accessible to British researchers and practitioners than has previously been the case. 1988 saw the first jointly sponsored AERC - SCUTREA conference at the University of Leeds.

There are also in existence various Postgraduate Certificates in the Education of Adults either validated by the Council for National Academic Awards (CNAA) or run by universities, and students on these courses are eligible for mandatory grant awards from the Department of Education and Science. The Advisory Committee on the Supply and Education of Teachers (ACSET) offers preparatory as well as in-service training to teachers of adults. The nursing profession requires a qualification in adult or further education of its nurse educators. The Advisory Council for Adult and Continuing Education (ACACE) report on Continuing Education: From Policies to Practice used a definition that would not appear out of place in most American texts on adult education:

> "we do not think that it is useful to draw artificial boundaries between education and training, between vocational and general education, or between formal and informal systems of provision. We include systematic learning wherever it takes place: in libraries, in the workplace, at home, in community groups and in educational institutions" (ACACE, 1982, p. 2).

In his Chairman's address to the 1984 SCUTREA conference Thomas (1984) declared that "there can be no doubt that the standard and range of publication has improved enormously in the last ten years" (p. 76), and the categories of research included in this expanded range are much closer to those evident in the United States than was formerly the case. For example, the steering committee for the 12 volume NIACE series on reviews of research in adult education decided that a monograph on historical research would not be included because "university adult education departments are well-stocked with such volumes and relevant bibliographies, so there is little difficulty in tracing and obtaining such work" (Charnley, 1984, p. 62). The twelve reviews of research published (on mature students, open learning and distance education, the voluntary field, information guidance and counselling, the disadvantaged, the elderly, training adult tutors, numeracy, adult education and unemployment, the economics of adult and continuing education, the psychology of adult learning and development, and adult education and the local community) are on themes familiar to American researchers and practitioners. It is not inconceivable that one important next stage in an American-British dialogue and exchange on adult education research might be some jointly organised and conducted research projects, in which a common research design is applied to investigating the same process or substantive theme in settings within the two countries. Publication outlets certainly exist for any such research which might be conducted. The Kellog Foundation has funded the publication of a transatlantic collection of papers on the theme of Dialogue on issues of Lifelong Learning in a Democratic Society (Conti and Fellenz, 1985) and a ready made forum for further publications exists in the International Journal of Lifelong Education which was created in 1982 as a forum "within which the principles and practices of lifelong education may be debated in both an international and an academic context" (from the editors' introduction to the first issue of the journal).

CONCLUSION

There will be many researchers, academics and practitioners of adult education in Britain and America who do not recognise themselves, or their programmes, within the five analytical categories discussed in the foregoing analysis. Individual adult educators will undoubtedly be able to cite instances from their own research and practice activities, and those of their colleagues, which contradict the typologies and generalisations made. The central argument remains, however, intact. Programmes of graduate study in adult education can only be understood from within their socio-cultural contexts. The curriculum, practice, literature and organisation of these programmes are reflective of certain dominant aspects of the wider culture. Programmes are not isolated psycho-social dramas comprising the interactions of person or situation specific actions, expectations and preferences. There is a fruitful area of research waiting for those analysts who wish to understand the manner in which adult education is a socio-cultural product, reflective of, and sustaining to, wider structures, dominant values and prevailing ideologies.

REFERENCES

Adams, F., 1975, "Unearthing Seeds of Fire," Winston-Salem; John F. Blair Publishers.

Adams, J. T., 1944, "Frontiers of American Culture: A Study of Adult Education in a Democracy," Scribner's Sons; New York.

Advisory Council for Adult and Continuing Education, (1982), "Continuing Education: From Policies to Practice,"

Leicester; Advisory Council for Adult and Continuing Education.

Adams, J. T., 1944, "Frontiers of American Culture: A Study of Adult Education in a Democracy," Scribner's Sons; New York.

Allcorn, S., 1985, The knowledge gap of adult education, Lifelong Learning, 8 (5), 12-16.

Apple, M. W., (1981), "Ideology and Curriculum," Routledge and Kegan Paul; London.

Apple, M. W., 1982), "Education and Power," Routledge and Kegan Paul; London.

Apps, J. A., (1973), Toward a broader definition of research, Adult Education, 23 (4) 59-64.

Armstrong, P. F., 1988, "Adult Education and Socialism, " Croom Helm; London.

Aronowitz, S., and Giroux, H. A., 1985, "Education Under Siege: The Conservative, Liberal and Radical Debate Over Schooling," Bergin and Garvey; South Hadley, Massachussetts.

Beder, H., ed., 1986, "Marketing Continuing Education," Jossey-Bass, San Francisco.

Beder, H., 1987, Dominant paradigms, adult education and social justice, Adult Education Quarterly, 37 (2) 105-113.

Bernstein, B. (1977), "Class, Codes and Control. Vol. 3: Towards a Theory of Educational Transmission," Routledge and Kegan Paul; London.

Blakely, R. J., 1958, "Adult Education in a Free Society," Guardian Bird Publications, Toronto.

Boone, E. J., Shearon, R. W., White, E. E., and Associates, 1980, "Serving Personal and Community Needs Through Adult Education," Jossey-Bass; San Francisco.

Boshier, R., 1977, Review of Register of Research in Progress, (C.D. Legge), Adult Education, 27(4) 231-232.

Boshier, R., 1985, Revolting soldiers: the origins of education in the armies in world war one, Adult Education Research Conference Proceedings, No. 26, Arizona State University; Tempe, Arizona.

Bourdieu, P., and Passerson, J., 1977, "Reproduction in Education, Society and Culture," Sage; Beverly Hills.

Bowles, S., and Gintis, H., 1976, "Schooling in Capitalist America," Basic Books; New York.

Bowles, S., and Gintis, H., 1986, "Democracy and Capitalism," Basic Books; New York.

Boyle, P. G., 1981, "Planning Better Programmes," McGraw Hill, New York.

Brookfield, S. D., 1982, Adult education research: A comparison of North American and British Theory and Practice, International Journal of Lifelong Education, 1 (2), 157-167.

Brookfield, S. D., ed., 1985a, "Self-Directed Learning: From Theory to Practice," Jossey-Bass; San Francisco.

Brookfield, S. D., 1985b, Training educators of adults: A comparative analysis of graduate adult education in the Unites States and Great Britain, International Journal of Lifelong Education, 4 (4), 295-318.

Brookfield, S. D., 1986, Review of University Adult Education in England and Wales, Studies in the Education of Adults, 18 (1), 52-54.

Brookfield, S. D., 1987, "Learning Democracy: Eduard Lindeman on Adult Education and Social Change," Croom Helm; London.

Bruce, R., Maxwell, D., and Galvin, P., 1986, Graduate study and the practice of adult education: A problem of congruence, Lifelong Learning, 10 (3), 4-7, 20.

Brunner, E., 1959, "An Overview of Adult Education Research," Adult Education Association of America; Chicago.

Bryson, L., 1936, "Adult Education," American Book Company; New York.

Cameron, C., 1987, Adult Education as a Force Toward Social Equity, Adult Education Quarterly, 37 (3), 173-177.

Cartwright, M. A., 1935, "Ten Years of Adult Education," The Macmillan Company; New York.

Charnley, A. H., 1974, "Research in Adult Education in the British Isles," National Institute of Adult Continuing Education; Leicester.

Charnley, A., 1984, Research and research documentation in adult education 1974-1984: A personal view, Studies in Adult Education, 16, 58-69.

Charnley, A. H., Osborn, M., and Withnall, A., 1982, "Training the Educators of Adults, "National Institute of Adult Continuing Education; Leicester.

Conti, G. J., and Fellenz, R. A., 1985, "Dialogue on Issues of Lifelong Learning in a Democratic Society," Texas A. and M. University; College Station, Texas.

Copeland, H. G., and Grabowski, S. M., 1971, Research and Investigation in the United States, Convergence, 4 (4), 23-32.

Corrigan, P., 1979, "Schooling the Smash Street Kids," Macmillan Press; London.

Cowburn, W., 1986, "Class, Ideology and Adult Education," Croom Helm; London.

Craver, S. M. 1984, Social and economic attitudes in the education of industrial workers in Richmond, Virginia, 1884 to 1904, Adult Education Research Conference Proceedings, No. 25, North Carolina State University; Raleigh.

Darkenwald, G., and Merriam, S. B., 1982, "Adult Education: Foundations of Practice," Harper and Row; New York.

Davis, L. N., 1974, "Planning, Conducting, Evaluating Workshops," Learning Concepts Ltd; Austin, Texas.

Day, M., and McDermott, W., 1980, Where has all the history gone in graduate programmes of adult education?, Paper presented to the 1980 National Adult Education Conference, St. Louis, November 1980.

De Crow, R., 1969, New Directions in Adult Education Research, Syracuse University Papers in Continuing Education for Adults, No. 139; Syracuse.

Deshler, D., 1984, "Evaluation for Programme Improvement," Jossey-Bass; San Francisco.

Dickinson, G., and Rusnell, D., 1971, A content analysis of adult education, Adult Education, 21 (3), 177-185.

Elias, J. L., and Merriam, S. B., 1980, "Philosophical Foundations of Adult Education," Robert Krieger; Malabar, Florida.

Elsdon, K. T., 1975, "Training for Adult Education," University of Nottingham, Department of Adult Education; Nottingham.

Elsdon, K. T., 1984, "The Training of Trainers," Huntington Publishers, Cambridge.

Ely, M. L., ed., 1936, "Adult Education in Action," American Association for Adult Education; New York.

Evans, B., 1987, "Radical Adult Education: A Political and Philosophical Critique," Croom Helm; London.

Ewert, M., 1982, Involving adult learners in programme planning, in: "Linking Philosophy and Practice," S. B. Merriam, ed., Jossey-Bass; San Francisco.

Farlow, H., 1979, "Publicising and Promoting Programmes," McGraw Hill, New York.

Field, B., 1980, The Southern Counties Adult Education Society: Some nineteenth century views on workers' education, Studies in Adult Education, 12 (2), 101-108.

Fieldhouse, R., 1983, The ideology of English adult education teaching, 1925-1950, Studies in Adult Education, 15, 11-35.

Fieldhouse, R., 1985, Conformity and contradiction in english responsible body tradition, Studies in the Education of Adults, 17 (2), 121-134.

Fine, M., 1982, "Examining Inequity: View From Urban Schools," University of Pennsylvania. Unpublished manuscript; Philadelphia.

Finlay, L. S., and Faith, V., 1979, Illiteracy and alienation in American colleges: Is Paulo Freire's Pedagogy Relevant? Radical Teacher, 16 (1), 28-37.

Gainey, L., 1986, Clandestine learning among slaves: evidence from the federal writers project 'Slave Narratives, 1936-1938', Adult Education Research Conference Proceedings, No. 27. Syracuse University; Syracuse.

Graham, T. B., Daines, J. M., Sullivan, T., Harris, P., and Baum, F. E., 1982, "The Training of Part-Time Teachers of Adults," Department of Adult Education, University of Nottingham; Nottingham.

Gelpi, E., 1979, "A Future for Lifelong Education," (Two volumes). Manchester Monographs in Education, No. 13. Department of Higher and Adult Education, University of Manchester; Manchester.

Gelpi, E., 1985, "Lifelong Education and International Relations," Croom Helm; London.

Giroux, H. A., 1983, "Theory and Resistance in Education," Bergin and Garvey; South Hadley, Massachussetts.

Goldstein, A. J., and Frary, A. C., (eds.), 1986, "Graduate Programmes in the Humanities and Social Sciences, 1986," Peterson's Guides; Princeton, New Jersey.

Grabowski, S. M., 1980, Trends in graduate research, in: "Changing Approaches to Studying Adult Education," H.M. Long and R. Hiemstra and Associates, eds., Jossey-Bass; San Francisco.

Grattan, H. C., 1965, "In Quest of Knowledge," Association Press, New York.

Griffin, C., 1983, "Curriculum Theory in Adult and Lifelong Education," Croom Helm; London.

Griffin, C., 1987, "Adult Education and Social Policy," Croom Helm; London.

Griffith, W. S., 1979, Adult education research: emerging developments, Studies in Adult Education, 11 (2), 130–142.

Guy, D. M. 1976, A review of articles in three adult education publications, 1970-1974, Continuing Education in New Zealand, 8 (2), 48–60.

Harrison, J. F. C., 1961, "Learning and Living, 1790-1960," Routledge and Kegan Paul; London.

Heaney, T., 1984, Action, freedom, and liberatory education, in: "Selected Writings on Philosophy and Adult Education," S. B. Merriam, ed., Robert Krieger; Malabar, Florida.

Hellyer, M. R., and Schied, F. M., 1984, Workers' education and the labor college movement: Radical traditions in American adult education, Adult Education Research Conference Proceedings, No. 25. North Carolina State University; Raleigh.

Hellyer, M., 1986, Adult education and government repression in the U.S; 1919-1920 Revolutionary Radicalism, Adult Education Research Conference Proceedings, No. 27. Syracuse University; Syracuse.

Hiemstra, R., 1976, "Lifelong Learning," Professional Educators Publications; Lincoln, Nebraska.

Houle, C. O., 1961, "The Inquiring Mind," University of Wisconsin Press; Madison, Wisconsin.

Houle, C. O., 1972, "The Design of Education," Jossey-Bass; Francisco.

Hugo, J. M., 1987, The elegant arts amid the coarser plants of daily necessity: A retrospective view of a women's study club, 1885-1957, Adult Education Research

Conference Proceedings, No. 28. University of Wyoming; Laramie.

Jarvis, P., 1978, Knowledge and the curriculum in adult education: A sociological approach, Adult Education, 51 (4), 221-26.

Jensen, G., Liveright, A. A., and Hallenbeck, W. C., eds., 1964, "Adult Education: Outlines of an Emerging Field of University Study," Adult Education Association of the United States; Washington D.C.

Jones, R. K., 1985, "Sociology of Adult Education," Gower Publishing Company; Brookfield, Vermont.

Joyce, P., 1973, Education for social change, Adult Education, 46 (3), 170-174.

Keddie, N., 1980, Adult education: an ideology of individualism, in: "Adult Education for a Change," J.L. Thompson, ed., Hutchinson; London.

Kelly, T., 1970, "A History of Adult Education in Great Britain," Liverpool University Press; Liverpool.

Kelly, T., 1974, "A Select Bibliography of Adult Education," National Institute of Adult Education; London.

Kennedy, W. B., 1981, Highlander Praxis: learning with Myles Horton, Teachers College Record, 83, 105-119.

Kidd, J. R., 1981, Research needs in adult education, Studies in Adult Education, 13 (1), 1-14.

Klevins, C., (ed.), 1982, "Materials and Methods in Adult and Continuing Education," Klevens Publications; Canoga Park, California.

Knott, E. S., 1983, A philosophical consideration of the relevance of Paulo Freire for the education of older adults, Lifelong Learning Research Conference proceedings, No. 5, Department of Agricultural and Extension Education, University of Maryland; Maryland.

Knowles, M. S., 1972, The relevance of research for the adult education teacher/trainer, Adult Leadership, 20 (8), 172-175.

Knowles, M. S., 1975, "Self-Directed Learning," Cambridge Books; New York.

Knowles, M. S., 1977, "A History of the Adult Education Movement in the United States," Robert E. Krieger; Malabar, Florida.

Knowles, M. S., 1980, "The Modern Practice of Adult Education," Cambridge Books; New York.

Knowles, M. S., 1984, "Andragogy in Action," Jossey-Bass; San Francisco.

Knox, A. B., and Associates, 1980, "Developing, Administrating and Evaluating Adult Education," Jossey-Bass; San Francisco.

Kozol, J., 1985, "Illiterate America," Doubleday; New York.

Kreitlow, B., and Associates, 1981, "Examining Controversies in Adult Education," Jossey-Bass; San Francisco.

Langerman, P. D., and Smith, D. H., 1979, "Managing Adult

and Continuing Education Programmes and Staff,"
National Association for Public Continuing and Adult
Education; Washington D.C.

Lauffer, A., 1977, "The Practice of Continuing Education in
the Human Services," McGraw Hill; New York.

Lawson, K. H., 1979, "Philosophical Concepts and Values in
Adult Education," Open University Press; Milton Keynes.

Lawson, K. H., 1982, "Analysis and Ideology: Conceptual
Essays on the Education of Adults," Department of Adult
Education, University of Nottingham; Nottingham.

Lawson, K. H., 1985, Deontological liberalism: The political
philosophy of liberal adult education, International
Journal of Lifelong Education, 4 (3), 219-227.

Legge, C. D., 1977, "Register of Research in Progress in
Adult Education, 1976 and 1977," Department of Higher
and Adult Education, University of Manchester;
Manchester.

Legge, C. D., 1981, The training of teachers of adults, in:
"Policy and Research in Adult Education: The First
Nottingham International Colloquium, 1981," B. Harvey,
J. Daines, D. Jones and J. Wallis, eds., Department of
Adult Education, University of Nottingham; Nottingham.

Lindeman, E. C., 1926, "The Meaning of Adult Education,"
New Republic; New York.

Lindeman, E. C., 1944, New Needs for Adult Education,
Annals of the American Academy of Political and Social
Sciences, 231, 115-122.

Livingstone, D. W., 1987, "Critical Pedagogy and Cultural
Power," Bergin and Garvey; South Hadley,
Massachussets.

Livingstone, R., 1945, "On Education," Cambridge University
Press, Cambridge.

Long, H. B., 1977, Publication activity of selected professors
of adult education, Adult Education, 27 (3), 173-186.

Long, H. B. 1982, Meta-research and research needs in
lifelong learning, Lifelong Learning Research Conference Proceedings, No.4. Department of Agricultural and
Extension Education, University of Maryland; College
Park, Maryland.

Long, H. B. 1983, "New Perspectives on the Education of
Adults in the United States," Croom Helm; London.

Long, H. B., and Agyekum, S., 1974, Adult Education
1964-1973: Reflections of a changing discipline, Adult
Education, 24 (2), 99-120.

Lovett, T., 1975, "Adult Education, Community Development
and the Working Class," Ward Educational; London.

Lovett, T., Clarke, C., and Kilmurray, A., 1983, "Adult
Education and Community Action," Croom Helm; London.

Lovett, T., ed., 1988, "Radical Approaches to Adult
Education".

Lumsden, D. B., 1977, The curriculum development process

in adult education, Adult Education, 49 (5), 279-284.

Marks, H., 1982, Unemployment and adult education in the 1930's, Studies in Adult Education, 14, 1-15.

Magee, S. R., and Alexander, D. J., 1986, Training and educating in continuing education, International Journal of Lifelong Education, 5 (3), 173-185.

Marriott, S., 1981, State Aid - The earliest demands for government support of university extra-mural education, Studies in Adult Education, 13 (1), 28-44.

McCall, R. T., and Schenz, R. F., 1969, Planning a balanced curriculum, in: "Administration of Continuing Education," N. C. Shaw, ed., National Association for Public Adult and Continuing Education; Washington D.C.

McIllroy, J. A., 1985, Adult Education and the Role of the client - the TUC Education Scheme 1929-80, Studies in the Education of Adults, 17 (1), 33-58.

Mee, G., 1978, Research Programmes for Adult Educators, Studies in Adult Education, 10 (2), 161-167.

Mee, G., and Wiltshire, H., 1978, "Structure and Performance in Adult Education," Longman; London.

Minich, C. E., 1969, Major curriculum areas and programme concerns, in: "Administration of Continuing Education," N. C. Shaw, ed., National Association for Public Adult and Continuing Education; Washington D.C.

Minkler, M., and Cox, K., 1980, Creating critical consciousness in health; applications of Freire's philosophy and methods to the health care setting, International Journal of Health Services, 10 (2), 311-322.

Monette, M., 1977, The concept of educational need: an analysis of selected literature, Adult Education, 27 (2), 116-127.

Monette, M., 1979, Paulo Freire and other unheard voices, Religious Education, 74, (2), 543-554.

Nel, J., 1987, The University of Wyoming's role in the historical development of adult education in Wyoming, 1886-1918, Adult Education Research Conference Proceedings, No. 28. University of Wyoming; Laramie.

Noble, P., 1983, "Formation of Freirean Facilitators," Latino Institute; Chicago.

Omolewa, M., 1984, Neglected themes in adult education historical research in Canada, Adult Education Research Conference Proceedings, No. 25. North Carolina State University; Raleigh.

Paterson, R. W. K., 1973, Social Change as an educational aim, Adult Education, 45 (6), 353-359.

Paterson, R. W. K., 1979, "Values, Education and the Adult," Routledge and Kegan Paul; London.

Paterson, R. W. K., 1987, Adult education and the individual, International Journal of Lifelong Education, 6 (2), 111-123.

Pell, O. A. H., 1952, Social Philosophy at the grass roots:

the work of the AEA's committee on social philosophy, Adult Education, 2 (1), 123-132.

Pennington, F. C. (ed.), (1980), "Assessing Educational Needs of Adults," Jossey-bass; San Francisco.

Peters, J. M., 1974, Developing a Curriculum that meets student needs, in: "You Can be a Successful Teacher of Adults," National Association for Public Adult and Continuing Education; Washington D.C.

Pilsworth, M., and Ruddock, R., 1975, Some criticisms of survey research methods in adult methods, Convergence, 8 (2), 33-43.

Rockhill, K., 1984, Between the wars: Liberalism and the framing of conflict in the framing of adult education, Adult Education Research Conference Proceedings, No. 25. North Carolina State University; Raleigh.

Rockhill, K., (1985), Ideological Solidification of liberalism in university adult education: Confrontation over workers' education in the USA, in: "University Adult Education in England and the USA," R. Taylor, K. Rockhill and R. Fieldhouse, Croom Helm; London.

Rubenson, K., 1982, Adult education research: In quest of a map of the territory, Adult Education, 32 (2), 57-74.

Ruddock, R., 1980 Perspectives on Adult Education, Manchester Monographs, No.2., Department of Higher and Adult Education, University of Manchester.

Sisco, B. R., 1985, From whence we came: a critical examination of selected historical literature of adult education, Adult Education Research Conference Proceedings, No. 26. Arizona State University; Tempe, Arizona.

Shor, I., 1980, "Critical Teaching in Everyday Life," South End Press; Boston.

Sork, T., (ed.,) 1979, "Research and Investigations in Adult Education: 1976-1978 Register," ERIC Clearinghouse on Adult, Career and Vocational Education; Columbus, Ohio.

Standing Conference on University Teaching and Research into the Education of Adults (SCUTREA), 1986, Guide to University Courses for Adult Educators in the United Kingdom and Eire.

Stewart, D. W., 1987, "Adult Learning in America: Eduard Lindeman and His Agenda for Lifelong Education," Robert E. Krieger; Malabar, Florida.

Strother, G. B., and Klus, J. P., 1982, "Administration of Continuing Education," Wadsworth; Belmont, California.

Taylor, R., Rockhill, K., and Fieldhouse, R., 1985, "University Adult Education in England and the USA," Croom Helm; London.

Thatcher, J. H., 1956, Curriculum areas, in: "Public School Adult Education: A Guide for Administrators," National Association for Public Adult and Continuing Education; Washington D.C.

Thomas, J. E., 1982, "Radical Adult Education: Theory and

Practice," Department of Adult Education, University of Nottingham; Nottingham.

Thomas, J. E., 1984, Adult Education, Research and SCUTREA, Studies in Adult Education, 16, 70-77.

Thomas, J. E. and Davies, J. H., 1984, "A Select Bibliography of Adult Continuing Education," National Institute of Adult Continuing Education; Leicester.

Thompson, J. E., (ed.), 1980, "Adult Education for a Change," Hutchinson; London.

Thompson, J. L., 1983, "Learning Liberation: Women's Response to Men's Education," Croom Helm; London.

Usher, R., 1987, The place of theory in designing curricula for the continuing education of adult educators, Studies in the Education of Adults, 19 (1), 26-35.

Youngman, F., 1986, "Adult Education and Socialist Pedagogy," Croom Helm; London.

Ward, K., and Taylor, R., (eds.), 1986, "Adult Education and the Working Class," Croom Helm; London.

Wallace, R. K., 1986, "The Americanisation Movement in the 1920's: A Neglected Aspect of Adult Education History," Adult Education Research Conference Proceedings, No. 27. Syracuse University Press; Syracuse.

Willis, P., 1977, "Learning to Labour," Saxon House; Westmead.

Wiltshire, H., 1976, The nature and uses of adult education, in: "The Spirit and the Form: Essays in Adult Education in Honour of Professor Harold Wiltshire," A. Rogers, (ed.),Department of Adult Education, University of Nottingham; Nottingham.

PART EIGHT

CONCLUSION

Chapter Twenty-Four

DEVELOPING CRITICALLY REFLECTIVE PRACTITIONERS:
A RATIONALE FOR TRAINING EDUCATORS OF ADULTS

Stephen Brookfield (1988)

Practice, if it is to be informed by thoughtful reflection and analysis, must be based upon some kind of rationale. This is as true for programmes of graduate adult education as it is for any other form of professional development. If adult education as an area of practice is to develop any measure of distinctive professional identity, then its practitioners need to have their activities informed by a sense of common purposes. They also need to have some agreement on the criteria by which the success of their efforts is to be judged. A critical rationale is not merely a statement of philosophical purpose. It is also a specification of the various methods and indicators through which these philosophical purposes and criteria are realised. In other words, a critical rationale should mix prescriptive and descriptive elements; it should elaborate central philosophical aims for a field of practice and it should describe ways and means by which these purposes can be operationalised and recognised.

In this chapter a critical rationale for practice in the training of adult educators is proposed. This critical rationale comprises the following three elements:

1. A statement of central philosophical purposes for the training of adult educators.
2. An elaboration of the ideas regarding adult learning informing the framing of these purposes.
3. A description of the methods appropriate to the achievement of these purposes and a justification for their adoption.

PHILOSOPHICAL PURPOSES OF GRADUATE ADULT
EDUCATION

The purposes of graduate adult education are several, and the extent to which each of the following applies depends partly on the relative experience of the learners involved. In programmes where the participants are new to the theory and practice of adult education, there will probably be a greater emphasis placed on training in basic techniques of facilitation, programme development, counselling and curriculum design. In programmes where participants already have substantial experience in working with adult learners, there will probably be a greater emphasis placed on exploring discrepancies between the theory and practice of adult education, on clarifying participants' own 'theories-in-use' and on critically appraising the assumptions and biases endemic to various theories and models of practice.

The following purposes are proposed as comprising a critical rationale for training educators of adults:

1. Participants should become familiar with the theoretical literature pertaining to the practice of adult education, particularly in the development of programmes for adult learners and in the facilitation of learning.

2. Participants should be encouraged to place the practice of adult education within a socio-political context. They should explore the extent to which the organisation, functioning and clientele of their programmes reflect the norms and structures of the broader culture. They should be able to make the connection between their personal actions and the wider cultural, economic and political context.

3. Participants should be able to articulate an informed rationale for their practice. They should be helped to develop a personal philosophy of adult education, comprising central aims, appropriate methods and curricula, and evaluative criteria and indicators.

4. Participants should be assisted to identify and elaborate the 'theories in use' (Schon, 1983, 1987) which inform their practice. A 'theory in use' is a collection of hunches, insights and intuitions which practitioners draw upon to guide their actions when they are faced with particular sets of circumstances. They are frequently contradictory to 'espoused theories' of practice, which are the publicly recognised givens (for example, that adults are self-directed learners or that adult education is collaborative) by which we organise our practice.

5. Participants should be helped to be critically reflective concerning the espoused concepts, models of practice and research conclusions they encounter in the literature of adult education research and theory. They should become sceptical of uncritically accepted givens of adult education practice, research and theory; for example, that all adults are self-directed learners, that discussion is the adult educational method par excellence, or that andragogy comprises the distinctive set of assumptions which inform our practice. These myths, givens and folk

wisdoms should be scrutinised critically for their congruence or discrepancy with participants' own experiences of adult education reality.

THE NATURE OF ADULT LEARNING

Any learner is a complex configuration of variables such as personality, accumulated experiences, cultural conditioning, inherited capacities, developed abilities and evolved learning style. Each individual develops idiosyncratic and unique mediatory structures through which new experiences are interpreted. These mediatory structures comprise frameworks of understanding and perceptual filters through which we try to understand and assign meaning to new experiences. The processes through which we make sense of, interpret and construct meaning where new experiences are concerned are similar in childhood, adolescence and the various stages of adulthood. I have argued elsewhere (Brookfield, 1985, 1986, 1987) that a major reason that concepts such as andragogy and self-directed have been accepted so uncritically by many adult educators is the promise they seem to hold regarding how a distinctive field of adult education practice can be identified. Because of our justified sense of professional insecurity and institutional marginality we are constantly seeking the Holy Grail of adult learning. If we could only discover something unique about adult learning, or about teaching adults, then our professional existence would be much easier to justify. We could point to this form of learning, or that pedagogical approach, and claim that it was appropriate only where adults were concerned, and not paralleled in children.

There may be, as developmental psychologists such as Kohlberg (1981), Kegan (1982), Perry (1970), Gould (1978) and Gilligan (1982) suggest, a capacity for moral reasoning which develops with chronological age. On the whole, however, the learning of children, adolescents and adults shares more similarities than it exhibits differences. Many of the tenets of andragogy (Knowles, 1980, 1984), for example, are paralleled in Dewey's analyses of How We Think (1910) and Experience and Education (1983). Children are frequently problem-centered in their learning, they may show a propensity for self-directedness, they often work best when new learning activities are evidently connected to past experiences, and they frequently like to see immediate application of what they are learning. Similarly, the pedagogic principles which govern the teaching of adults (vary instructional approaches, build curricula on learners' experiences, create a relaxed psychological climate for learning, use a mixture of resource materials, involve learners actively in planning, conducting and evaluating their own learning) are equally

319

applicable to teaching children. Indeed, whenever I have outlined these principles at a workshop on facilitating adult learning, there are invariably several schoolteachers who claim that these are precisely the principles they follow in their own teaching.

What, then, can we claim is in any way distinctive about adult learning? Here, the central concern is that of the adult's accumulated life experiences. We must be very cautious in any generalisations we make about the generic nature of adulthood compared to childhood, or indeed about adulthood as a phase of life when there are so many distinctive passages (Sheehy, 1976, 1981) transition points (Schlossberg, 1984) and developmental stages (Levinson, 1978, Gilligan, 1982) in adult life. Notwithstanding this caution, however, it is evident that passing through experiences which become increasingly varied in their breadth, form and intensity, affects fundamentally how we perceive the world and how we interpret new happenings and stimuli. As we develop intimate relationships and experience their dissolution, as we leave the confines of the formal school system and enter the world of work or face the reality of unemployment, and as we become involved in developing political involvements within our communities and societies, we realise the contextuality of the world. We become sceptical of those who proclaim that they have the final answer or ultimate truth regarding the dilemmas and crises of adult life.

Hostler (1977) has outlined the components of intellectual and personal maturity which he feels mark the attainment of adulthood. Intellectually, adults' acquaintance with the realities of existence means that they can accept notions of complexity, doubt, ambiguity and uncertainty as endemic to intellectual inquiry. It means that they can comprehend the concept of relative truth and that they appreciate the importance of contextuality. Hence,

"The adult's experience fosters the ability to make subtle discriminations between varying degrees and kinds of truth, which itself permits a more faithful understanding of reality" (p. 61).

Personally, adults experience relationships which are more permanent, deep and comprehensive than those involving children. This means that adults are able to appreciate art treating the facets of human existence, and to formulate values and ethical principles based on emotional and spiritual realities. Hostler argues that adults' wide experiences of the world make it impossible for educators to select subjects on behalf of these learners. Hence, "the adulthood of our students imposes no restrictions upon what we teach them, but rather argues for as wide a choice of subjects as possible" (p. 63).

Pedagogically, he believes that the equality of status existing between adult learners and their teachers necessarily requires that adult education be conducted on a voluntary, collaborative basis.

This theme of how the nature of adulthood determines the nature and form of adult education is taken up by Paterson (1979) who maintains that adult education is,

"a purposive activity directed to the fuller development of adults as persons in their personhood by the taking of measures which are proper for this purpose" (p. 36).

'Personhood', according to Paterson, takes two forms;

(1) the enlargement of awareness and
(2) the development of experience and knowledge characterised by breadth and balance.

Developing the qualities of personhood requires adult education to,

"be marked by qualities of wittingness, voluntariness, conscious control, interpersonal encounter, and active participation by the educand" (p. 36).

The presumption underlying Hostler's and Paterson's analyses is that chronological age is correlated with increased maturity, however such maturity might be defined. Paterson (1979) writes that,

"it is clearly more appropriate that adults should be entrusted with a greater degree of responsibility for the shape of their own education, since it is on the presumption of precisely such attributes as responsibility and independence of judgment that their status as adults rests" (p.33).

But how empirically sound is the assumption that chronological age is correlated with an increased maturity of outlook as defined by such traits as an acceptance and understanding of contextuality, an awareness of relativism, and a familiarity with multiple and ambiguous interpretations of reality? It is here that we need to turn to the literature of developmental psychology.

One of the most provocative themes explored by developmental psychologists concerns the development of critical consciousness in adults. As Daloz (1986) puts it, "the struggle to be something more than the person others have made, to construct and then live up to a set of our own expectations, is one of the most compelling struggles of our adult lives" (p. 154). Kohlberg (1981), Loevinger (1976), Levinson (1978), Gould (1978), Gilligan (1982) and Kegan (1982) identify as a central focus of adult development the individual's becoming critically reflective regarding assumptions, values and behavioural norms which were uncritically assimilated in childhood. Hence, in coming to terms with the transitions, dilemmas and crises of adult life, the person learns,

"to question and reappraise the existing structure, to search for new possibilities in self and world, and to modify the present structure enough so that a new one can be formed" (Levinson, 1978, p. 53).

Gould (1980) posits a maturational push throughout adult life by which people become critically aware of inhibitions acquired in childhood. He writes that,

"during the adult years we strive to become more liberated from ideas that were generated in childhood and persevere in adulthood even though they constrain us ... we are continuously transforming ourselves - within a community, out of the past into the future, with and within a complex mind, trying always to gain a little more liberty to be what we are becoming" (p. 23').

Critical reflection is problematic in childhood since we are learning new rules, values and assumptions; we have no way of judging the accuracy or validity of the norms since our experience is one dimensional. Argyris, Puttnam and Smith (1985) write that,

"in adulthood this early learning returns to roost, as the learning frames and strategies we developed in childhood begin to jeopardise the very growth and learning they were initially designed to ensure" (p. 289).

As we develop relationships and enter the work and political worlds, we become aware of ambiguities and of how context distorts the validity of general truths. Thinking critically in the context of adult life involves our scrutinising the stock of comfortable and familiar assumptions, values and norms we have developed in childhood. Mezirow (1981) describes this process as perspective transformation;

"the learning process by which adults come to recognise their culturally induced dependency roles and relationships and the reasons for them and take action to over-come them" (p.7).

Labouvie-Vief's (1977, 1980) work on adults' cognitive styles emphasises how adults become aware of the over-whelming importance of context. She argues that,

"as a tool, logic is embedded in a social context with all the constraints society brings, and it is the major task of adulthood to achieve this cognitive subordination of logic to social-system needs" (1980, p. 13).

Adults conduct logical reasoning within a context of pragmatic constraints at work, within their political involvements, and in their intimate relationships. Hence,

"one of the structural transitions of adulthood should be to achieve a new integration in which logic, initially decontextualised, is reembedded in its social context" (1980, p. 16).

Perry's research into the intellectual and ethical development of Harvard male students has been applied to the investigation of adult cognitive styles by Cameron (1983) and Zachary (1985). Perry identifies nine intellectual stages, or positions, which represent intellectual and ethical development in early adulthood. This process entails moving from a dualistic to a multiplistic perspective on the world, and then to the making of conscious commitments to identities while being aware of the relativistic nature of these. The Syracuse Rating Group (Cameron, 1983) argue that the ninth position of 'developing commitments' is recognised in adult life by people embracing risk taking and challenge as a motif central to their lives. This search for challenge is taken in the full knowledge that it entails risk to self-esteem and the likelihood of failure. Adults at this stage recognise that they are mistaken if they pursue a final, static or ultimate life style. In working through the eight positions leading up to this stage adults learn to view knowledge as contextual, to take on the perspective of others, and to become aware of the culturally constructed nature of values. Attainment of this ninth stage is marked by the adults' realisation that only through making an informed and thought-through commitment to values, identities and ideals will a sense of responsibility for creating and re-creating their personal and social worlds emerge.

ADULT LEARNING AND CRITICAL THINKING

As a concept, critical thinking has been interpreted in a number of ways. It has been equated with the development of logical reasoning abilities (Hallet, 1984), with the application of reflective judgment (Kitchener, 1986), with assumption hunting (Scriven, 1976) and with the creation, using and testing of meaning (Hullfish and Smith, 1961). Ennis (1962) lists twelve aspects of critical thinking including analytical and argumentative capacities such as recognising ambiguity in reasoning, identifying contradictions in arguments, and ascertaining the empirical soundness of generalised conclusions. D'Angelo (1971) specifies ten attitudes which are necessary conditions for being critical including curiosity, flexibility, scepticism and honesty. To Halpern (1984) critical thought is a rational and purposive attempt to use reasoning to move towards future goals.

Critical thinking has, however, generally been conceptualised as an intellectual ability most evident in formal higher educational settings (Drake, 1976; Young, 1980; Meyers, 1986; Stice, 1987). Empirical studies of the development of critical thinking focus on young adults (Kitchener, 1986) or college students (Perry, 1970). While this setting for critical thinking is undoubtedly crucial, it is but one of the many settings in which critical thinking is practised, particularly in adult life. In personal relationships, at the workplace, in community and political involvements, and in perceptions of mass media of communication, critical thinking is evident. An interpretation of the concept of critical thinking which places critical thinking squarely in the context of adult life is that of emancipatory learning. Derived from the work of Habermas (1979) and developed by adult educators such as Mezirow (1981), Apps (1985), Hart (1985) and Collins (1985), emancipatory learning is recognised by learners becoming aware of the forces which have brought them to their current situations and taking action to change some aspects of these situations. To Apps (1985),

> "emancipatory learning is that which frees people from personal, institutional, or environmental forces that prevent them from seeing new directions, from gaining control of their lives, their society and their world" (p. 151).

Another concept closely related to critical thinking is dialectical thinking (Riegel, 1975; Basseches, 1984). Dialectical thinking focuses on the understanding and resolution of contradictions;

> "dialectical analysis shows us that the management of organisation, of society, and of personal life ultimately involves the management of contradiction" (Morgan, 1986, p. 266).

It fuses elements of relativistic thought (for example, assuming that moral judgments can only be made in the context of the culture concerned) with elements of universalistic thought (for example, believing that universal moral judgments are possible). Dialectical thinking entails a continuous process of making judgments, identifying the assumptions implicit in these judgments, modifying the original judgments in the light of the accuracy and validity of these revealed assumptions, and so on. To Deshler (1985),

> "dialectical thinking is thinking which looks for, recognises, and welcomes contradictions as a stimulus to development" (p. 6).

Change is viewed as a fundamental reality, forms and structures are perceived as temporary, relationships are held to involve developmental transformations, and openness to new ways of perceiving and acting is welcomed. Dialectical thinkers are involved in a continuous process of trying to create order in the world - to discover what elements are missing from our existing ordering, and to create new orderings which include these. Daloz (1986) echoes this idea in his belief that dialectical thinking,

> "presumes change rather than a static notion of 'reality'. As each assertion is derived from the one before, truth is always emergent, never fixed; relative, not absolute" (p. 141).

As a form of adult learning, critical reflection entails more than purely cognitive activities such as logical reasoning, or scrutinising arguments for assertions unsupported by empirical evidence. It involves our recognising the assumptions underlying our beliefs and behaviours. It means we can give justifications for our ideas and actions. Most importantly, perhaps, it means we try to judge the rationality of these justifications. We do this by comparing them to a range of varying interpretations and perspectives. We can think through, project and anticipate the consequences of our actions which are based on these justifications. And we can test the accuracy and rationality of these justifications against some kind of objective analysis of the 'real' world as we understand it.

Four component elements have been identified as central to critical reflection in adult life (Brookfield 1987); assumption analysis, contextual awareness, imaginative speculation, and reflective scepticism. Assumption analysis describes the activity of becoming aware of the assumptions underlying our habitual beliefs, values, behaviours and social structures and then assessing the accuracy and validity of these assumptions against our lived experiences. Contextual awareness is evident when we come to realise that these assumptions are historically and culturally specific. When people realise that actions, values, beliefs and moral codes can be fully understood only as products of a particular historical and cultural context, then they are contextually aware. Contextual thinkers view their dearly held beliefs and values as, to some extent, social constructs. They understand that value systems and behavioural codes are socially transmitted as well as being personally generated and sharpened by individual experience. Public and private knowledge are seen as provisional, relative and contextual.

Imaginative speculation is present when adults are exploring alternatives to their current ways of thinking and living. Imagining and exploring alternatives can be both liberating and threatening. It is liberating to realise that the world is malleable, and can be acted upon; that we can effect change in our personal relationships, workplaces and communities. We can contemplate jettisoning unsatisfactory beliefs and behaviours in favour of ones which are more congenial and satisfactory. Imaginative speculation suggests that if we find economic or social arrangements to be obsolete, irrational or oppressive, we can replace them with more contemporary, rational or just alternatives. This realisation can be threatening, however, because it implies that we may have been taking on trust stereotypes, social norms and moral codes which are meaningless, obsolete or harmful. As this suspicion begins to nudge at our consciousness our immediate reaction may be to dismiss such misgivings as irrational and unfounded. But when the circumstances of our daily existences are such that suspicions and misgivings arise repeatedly, forcing themselves on our unconsciousness and destroying our prized mental equilibrium, then we are forced eventually to acknowledge their legitimacy.

Imagining and exploring alternatives frequently lead to the development of a particularly critical cast of mind which might be described as reflective scepticism. Reflective scepticism is evident when claims made for the universal validity or truth of an idea, practice or institution are doubted. Adults are reflectively sceptical when they do not take for granted the universal truth of statements, policies or justifications, simply because of the authority ascribed to the source of these supposed truths. Reflective scepticism is apparent when adults call into question the belief that simply because some idea or social structure has existed unchanged for a period of time that it must therefore be a) right and b) the best possible arrangement. Being reflectively sceptical is to be wary of claims to universal truth or of access to some otherwise inaccessible fount of wisdom. This is not to be equated, however, with avoiding commitment to beliefs or causes. We can commit ourselves wholeheartedly to an idea, social structure or cause and still be critically reflective. The point is that this commitment is informed; we have arrived at our convictions after a period of critical questioning, analysis and reflection. We have examined ideas, structures and causes in terms of our experiences of the world, and have concluded that they are the closest 'fit' with reality as we understand it best. Being reflectively sceptical of universal rules or divinely ordained givens is not the same as being completely cynical about making any commitments in life. Pure scepticism entails a knee-jerk dismissal of any and all claims to insight. The point is that any commitments which are made take place after a period of critically reflective analysis. During this period the validity of the apparently ultimate or final truth is established through the person concerned examining its congruence with reality as he or she perceives it.

METHODS OF GRADUATE ADULT EDUCATION

The orienteering concept informing the actual conduct of graduate adult education programmes is that of the critically reflective practitioner (Schon, 1983, 1987). The purpose of graduate adult education should be to develop critically reflective practitioners; that is, adult educators who can recognise their own theories in use in adult learning and education, who can articulate a clear and informed rationale as to why their practice is organised the way it is, and who are open and ready to evolve new forms of practice appropriate for the different contexts in which they are called on to facilitate adults' learning. The model of the clinical professor (or scholar-practitioner) used in some training for the mental and physical health professions is perhaps the closest parallel from an allied field to the organising concept of the critically reflective practitioner which I am proposing. The following suggestions are an attempt to give some methodological flesh to this skeletal notion of the critically reflective practitioner. They derive from some of my own writings (Brookfield, 1986, 1987) as well as from Schon's work and that of the Nottingham Andragogy Group (1983).

1.   Interactional Encounters
Graduate programmes of adult education should be conceived as interactional encounters; that is, as educational events in which the content, purposes and methods are in a process of continual negotiation, revision and alteration according to the expressed preferences of learners and facilitators. Hence, the decisions regarding what are appropriate educational needs, problems to be addressed, substantive curricula, methods of teaching and learning, evaluative approaches, and criteria of assessment arise out of a process of continuous negotiation

between participants in the educational encounter. In a sense, the graduate programme should be run as if it is a deliberate effort in formative evaluation, so that discussion and decisions regarding what has happened in the past and what is to happen in the future take place regularly and are perceived as part of the normal modus operandi of the programme.

One danger of advocating this interactional approach is that it may be interpreted as presuming that learners' voices regarding appropriate methods, content and evaluative criteria should always hold sway. This is misconceived for two reasons. Firstly, no one group of graduate students are likely to articulate a commonly shared and coherent set of learning needs. Secondly, the voices of facilitators are central to these interactions, and there will be many times when learners and facilitators disagree about what should be happening. The point is that opportunities for discussion and negotiation on these matters should be central to graduate programmes (as they should to all adult education encounters) and treated as central to the operational procedures of the programme, not as a sop to the principles of democratic, collaborative learning we so frequently espouse. But having initiated these negotiations, professors of adult education should not feel reticent about challenging learners' perceptions of suitable curricula, activities and evaluative criteria. Central to the adult educator's role is being ready and willing to challenge learners' assumptions, arguments and desires. Central to adult education is the recognition that disagreement, divergence and challenge are endemic to learning; that we are all enclosed in our own paradigms and histories and that we can frequently only be prompted to examine these critically by an external source challenging our habitually accepted and comfortable ways of thinking and acting.

2.   Peer Learning

The importance of learning from peers in a graduate adult education programme can hardly be overstated. Participants in such programmes typically have a breadth and depth of remarkably contrasting experiences in facilitating adults' learning. If the purpose of graduate adult education is to develop critically reflective practitioners who are ready to challenge assumptions underlying their practice and to explore alternatives to the conventionally accepted wisdoms regarding adult education, then the experiences of fellow learners represent an invaluable resource. Through learning how other adult educators have tried to facilitate learning in their particular settings, and of how contextual factors have distorted their neat application of general principles, students are likely to become attuned to the importance of context. As well as developing contextual awareness they will also likely

develop reflective scepticism regarding the universal applica-
bility of textbook models of practice, or the universal truth
of espoused conventional wisdoms regarding the nature of
adult learning and the most effective ways of facilitating that
learning. When adult educators meet to discuss the nature of
learning and education, then their own contrasting experiences as learners and facilitators of learning are likely to
provide ample experiential evidence of the contextual nature
of these activities.

Three examples of how peer learning is deliberately
fostered in the graduate programme in which I work may make
this point clearer. The first has to do with how new entrants
to the AEGIS doctoral programme in adult education at
Teachers College (the acronym refers to Adult Education
through Guided Independent Study) are welcomed. All new
entrants to the programme are invited to a 3 week orientation
at the outset of their studies at which we try to cluster them
into peer support groups on the basis of geographical
proximity, professional orientation and research interests.
The intent is for these initial interest groups to solidify into
support groups which will last the length of a student's
doctoral programme. A second attempt to encourage peer
learning is through the mechanism of a group coordinated
dissertation. In the writing of dissertations, graduate
students form themselves into clusters organised around
common dissertation themes. These groups explore themes
such as 'Learning at the Workplace' or 'Programme Development in Continuing and Higher Education' and they collaborate
on developing dissertation proposals, conducting literature
reviews, designing data collection instruments, field testing
instruments and analysing results. Although each student
conducts his or her own individual research project in a site
he or she has chosen, and each student writes and defends
an individual dissertation, participation in the group means
that individual members have a readymade forum. They can
use this forum to test out their ideas, conduct collaborative
literature reviews in areas of common concern, gain advice on
their instrument designs, and compare findings. Having five
or six students writing a dissertation on the same general
theme prompts an enormous amount of information exchange,
emotional support and idea generation and refinement within
the group.

Thirdly, courses can be taught in ways which encourage
peer learning. In a course I teach on Adult Education for
Social Action participants construct individual inventories of
learning needs in the field of social action and then assign
themselves to small work groups which design and conduct
class sessions on specific topics they have themselves chosen.
The pass-fail option is the chief grading mechanism used, and
this removes from participants the feeling that they are in
competition with other learners for the highest grades on a

Bell curve. Learning contracts are used to determine the content and format of any papers required for the course and at the end of the course participants write a self-evaluation of the learning they have undertaken as a result of course participation. During the first two course meetings participants clarify their interests in adult education for social action, identify their learning needs in this area, list the previous experiences they have had in this activity and indicate the resources they can bring to the group. These individual interests, needs and resources are synthesised and published for the whole group, and the third session is devoted to negotiating, as a group, the provisional allocation of time for the rest of the course. At this session participants also sign up for membership in planning groups for each of the topic areas that they have determined will be explored in the course. These small groups have complete responsibility for managing the sessions, and the role of the faculty member is that of consultant on planning and resource person. If asked, I can supply supplementary readings, react to role plays, simulations, or case studies that the groups are considering using, and suggest outside speakers and other resources that might be useful to them.

In another course on Qualitative Methods for Educators learners undertake a small scale research project between each class (for example, drafting an interview schedule, conducting an observation, administering critical incidents, or coding and analysing data) and bring along multiple copies of their efforts to the next class meeting. This means that in every class each learner has a collection of the research exercises conducted by the other members of the group. The class time is then devoted to the group analysing each other's research efforts, and to learning about qualitative research methods from seeing how various group members conducted the research task assigned. Again, this course is taken only for a pass-fail grade, meaning that learners are not in competition for the limited number of higher grades on a Bell curve. Course members become used to critically analysing each other's (and their own) research activities in pairs, small groups, or in class wide discussion. At the end of the course learners submit a "Participant Qualitative Research Portfolio" in which they present the research exercises they have undertaken during the course, revised according to what they have learned from observing how fellow learners undertook the same exercises during the course. Participants are encouraged to alter their research instruments to incorporate those features drawn from other learners' efforts which participants feel are useful. In this way learners realise that working collaboratively and learning from other course members is not a form of stealing, cribbing or plagiarising; rather, it is the way of conducting research which is most frequently found in the real world. Most educational research activities (such as foundation sponsored research efforts, or course or programme evaluations) are collaborative team efforts, rather than individually conducted projects. To train researchers in graduate schools of education only in individual research modes, and to condemn group coordinated dissertations as somehow not being intellectually respectable, is to do a disservice to students. It does not prepare them properly to participate in the collaborative research activities they are almost certain to encounter in their daily practice.

3. Learning Contracts
One of the most effective ways of operationalising the continuous interactional negotiation of purposes, methods and content of graduate adult education is to use learning contracts (Berte, 1975; Knowles, 1986). Contracts are devices through which learners and facilitators negotiate appropriate activities in an educational programme and then enshrine these agreements in some public medium. A learning contract typically consists of:

(1) a statement of purposes regarding what is to be learned,
(2) a description of human and material resources to be consulted in carrying out these purposes,
(3) an outline of the different methods to be used in accomplishing these purposes, and
(4) a statement of the evaluative criteria and indicators to be applied in judging the merit of the work presented by the learner.

This evaluation of learners' accomplishments should combine several sources of evaluative data such as the facilitator's judgment of what has been accomplished, a self-evaluation by the learner, and an evaluation conducted by an external expert to be nominated by the learner. One description of how learning contracts are used within a graduate adult education programme to organise students' learning activities is contained in Bauer (1985).

4. Assignments
Assessed work within a graduate programme of adult education which is focused on developing critically reflective practitioners should allow learners to explore the theory-practice congruences and discrepancies they observe within their experiences. In particular, assessed work should be organised to help learners scrutinise critically the espoused theories of adult education. Examples of espoused theories currently extant within the field are that teaching adults differs significantly from teaching children, that adults learn

331

differently from children, that adults have a natural tendency toward self-directedness, that collaborative modes of learning are most appropriate to working with adult learners, and that methods and content of adult education activities should build on learners' experiences. Assignments which analysed critically the accuracy and validity of these theories in terms of learners' own experiences (as both teachers of adults and adult learners themselves) would be crucial in helping these learners identify and assess their own theories-in-use of learning and education.

Some examples of assignments which might assist this process are the following, all of which are drawn from courses I teach on adult learning, programme development in adult and continuing education and theory and philosophy of adult and continuing education.

Assignment Example (1): "Analysing Adult Learning"

Think back over the last year. Identify the single most important learning episode in which you were involved. This episode will most likely be remembered as a mix of activities (for example, solitary reflection, group participation, deliberate seeking after information) and consequences (for example, skills developed or improved, knowledge acquired, insights realised). This learning can be in any setting you choose - the workplace, your intimate relationships, your community, recreational pursuits etc.

Describe in detail:-

(a) The consequences you identify; for example, the skills you developed, the knowledge you acquired, the insights you realised.

(b) The general approaches you used; for example, did you enrol in a course of instruction? seek out an expert? join an enthusiasts group? engage in extended personal reflection? undertake a programme of independently conceived reading?

(c) The methods you used; for example, did you use trial and error methods? did you consciously experiment with different activities? did you try to solve a series of progressively difficult problems? did you follow a closely specified plan of short, medium and long range goals? did you follow your instincts in as natural a way as possible?

(d) Why you undertook this learning; for example, was it to solve a problem you were facing? was it because someone told you to do this? was it because of the innate fascination of the area to be explored? was it to improve your job prospects? was it to help you make sense of a crisis in you life?

(e)   The most pleasurable, enjoyable aspects of the learning episode.

(f)   The most distressing, problematic aspects of the learning episode.

Now, compare your description of this learning episode with the tenets of adult learning as prescribed in the course reading. Take the chief features of adults' preferred learning styles as identified by Cross, Knox, Knowles, Brookfield, Kidd, Smith, Lovell and Long, and comment on the extent to which your experiences parallel, or contradict, what this literature identifies as characteristically adult learning styles.

Assignment Example (2): "A Critical Review of Adult Education Programme Development Literature"

This assignment asks you to review critically the espoused theories of programme development in adult education, as represented by the literature of the course. The assignment has two purposes:

(a)   to familiarise you with the basic literature on programme development in adult education, and

(b)   to help you identify assumptions, omissions, oversimplifications, contradictions and ambiguities in this body of literature.

For the assignment, please choose at least two of the following themes to explore in your critical review. You may choose more than two if you wish:

(i)   To what extent does the literature of programme development contain hidden assumptions regarding the nature of adult education and adult learning? Does the literature acknowledge that programme developers need to make value judgments regarding appropriate offerings and appropriate ways of undertaking needs assessments, curriculum development and evaluation?

(ii) Does the literature of programme development acknowledge the complexity of the concept of need, in particular the essential difference between felt and prescribed needs?

(iii) Does the literature acknowledge the distorting influence of context on programme development? Are contextual variables (such as budgetary constraints, the political ethos of the institution, the political climate of the country, the programmers' personal values and philosophy, the personality conflicts and differences which arise among major administrators and teachers) discussed for the ways in which they affect how programmes are chosen, designed and conducted?

(iv) Does the literature of programme development discuss the ethical dilemmas faced by educators in their practice? for example, when is it ethical to refuse to mount certain programmes because educators consider them to be frivolous or harmful? should learners' felt needs always be satisfied? do the ends of learners' development justify any instructional means such as those which prompt painful and anxiety-producing self-scrutiny? is it ever justified to keep evaluative results secret from participants in programmes? do educators and learners always have to be informed that they are being evaluated?

(v) Does the literature acknowledge and discuss the chief theory-practice disjunctions which participants perceive between their own experiences of programme development (as both developers and learners) and the models and images of programme development included within textbooks and articles?

Assignment Example (3): "Case Study of a Theorist of Adult Education"
Critically examine either the work of Paulo Freire or Eduard Lindeman. Your paper should address the following themes:

(i) An elaboration of the theorist's chief ideas, arguments and suggestions for adult education practice.

(ii) An analysis of those elements of the theorist's ideas which you find most relevant, appropriate and applicable when viewed from within the context of your own practice.

(iii) An analysis of those elements of the theorist's ideas which you find most irrelevant, inappropriate and unsuitable when viewed from within the context of your own practice.

CONCLUSION

One of the most frequent complaints made by participants in graduate programmes of adult education is that such programmes exhibit a severe theory-practice disjunction. The focus of these complaints is on such matters as the competitive grading system frequently used in such programmes, the prevalence of teacher direction and authority, the use of didactic teaching methods, and the lack of evaluative criteria grounded in learners' concerns rather than institutional necessity. Students read the literature regarding the collaborative nature of adult education, the need to develop self-direction in learning, or the importance of critical reflection in adult education, and then they find themselves unable to renegotiate central features of the curriculum, prevented from challenging institutional evaluative norms, or penalised for criticising lecturers and professors' ideas. The recommendations and suggestions contained within this chapter, if adopted, might go some way to reducing the sense of discrepancy and anomaly felt by students in graduate programmes of adult education. At the very least, they might comprise an adult education experience which would directly inform students' practice, instead of being an exercise in credentialing.

REFERENCES

Allman, P., 1985, Dialectical thinking: Our logical potential, in: "Dialogue on Issues of Lifelong Learning in a Democratic Society," G.J. Conti and R.A. Fellenz, eds., Texas A & M University; College Station, Texas.

Apps, J. W., 1985, "Improving Practice in Continuing Education," Jossey-Bass; San Francisco.

Argyris, C., Putnam, R., and Smith, D. M., 1985, "Action Science: Concepts, Methods and Skills for Research and Intervention," Jossey-Bass; San Francisco.

Bassaches, M., 1984, "Dialectical Thinking and Adult Development," Ablex Publishing Corporation; Norwood, New Jersey.

Bauer, B. A., 1985, Self-directed learning in a graduate adult education programme, in: "Self-Directed Learning: From Theory to Practice," S. Brookfield, ed., Jossey-Bass; San Francisco.

Berte, N. A., ed., "Individualising Education by Learning Contracts," Jossey-Bass; San Francisco.

Brookfield, S. D., 1985, "Self-Directed Learning: From Theory to Practice," Jossey-Bass; San Francisco.

Brookfield, S. D., 1986, "Understanding and Facilitating Adult Learning," Open University Press; Milton Keynes.

Brookfield, S. D., 1987, "Developing Critical Thinkers," Open University Press; Milton Keynes.

Cameron, S. W., 1983, The Perry Scheme: A new perspective on adult learners, Adult Education Research Conference Proceedings, No. 24, Concordia University; Montreal.

Collins, M., 1985, Jurgen Habermas's concept of communicative action and its implications for the adult learning process, Adult Education Research Conference Proceedings, No. 26, Arizona State University; Tempe, Arizona.

D'Angelo, E., 1971, "The Teaching of Critical Thinking," B.R. Gruner; Amsterdam.

Daloz, L. A., 1986, "Effective Teaching and Mentoring," Jossey-Bass; San Francisco.

Deshler, D., 1986, Moral faith and cognitive development: Aspects of critical awareness on the part of professors of adult education, Paper presented to the Annual Conference of the Commission of Professors of Adult Education, Milwaukee, November, 1985.

Dewey, J., (1910), "How We Think," University of Chicago; Chicago.

Dewey, J., 1938, "Experience and Education," Macmillan; New York.

Drake, J., 1976, "Teaching Critical Thinking," Interstate Publishers; Danville, Illinois.

Ennis, R. H., 1962, A concept of critical thinking, Harvard Educational Review, 32 (1), 81-111.

Gilligan, C., 1982, "In a Different Voice: Psychological Theory and Women's Development," Harvard University Press; Cambridge, Massachussetts.

Gould, R. L., 1978, "Transformations: Growth and Change in Adult Life," Simon and Schuster; New York.

Gould, R. L., 1980, Transformations during early and middle adult years, in: "Themes of Work and Love in Adulthood," N.J. Smelser and E.H. Erikson, eds., Harvard University Press; Massachussetts, Cambridge.

Habermas, J., 1979, "Communication and the Evolution of Society," Beacon Press; Boston.

Hallet, G. L., 1984, "Logic for the Labyrinth: A Guide to Critical Thinking," University Press of America; Washington D.C.

Halpern, D. F., 1984, "Thought and Knowledge: An Introduction to Critical thinking," L. Earlbaum Associates; Hillsdale, New Jersey.

Hart, M., 1985, Thematization of power, the search for common interests, and self-reflection: Towards a comprehensive concept of emancipatory education, International Journal of Lifelong Education, 4 (2), 119-134.

Hostler, J., 1977, The education of adults, Studies in Adult Education, 9 (1), 58-64.

Hullfish, H. G., and Smith, P. G., 1961, "Reflective Thinking," Greenwood Press; Westport, Connecticut.

Kegan, R., 1982, "The Evolving Self," Harvard University Press; Cambridge, Massachussetts.

Kitchener, K. S., 1986, The reflective judgment model: Characteristics, evidence and measurement, in: "Adult Cognitive Development: Methods and Models," R.A. Mines and K.S. Kitchener, eds., Praeger; New York.

Knowles, M. S., 1980, "The Modern Practice of Adult Education," Cambridge Books; New York.

Knowles, M. S., 1984, "Andragogy in Action," Jossey-Bass; San Francisco.

Knowles, M. S., 1986, "Using Learning Contracts," Jossey-Bass; San Francisco.

Kohlberg, L., 1981, "The Philosophy of Moral Development," Harper and Row; New York.

Labouvie-Vief, G., 1977, Adult cognitive development: In search of alternative interpretations, Merril-Palmer Quarterly, 23 (4) 227-263.

Labouvie-Vief, G., 1980, Beyond formal operations: Uses and limits of pure logic in life-span development, Human Development, 23 141-161.

Levinson, D. J., 1978, "The Season's of a Man's Life," Alfred A. Knopf; New York.

Loevinger, J., 1976, "Ego Development: Conceptions and Theories," Jossey-Bass; San Francisco.

Mezirow, J., 1981, A critical theory of adult learning and education, Adult Education, 32 (1), 3-27.

Meyers, C., 1986, "Teaching Students to Think Critically," Jossey-Bass; San Francisco.

Morgan, G., 1986, "Images of Organizations," Sage; Beverly Hills.

Nottingham Andragogy Group, 1983, "Toward a Developmental Theory of Andragogy," Department of Adult Education, University of Nottingham; Nottingham.

Paterson, R. W. K., 1979, "Values, Education and the Adult," Routledge and Kegan Paul; London.

Perry, W. G., 1970, "Forms of Intellectual and Ethical Development in the College Years: A Scheme," Holt, Rinehart and Winston; New York.

Riegal, K. P., 1975, Toward a Dialectical theory of development, Human Development, 18, 50-64.

Schlossberg, N. K., 1984, "Counselling Adults in Transition: Linking Practice with Theory," Springer; New York.

Schon, D. A., 1983, "The Reflective Practitioner," Basic Books; New York.

Schon, D. A., 1987, "Educating the Reflective Practitioner," Jossey-Bass; San Francisco.

Scriven, M., 1976, "Reasoning," McGraw Hill; New York.

Sheehy, G., 1976, "Passages: Predictable Crises of Adult Life," E.F. Dutton; New York.

Sheehy, G., 1981, "Pathfinders: Overcoming the Crises of Adult Life and Finding Your Own Path to Well-Being," Bantam Books; New York.

Stice, J., ed., 1987, "Developing Critical thinking and Problem Solving Abilities," Jossey-Bass; San Francisco.

Young, R. E., ed., 1980, "Fostering Critical Thinking," Jossey-Bass; San Francisco.

Zachary, L., 1985, An analysis of the relevance of the Perry scheme of intellectual and ethical development to the practice of adult education, Unpublished doctoral

dissertation, Department of Higher and Adult Education,
Teachers College, Columbia University; New York.

All institutions and organisations in this index are American unless otherwise stated.